Welcome to the EVERYTHING® series!

These handy, accessible books give you all you need to tackle a difficult project, gain a new hobby, comprehend a fascinating topic, prepare for an exam, or even brush up on something you learned back in school but have since forgotten.

You can read an *EVERYTHING®* book from cover-to-cover or just pick out the information you want from our four useful boxes: e-facts, e-ssentials, e-alerts, and e-questions. We literally give you everything you need to know on the subject, but throw in a lot of fun stuff along the way, too.

We now have well over 100 *EVERYTHING®* books in print, spanning such wide-ranging topics as weddings, pregnancy, wine, learning guitar, one-pot cooking, managing people, and so much more. When you're done reading them all, you can finally say you know *EVERYTHING®*!

FACTS
Important sound bytes of information

ESSENTIALS
Quick handy tips

ALERT
Urgent warnings

QUESTIONS?
Solutions to common problems

Dear Reader,

When I was growing up, I belonged to an English Christian organization called The Boy's Brigade. I still have the Holy Bible every boy was presented with on his eleventh birthday. It's pretty dog-eared now, due mainly to the daily reading schedule we were given to follow. I'm guessing more than a few of you have a similar story.

When I discovered there were more religions in the world than just Christianity, my natural curiosity led me to take a closer look at them. That opened up a whole new world for me, as I came to realize that there were many other ways people choose to live their lives. It became an exciting study, not only about religions but also about the historical and geographical differences that affect the way we all live. The more I got to know, the greater my respect became for the beliefs of others.

When I came to write this book, it was wonderful to relive and renew those earlier studies.

I got a tremendous amount of enjoyment researching and writing this book. I hope some of that enjoyment has found a way into the content and with luck will rub off on you, who are, after all, the most important element, for readers bring all that they are to a book.

THE
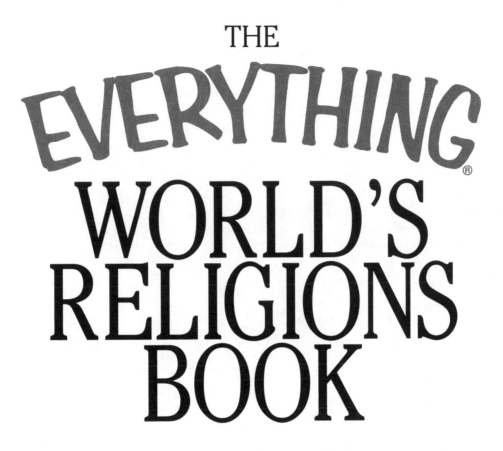

EVERYTHING®
WORLD'S
RELIGIONS
BOOK

Discover the beliefs, traditions, and
cultures of ancient and modern religions

Robert Pollock

Adams Media Corporation
Avon, Massachusetts

This book is dedicated to Susan E. Craig, M.D.

• • •

EDITORIAL
Publishing Director: Gary M. Krebs
Managing Editor: Kate McBride
Copy Chief: Laura MacLaughlin
Acquisitions Editor: Bethany Brown
Development Editors: Lesley Bolton,
            Julie Gutin,
            Michael Paydos

PRODUCTION
Production Director: Susan Beale
Production Manager: Michelle Roy Kelly
Series Designer: Daria Perreault
Layout and Graphics: Brooke Camfield,
Colleen Cunningham, Rachel Eiben,
Michelle Roy Kelly, Daria Perreault
Cover Layout: Paul Beatrice and Frank Rivera

An Everything® Series Book.
Everything® and everything.com® are registered trademarks of F+W Publications, Inc.

Published by Adams Media, an F+W Publications Company
57 Littlefield Street, Avon, MA 02322 U.S.A.
www.adamsmedia.com

ISBN: 1-58062-648-3
Printed in the United States of America.

J I H G F E D

Library of Congress Cataloging-in-Publication Data
available from the publisher

This publication is designed to provide accurate and authoritative information with regard to the subject matter covered. It is sold with the understanding that the publisher is not engaged in rendering legal, accounting, or other professional advice. If legal advice or other expert assistance is required, the services of a competent professional person should be sought.
—From a *Declaration of Principles* jointly adopted by a Committee of the American Bar Association and a Committee of Publishers and Associations

Illustrations by Barry Littmann.
Photographs © 2001 brand X pictures.

This book is available at quantity discounts for bulk purchases.
For information, call 1-800-872-5627.

Visit the entire Everything® series at everything.com

Contents

Introduction

The question might be asked, "Why bother to learn about other people's religions?" The most obvious answer would be that as we live in a world that seems to be getting smaller and smaller, it would benefit all of us to find out more about what our world neighbors believe in. That is what this book endeavors to offer, a factual overview of the world's religions.

The belief in unseen powers has been around for centuries. As far back as around 5,000 years ago, the Egyptians, Hittites, Phoenicians, and Scandinavians worshipped divinities. In Sumer, an ancient country in Mesopotamia, the victory of the god of spring over the goddess of chaos was celebrated. Once the early people discovered that there were places beyond the land in which they lived, adventurers went exploring and took their beliefs with them to far away places.

Charismatic leaders emerged to not only lead their people into battle but also to provide them with gods who would offer help and guidance in the difficult process of living their lives. These gods demanded obedience and worship. When things went well, people would thank the gods; when things went badly, they sought help and forgiveness. In both instances, sacrifices were offered, either in thanks or to assuage the wrath of the gods.

Not everyone accepted the beliefs prevalent in their time. Throughout history new spiritual leaders sprang up and preached or taught different philosophies or theologies. Jesus Christ, Buddha, and Muhammad each offered people a new way of life. This process continues today.

A wonderful fascination develops when a person takes a look at how the world's religions came into existence, developed, and spread. As author Lloyd C. Douglas said, "It becomes a magnificent obsession." It's also fun. It might seem facetious to use the word fun in the context of religion, but certainly joy would not be out of place, for it is joy that many adherents feel their religion gives to them, almost as a gift. Adherents contribute in many ways to their faiths and not just in terms of money. They often become part of what they consider to be a special community, one that has a major focus on helping others. All the major leaders of religious faiths teach, in their own ways, the Golden Rule—Do unto others as you would have them do unto you.

In this book, the conversational style is intended to make reading it a pleasure. The information has been taken from authentic documentation and from personal interviews with leading authorities. No opinions are given; they are left up to the reader. However, readers could change their opinions once they know the facts—some of which might surprise them.

It will be seen that the opinions that some people held in the past gave rise to a splitting off from a mainstream religion to form separate alliances or sects. Christianity is an example of this, but certainly is not the only one.

It is probably true to say that religion has produced a greater mass of literature, opinion, hate, strife, wars, persecution, absolute drama, and love than almost any other subject. All of these elements will be found in this book. Even so, from religion has come the glue that holds people together; it has produced mighty spiritual leaders and educators from whom the world has benefited immeasurably, for it is the solemn belief in a faith that gives humankind its essence and the will to go on.

CHAPTER 1
Religion Through the Ages

What can be said with confidence about the world's religions is that no one knows exactly how many there are, although the best estimate is 4,200. One religion is certainly not superior to another. What might still be true are the words of the great French writer Voltaire (1694–1778): "If God did not exist, it would be necessary to invent him."

Defining Religion

Here is what Charles Dickens wrote to the Reverend Frederick Layton in 1847, in answer to a query regarding his religious beliefs: "As I really do not know what orthodoxy may be, or what it may be supposed to include—a point not exactly settled, I believe, as yet, in the learned or unlearned world—I am not in a condition to say whether I deserve my lax reputation in that wise. . . ."

Dickens wasn't, and still isn't, alone in his opinion. No single definition has yet been satisfactorily stated on the subject of the varied sets of traditions, practices, ideas, and faiths that could constitute a simple definition of religion. There has rarely been unanimity about the nature of the subject among scholars partly because the subject itself has been so involved in controversy throughout its history.

FACTS

The Concise Oxford Dictionary defines religion as "the belief in a superhuman controlling power, especially in a personal God or gods entitled to obedience and worship." This is a loose definition that encompasses many beliefs and traditions.

Fundamentals of Religion

In any study of religion, the student will come across a word that seems to be used almost endlessly, and, in fact, is used in virtually every religion: schism. *The Concise Oxford Dictionary* defines schism as "the division of a group into opposing sections or parties; the separation of a church into two churches or the secession of a group owing to doctrinal, disciplinary differences." What this shows is that people in a group will differ, which isn't exactly news. However, if they differ enough, they will pick up, go off, and start their own groups, creating different religions or variations of a religion.

Even in modern times, the questions raised when debating religion versus politics, religion versus science, and religion versus secular systems of government continue to create religious belligerence throughout the world, which is often violently expressed. It seems unlikely that any kind of common resolution will come about soon. What does seem certain, however, is that all peoples, regardless of caste, creed, or nationality, require and often seek out some kind of belief system to sustain themselves in their daily lives, giving them hope and comfort.

A Western Interpretation

This book provides an examination of the major religions of today—how they evolved and what they are about—from a Western perspective. Muslims contend that Islam is not a religion; it is a way of life. Similarly, Taoism is considered by many not to be a religion but "The Way." Buddhism, which does not serve a god, believes in "The Path."

Nevertheless, it would seem that whatever name or designation is given to a particular faith or belief, the needs of the adherents do not differ; in that, there is universal agreement.

For those readers who, through their reading here, seek information of greater depth, it is suggested that they consult books that specialize in whichever religion happens to attract their attention. It is not the intention of this book to provide extensive, scholarly data, but to provide accurate information to inform the inquiring mind. There is a list of further recommended reading in Appendix A.

In this book the great five religions are in order of number of adherents, not chronological order. If they were in chronological order, then Judaism, for instance, would be before Christianity, which evolved from Judaism. However, Christianity is now the largest religion in the world, consisting of one third of the earth's population, and therefore will be explored first.

FACTS

In the religious calendar, the years prior to Jesus' birth were counted down from year one and designated "Before Christ," abbreviated B.C. The years following his birth were designated A.D. *(Anno Domini,* "The year of our Lord"). However, as non-Christian countries adopted the Gregorian calendar, it was deemed appropriate that the meaning of the years be changed to "Common Era," abbreviated C.E., and "Before Common Era," abbreviated B.C.E.

The Study of Religions

Most scholars agree that the nineteenth century was the formative period when the study of modern religions got under way. Many disciplines were involved, including the philological sciences, literary criticism, psychology, anthropology, and sociology. Naturally, all of the scholars brought their own academic biases into play. Their task was formidable because so many aspects of religion had to be evaluated—history, origins, development, philosophy—to name just a few. It comes as no surprise to learn that unanimity among them was rare. The very nature of the subject was loaded with problems; different scholars had differing views even about the nature of their subjects, be it Christian, Muslim, or Jewish. The subject is, after all, vast and must include not only getting the information together but interpreting it in an endeavor to understand its meaning.

Questions immediately come up that go beyond the recorded facts. What, for example, is the religious experience and how is it exhibited? What are the principles at work in the various religions? Are there laws in place in the religions, and how do they affect the adherents? In addition, there were the questions of truth or falsity, and the reliability of the recorded history of each religion. In short, it would be fair to say that the whole subject was fraught with controversy.

Classifying Religions

The whole issue of true and false religions and a classification that demonstrated the claims of each led to the necessity to defend one religion against another. Unfortunately, this type of classification, which is arbitrary and subjective, continues to exist.

For example, in the sixteenth century, Martin Luther, the great Protestant Reformer, went so far as to label Muslims, Jews, and Roman Catholic Christians to be false. He held that the gospel of Christianity understood from the viewpoint of justification by grace through faith was the true standard. Another example would be Islam, in which religions are classified into three groups: the wholly true, the partially true, and the wholly false. That classification is based in the Qur'an

(Koran, the Islamic sacred scripture) and is an integral part of Islamic teaching. It also has legal implications for the Muslim treatment of followers of other religions.

Of course, such classifications express an implied judgment, not only on Protestants, Jews, Roman Catholics, and Muslims, but all religions. This judgmental nature arises from the loyalties that exist in every society and religious culture. It is human nature for people to defend their own "tribe," and by association decry other "tribes." A simple secular example would be on the east coast of America where baseball fans are either for the New York Mets and against the New York Yankees or the other way around.

In the field of psychology, it is stated that in the religious person, emotions such as wonder, awe, and reverence are exhibited. Religious people tend to show concern for values—moral and aesthetic—and to seek out actions that have these values. They will be likely to characterize behavior not only as good or evil but also as holy or unholy, and people as virtuous or unvirtuous, even godly or ungodly.

The Greek philosopher Plato saw that in performing every good act, humans realize their link with eternity and the idea of goodness. He likened the human condition to the image of a man in a cave, chained by his earthly existence so that he cannot see the light outside, only the shadows on the wall. In order to see the light, man has to throw off his chains and leave the cave.

FACTS

Most religions incorporate love in their beliefs—love of others. Many have said that if people, of whatever faith, would take heed of a few verses from the Sermon on the Mount (from the New Testament of the Bible), the world would be a better place for all.

The Future of Religion

There is a universality contained in the answers, from whichever source one goes to, to the question, "what is the future of religion?" In essence, the respondents advised that a considerable increase of mutual understanding around the world needs to come about—an understanding that the earth is occupied by a vast number of people with an equally vast number of beliefs, and respect should be paid to all. It might seem a tall order to ask a Roman Catholic, for instance, to get an understanding of Buddhism or Deism, or the other way around. It is hoped that this book might help promote such an understanding. Of course, to become a student of the world's religions is not everyone's cup of tea; nevertheless, the philosophy of the Golden Rule is implicit in virtually every religion.

It will be inevitable that someone is going to ask why a certain religion has not been included here. As it is virtually impossible to discuss all the world's religions—over 4,000—in the space of a single book, we apologize in advance if the one you wanted to read about is missing.

It is well known that in times of trouble, either personal, national, or international, that the number of people who embrace a religion increases. It could, therefore, be said that as trouble isn't going to go away, neither is religion. Both are here to stay.

CHAPTER 2
Christianity

Christianity arose out of Judaism and rapidly developed as a faith with a separate identity, based on the teachings of Jesus of Nazareth, referred to as the Christ. There are many different denominations within Christianity. These have evolved over the years often because of disagreements about teachings or through different ways of worshiping. Most, however, agree on the basic tenets of the faith. The story about Jesus Christ's ministry and an early history of Christianity are contained in the New Testament of the Holy Bible.

Origins and Development

In Palestine at the time of Jesus, the political situation of the Jews was chaotic. They had been in servitude for nearly 100 years, were being extensively taxed by their masters the Romans, and were suffering from increased internal conflict within their own ranks. The main source of this conflict was the rivalry between the Sadducees and the Pharisees.

The Sadducees were a priestly sect that had flourished for about two centuries before the Second Temple of Jerusalem was destroyed by fire in August 70 C.E. The sect was made up of aristocratic families and merchants, the wealthy elements of the population who clung to birthright and social and economic position. They tended to have good relations with their Roman rulers and generally represented the conservative view within Judaism.

Their immediate rivals, the Pharisees, claimed to be the authority on piety and learning. They were seen as a political party concerned with the laws of rabbinic traditions, especially its holiness code—including dietary laws about the purity of meals and agricultural rules governing the fitness of food for Pharisaic consumption—and the observance of the Sabbath and festivals.

The core of the differences between the Sadducees and the Pharisees was over the interpretation of the content and extent of God's revelation to the Jewish people. It is notable that the Sadducees, because of their willingness to compromise with the Roman rulers, aroused the hatred of the common people.

FACTS

Historically, the Essenes are probably best known for the discovery in the late 1940s of the Dead Sea Scrolls, which a Bedouin of the Taamireh tribe found in caves in the Judean desert. These became known as the Qumran Scrolls, considered by scholars to be of Essene origin.

A third group of Jews, the Essenes—a virtual monastic brotherhood of property-sharing communities devoted to lives of disciplined piety—

considered the world too corrupt to allow for Judaism to renew itself, so they dropped out of any conflict.

It was into this complex political/religious cauldron that Jesus added a further element of dissension.

Jesus Christ

Jesus was born Jewish in the Roman province of Palestine (present-day Israel, Palestine, and Jordan) probably just before the first century C.E., during the reign of Herod the Great. The term *Christ* comes from the Greek word *Xristos*, which can be translated as "the anointed one." It has the same meaning as *meshiach* or *messiah* in Hebrew. *Christ* is applied to Jesus as a title to indicate his status. It is not Jesus' surname; his full name is Jesus of Nazareth.

The Early Years

Jesus was born in a stable to a Jewish couple, Mary and Joseph of Nazareth, in Galilee. They had traveled to Bethlehem, near Jerusalem, because of a Roman census. Their son, Jesus, grew up as a Jewish boy and followed Jewish traditions. There is virtually nothing on record about his young life except that his father was a carpenter; it is presumed that Jesus took up his father's profession. In the book of Luke, one of the books of the Bible, Jesus was presented at the temple and interacted with the teachers there when he was twelve.

It wasn't until he was about thirty years old that he emerged as a teacher himself. It was then that he left his life with his parents in Nazareth and began three years of traveling throughout Judea. He never went more than ninety miles from his birthplace; he owned nothing, attended no college, and produced no written works. Nor are there objective records of his life. The records that are available in the New Testament, for instance, are often contradictory. What does seem to be reliable is that the ministry of Jesus commenced with his baptism by John the Baptist.

In the Authorized King James Version of the Bible, the Gospel According to Saint Luke 3:21–23, it is written: "Now when all the people were baptized, it came to pass, that Jesus also being baptized, and praying, the heaven was opened. And the Holy Ghost descended in a bodily shape like a dove upon him, and a voice came from heaven, which said, Thou art my beloved Son; in thee I am well pleased. And Jesus himself began to be about thirty years of age . . ."

John the Baptist was a Jewish prophet of priestly origin who preached the imminence of God's final judgment and baptized those who repented in preparation for it. He is revered in Christianity as the forerunner of Jesus.

The Teachings of Jesus

Following his baptism, Jesus began to preach, teach, and perform miracles throughout Judea, and as he did so, he recruited many disciples including a core group of twelve who are now referred to as the apostles. At the beginning of his ministry, Jesus restricted his work to his fellow Jews.

As Luke 4:16–21 states:

And he came to Nazareth, where he had been brought up; and, as his custom was, he went into the synagogue on the Sabbath day, and stood up for to read.

And there was delivered unto him the book of the prophet Isaiah. And when he had opened the book, he found the place where it was written,

'The spirit of the Lord is upon me, because he hath anointed me to preach the gospel to the poor; he hath sent me to heal the broken-hearted, to preach deliverance to the captives and recovering of sight to the blind, to set at liberty them that are bruised.'

To preach the acceptable year of the Lord.

And he closed the book, and he gave it again to the minister, and sat down. And the eyes of all them that were in the synagogue were fastened on him.

And he began to say unto them, This day is this scripture fulfilled in your ears.

But it wasn't long before Jesus broadened his preaching to include non-Jews, known as Gentiles. His style of delivery was known to be charismatic with great moral authority. He spoke in the form of parables and of the coming of the kingdom of God. He was also a healer—raising Lazarus from the dead and curing a woman of an effusion of blood. The gospels record that he was a miracle worker, that he calmed the sea, changed water into wine, and fed the multitudes with only a few loaves of bread and fishes. He was accused of challenging existing laws, while he insisted that he fulfilled the law. However, he often performed miracles on the Sabbath, which was a violation of Jewish laws.

His message of moral reform was outlined in the Sermon on the Mount, which is recorded in the first book of the New Testament, the Gospel According to Matthew, Chapters 5–7. In the sermon, Jesus stresses selflessness and repentance.

The Sermon on the Mount contains the Lord's Prayer, which is preceded by a dictum in Chapter 6, verses 6–9:

But thou, when thou prayest, enter into thy closet, and when thou hast shut thy door, pray to thy Father which is in secret; and thy Father which seeth in secret shall reward thee openly.

But when ye pray, use not vain repetitions, as the heathen do: for they think that they shall be heard for their much speaking.

Be not ye therefore like unto them: for your Father knoweth what things ye have need of, before ye ask him.

After this manner therefore pray ye:

The Lord's Prayer then follows.
The sermon concludes:

And it came to pass when Jesus had ended these sayings, the people were astonished at his doctrine:

For he taught them as one having authority, and not as the scribes.

The Crucifixion

As his fame and reputation grew, so did the resentment of the authorities. Perhaps it was Jesus' dramatic visit to a Jerusalem temple that sparked the authorities to take direct action. Merchants were using the temple to conduct their business, and Jesus cast them out, saying that the temple was a house of prayer and not a den of thieves. When Jesus was questioned by Jewish leaders, his answers riled them. He claimed that he was the Son of God and that the highest commandment is to love God.

Jesus entered Jerusalem for the last time riding a donkey, which was a symbolic act and evoked messianic traditions of Judaism. The most important celebration for Jews at that time was the Passover meal on the first evening of the festival. Supporters of Jesus had made arrangements for him and his followers to hold their celebration in an upper room that they had prepared and made ready. At that meal, now called The Last Supper, Jesus had his twelve disciples around him. It was there that he established the new covenant by instituting the Eucharist, also called Holy Communion or The Lord's Supper, by sharing bread with the words "This is my body," and with wine "This is my blood." He told the disciples to do this in his memory. (The Eucharist is recognized by every Christian denomination as the central symbol of the death of Jesus on the cross.)

Was Jesus Christ ever married?
No. But, some people propose that he married Mary Magdalene and had a son named Bar-Abbas. However, not too many people would agree with this theory.

In an effort to deal with Jesus and have him delivered to the Roman justices, the Jewish authorities, who claimed Jesus was guilty of violating the law of Moses and preaching blasphemy, approached Judas Iscariot, one of the twelve disciples, and offered him thirty pieces of silver to betray Jesus. As arranged, Judas identified Jesus to the authorities by kissing him on the cheek in the garden of Gethsemane, where he was praying with his disciples.

Jesus was seized, arrested, and brought to trial before Pontius Pilate, the Roman governor. On examination, Pilate couldn't find sufficient evidence against Jesus, but the large, demonstrative crowd demanded his execution, and Pilate could find nothing else to do but agree that Jesus be crucified. According to the gospels, Pilate then took water and washed his hands before the multitude, saying, "I am innocent of the blood of this just person; see ye to it."

The Resurrection

As written in the gospels, Jesus was hanged on a cross to die. One of Jesus' followers requested and received from the Roman governor permission to bury him. So he laid Jesus' body in a cave and covered the opening with a heavy stone. This took place on a Friday, the day before the Sabbath. On the day after the Sabbath, women followers of Jesus went to prepare his body. They discovered that the stone had been rolled away from the entrance to the cave. An angel then appeared and told them Jesus was alive, that he had risen from the dead.

Jesus revealed himself first to Mary Magdalene. Later, at Pentecost, a Jewish festival seven weeks after Passover commemorating Moses delivering the law from Mount Sinai, also known as Shavuot, Jesus appeared to his disciples and commanded them to make disciples of all nations, baptizing them in the name of the Father, the Son, and the Holy

Spirit. During the weeks that followed, many who had known Jesus reported seeing him alive; they believed he had risen from the dead. Forty days after his resurrection, the disciples said they saw Jesus lifted up into heaven. That was the last time they saw him.

Central Beliefs

The belief that Jesus rose from the dead is central to Christians.

As the Son of God, Jesus represents the person that all Christians must strive to be like. Christians believe that he was perfect and that he came to earth to teach God's plan. God is almighty and rules over all. He is the one who created the earth, and he will be the one to cast judgment over it. Christians, as well as Jews and Muslims, believe in one all-powerful creator, God. Thus, the most important belief for Christians is that the world and everything in it is an expression of God's power and love.

FACTS

Christians believe that Jesus died for our sins and that God's love has the strength to overcome the worst of human sin. God can forgive the sins of anyone who repents and wishes to lead a new life, hence the expression "born again."

From the beginning of Christianity, followers have attempted to agree on statements of beliefs, called creeds. A creed is a set of principles or opinions especially as it refers to a religious philosophy of life. Creeds attempt to verbalize what cannot really be expressed in words. For instance, most Christians agree that God is three persons in one: God the Father, God the Son (Jesus), and God the Holy Spirit, creating the Holy Trinity.

Creeds developed throughout religious history. According to tradition, Jesus' twelve disciples wrote the Apostles' Creed, but it was actually developed in the early church to use with persons receiving instructions before they were baptized. The present text of the Apostles' Creed is similar to the baptismal creed used in the Church of Rome in the third and fourth centuries. In 325 C.E., a formal doctrine of Christian faith was adopted in Nicaea, referred to as the Nicene Creed. It gradually replaced other forms of baptismal creeds and was acknowledged as the official statement of faith that is used in the Roman Catholic, Anglican, and many Protestant churches.

Here is a modern English version of the Apostles' Creed:

I believe in God, the Father almighty, creator of Heaven and earth.
I believe in Jesus Christ, his only Son, our Lord.
He was conceived by the power of the Holy Spirit and born of the Virgin Mary.
He suffered under Pontius Pilate, was crucified, died, and was buried.
He descended to the dead.
On the third day he rose again.
He ascended into heaven, and is seated at the right hand of the Father.
He will come again to judge the living and the dead.
I believe in the Holy Spirit, the holy catholic church, the communion of saints,
the forgiveness of sins, the resurrection of the body, and the life everlasting.
Amen.

The Spread of Christianity

Christianity owes its initial dissemination to two men of vastly different backgrounds and personalities: Peter and Paul.

Peter

Peter's original name was Simon. He was a fisherman called to be a disciple of Jesus at the beginning of his ministry. He lived in

Capernaum at the northwest end of the Sea of Galilee, where he and his brother Andrew were in partnership as fishermen with James and John, the sons of Zebedee. It appears that Peter was not a well-educated man; he was untrained in Mosaic Law and it's doubtful that he knew Greek.

The story of how Jesus named Peter was reported in Matthew 16:18: "And I say also unto thee. That thou art Peter, and upon this rock I will build my church; and the gates of hell shall not prevail against it."

From all accounts in the New Testament, Peter was a man of strong emotions. He is depicted as rash, hasty, capable of anger, and often gentle, but firm. He professed love for Jesus and was capable of great loyalty. Peter is invariably mentioned first in lists of the disciples and designated as the spokesman for the group.

Given the information from the gospels, it's not surprising that Peter should emerge immediately after the death of Jesus as the leader of the earliest church. Peter dominated the community for nearly fifteen years following the Resurrection. It was he who raised his voice and preached at Pentecost, the day when the church came into being. It was he who served as an advocate for the apostles before the Jewish religious court in Jerusalem. It was he who led the others in extending the church, going first to the Samaritans, then to the Mediterranean coast where he introduced Gentiles into the church. When he accepted Gentiles and baptized them in the name of Jesus Christ without requiring the men to be circumcised, he encountered opposition from Jewish Christians and others. It didn't take long after that for his leadership in Jerusalem to come to an end.

How Peter's leadership ended is shrouded in uncertainty. Evidence that he lived in Rome and claims that Peter founded the Church of Rome or that he served as its first bishop or Pope are in dispute. The date of his death is unknown, and archaeological investigations have not located Peter's tomb.

Paul

Paul, on the other hand, it might be said, was the powerhouse who fueled the growth of Christianity. It is not going too far to say that it was due to Paul more than anyone else that Christianity grew from a small sect within Judaism to a world religion.

He was first and foremost an enigma. His original name was Saul of Tarsus. A Jew, he inherited Roman citizenship, perhaps granted by the Romans as a reward for mercenary service. This might explain why he had two names: He used his Jewish name, Saul, within the Jewish community and his Roman name, Paul, when speaking Greek.

He had a strict Jewish upbringing, and as part of his education, he mastered idiomatic Greek. According to Acts, he received training as a rabbi in Jerusalem under Gamaliel. His knowledge of the law and of rabbinic methods of interpreting it shows in his letters. Like most rabbis, he supported himself with a manual trade; in his case tent making, learned from his father. He obviously grew into a man of some sophistication.

Although it is fairly certain that he never met Jesus while in Jerusalem, he learned enough about him and his followers to regard the Christian movement as a threat to Pharisaic Judaism, of which he was an enthusiast. He had become a member of the Pharisees, the Jewish sect that promoted purity and fidelity to the Law of Moses.

Following the stoning to death of one Christian, Stephen, it is written in Acts 8: "And Saul was consenting unto his death. And at that time there was great persecution against the church which was at Jerusalem; and they were all scattered abroad throughout the regions of Judea and Samarian except the apostles."

Paul's first appearance on the historical Jewish/Christian landscape was as an oppressor of the members of the newly found church. Serious persecutions of Christians started with converts in Jerusalem, and Saul was a fierce advocate of the regime of persecution.

So eager was Saul to pursue, threaten, and slaughter Christians that he went to the high priest to request letters to the synagogues of Damascus so that if he discovered Christians, whether they were men or women, he might bring them bound to Jerusalem. As he came near to Damascus, it is written in Acts 9:

. . . suddenly there shined around about him a light from the heavens: And he fell to the earth, and heard a voice saying unto him, Saul, Saul, why persecutest thou me? And he said, Who art thou, Lord? And the Lord said, I am Jesus whom thou persecutest: it is hard for thee to kick against the pricks. And he trembling and astonished said, Lord, what wilt thou have me do? And the Lord said unto him, Arise and go into the city, and it shall be told thee what thou must do.

Thus did the conversion of Saul the prosecutor of Christians to Saint Paul the Apostle take place.

Three years after his conversion, Paul went to Jerusalem to meet Peter and James, Jesus' brother. At the meeting they recognized Paul as an apostle together with the founders of the church. In Jerusalem, Paul was accused of bringing a Gentile into the inner courts of the temple, beyond the barrier excluding non-Jews. He was arrested, partly to save his life from the mob. As a citizen of Rome, he was able to avoid trial and appeal to Caesar; he was taken to Rome and kept under house arrest for two years.

Paul was eventually convicted of the charges against him. No reliable account of his death exists.

His letters, which were collected for general circulation, have become a standard reference for Christian teaching. In addition, Saul of Tarsus is probably the first example in religious history of a sinner who was truly born again.

Holy Writings

The holy book of Christianity is the Bible. It is divided into two segments: the Old Testament and the New Testament. (The word testament means witness.)

Generally speaking, the average Christian looks at the Old Testament—also known as the Hebrew Bible—as the part that concerns the Jews, their history, and their prophecies, and at the New Testament as the part that concerns Jesus and the apostles. While that could be looked at as an oversimplification, it is nonetheless essentially a very adequate way of approaching the Bible. Regardless of viewpoint, there is no question that the Bible's impact has been, and is, immeasurable. The survival of the Jewish religion, for instance, and its subsequent influence in the history of Western culture are direct results of Biblical writings.

The first complete Bible in English appeared in the late fourteenth century and it has been retranslated into English dozens of times. In the modern world, missionaries have translated the Bible into nearly every written language in existence.

FACTS

It has been said that the King James Authorized Version of the Holy Bible had among its group of fifty-four translators and editors the services of William Shakespeare, John Donne, and Ben Jonson.

Some of the early Christian thinkers leaned toward the view that there was no need to have an Old Testament, but the dominant position conceded that Christianity needed to know about God's work on earth prior to Jesus and the only place to get that knowledge was from the Old Testament. (The Hebrew Bible will be dealt with in depth in Chapter 9.)

As for the New Testament and the way it evolved, it took several centuries for religious leaders to come to agreement on what information would be included. During the early years, there were many different versions and theologies of Christianity throughout the Mediterranean world and dozens of written gospels. Of the writings that Christian groups considered sacred, twenty-seven were chosen that would become the New Testament around 380 C.E. These twenty-seven books were the four gospels—Matthew, Mark, Luke, and John—Acts, twenty-one letters or epistles, and the Revelation of St. John the Divine. Many of the twenty-one letters or epistles were attributed to Paul. John, a close friend of Jesus, is credited as the author of Revelation, the last book in the New

Testament. It describes his vision about the end of time—the Apocalypse and Jesus' return.

FACTS

In the early times of Christianity, various sects were vying for recognition. In this setting, much of what was written was later judged to be apocryphal, meaning of doubtful origin, invented, or mythical. These writings were subsequently denounced.

Many Christian worship services include a reading from the Bible, often called the lesson. Often, members of the congregation will take turns in reading it from the pulpit or lectern.

Most formal churches, for example, Orthodox, Roman Catholic, and Anglican, will include in their services the celebration of The Last Supper, sometimes called the Eucharist, Mass, or Holy Communion. Only a minister or priest is authorized to perform the ceremony.

Rituals and Customs

Different denominations celebrate varying rites, festivals, and sacraments. The Protestant churches tend to be less formal than the Orthodox and Roman Catholic ones. The following are the common rituals and customs performed in Christianity.

Prayer

It is prayer that forms the backbone of the Christian religious life. Saint Teresa of Avila, a sixteenth-century Spanish mystic, described prayer as "an intimate friendship, a frequent conversation held alone with the Beloved."

Although specified periods for communal prayer are not set (unlike in some other religions), Sunday is usually the chosen day for Christians. This is not only the first day of the week, but also the day on which Jesus rose from the dead. The typical place for prayer is the church. However, Christians are urged to pray regularly either in public or in private as a personal act.

Prayer has been described as a pilgrimage of the spirit; many people consider it the purest form of religious expression. It expresses the desire to enter into a personal and constant intimate relationship with God.

QUESTIONS?

Are prayers categorized, such as prayers for someone who is ill? Yes, in a way they are. Whether by a group or an individual, prayers can cover almost every kind of possible need or occasion. They are used to thank God for his gifts, to ask for forgiveness, and to petition for blessings and favors.

Baptism

Baptism marks the beginning of life as a Christian. It is the emergence of a new person upon whom a new name is conferred. It is the total annulment of the sins of the person's past, from which an innocent person emerges. At the baptism, the person becomes a member of the church and is incorporated into the body of Jesus Christ. Most Christian churches baptize babies, but some denominations baptize only adults. Some churches hold that when children who were baptized as infants reach adulthood they must confirm their beliefs.

Historically, baptism was meant for adults, who were capable of accepting the ancient liturgies themselves. The Roman Catholic Church in more modern times asked adults, parents or godparents, to make the decision on behalf of the infant, with the expectation that the child will accept the decision made.

Confirmation

Confirmation usually takes place in adolescence or in adulthood. In some traditions it is seen as a confirmation of vows that the candidate could not make for him or herself as a child.

In both Anglicanism and Lutheranism, confirmation is generally preceded by instruction in the catechism. Other Protestants deny that confirmation is a sacrament, but they do sometimes use the term to mark the transition of baptized members into full membership of the church, including the right to receive Holy Communion.

Marriage

Christianity has contributed to a spiritualization of marriage and family life. Marriage can be called the most intimate form in which the fellowship of believers is realized. In many traditions there is respect for those who choose not to marry—monks, nuns, and Roman Catholic priests, for instance. But all Christians regard marriage as a serious step to take and a commitment as marriage vows are made before God.

Death

Christians believe that death is not the end of life because Jesus taught and promised eternal life for all believers. At the funeral service, the body of the dead person is commemorated and comfort is offered to the bereaved. The deceased is committed into God's care. Thereafter, the body is either buried or cremated, frequently depending on the wishes of the deceased as instructed in his or her will or in the particular tradition of the church.

Religious Festivals and Holy Holidays

Christmas Day, December 25
Epiphany, January 6
Ash Wednesday, the start of Lent—the period of preparation for Easter
Easter, dates vary between March 23 and April 24 (other churches have different dates)
Palm Sunday, also called Passion Sunday, the start of Holy Week
Easter Sunday
Ascension Day
Pentecost
Assumption of the Virgin Mary, August 15
All Hallows' Eve, October 31
All Saints' Day, November 1

CHAPTER 3
Catholicism

Catholicism is a branch of Christianity. Today, Roman Catholics throughout the world outnumber all other Christians combined. While Catholicism has its own rituals and customs, it is a form of Christianity and therefore follows the basic tenets outlined in the previous chapter.

History of Catholicism

Christianity became an accepted religious path when Constantine emerged as the political power of the Roman Empire. Constantine was sympathetic to the Christians because his mother was a member of the faith. It has been reported that Constantine, himself, experienced a conversion experience during a battle in 312 C.E. when he had a vision of a cross with the message "IHS," meaning "by this sign" in Latin. Constantine was victorious in the battle after receiving this vision. His rise to power continued until 323 when he became emperor and established his seat of power in Byzantium, later known as Constantinople (now Istanbul).

As Christianity spread throughout the empire theological interpretations began to differ in the East and West. Councils were held to establish orthodoxy and to try to eliminate heresy. These councils became increasingly politicized. In 1054, the divide between Rome and the Eastern churches became permanent. The Eastern part became the Eastern Orthodox Church, the Western part became the Roman Catholic Church with headquarters eventually in the Vatican in Rome, Italy.

But, probably the most decisive era in the history of Roman Catholicism was during the Protestant Reformation, which started on October 31, 1517, when Martin Luther posted his Ninety-five Theses on the door of Castle Church in Wittenberg, Germany. During the years after, several groups broke away from Roman Catholicism to form their own churches.

The historical development of the Catholic Church has been fraught with complicated dissension, not the least of which was the claim that it was the successor of the church started by the apostle Peter. However, the references to Peter in the New Testament and his identification with the Church of Rome show so many contradictions that even among scholars there is no consensus regarding his role in the early church.

The Roman Catholic Church conducted its liturgy in Latin well into the twentieth century. Sweeping changes were made at the Second Vatican Council. Officially known as the twenty-first ecumenical council of the Roman Catholic Church, it was announced by Pope John XXIII on January 25, 1959. The work of the council continued under Pope Paul VI up until its completion on December 8, 1965. The council enacted sixteen documents that detailed how the church would function going forward. One of the documents titled "The Pastoral Constitution on the Church in the World of Today" acknowledged the changes that had taken place and the requirement for the church to relate to the needs of a modern culture. In other words, the church was, and still is, seeking to update itself.

FACTS

Major changes were authorized in another of the sixteen documents, the "Constitution on the Sacred Liturgy." It allowed for church members' participation in the celebration of the Mass and sanctioned significant changes in the texts, forms, and language used in the celebration of the Mass and the administration of the sacraments.

The Hierarchy in Catholicism

Jesus Christ is the invisible head of the church, and by his authority, the Pope is the visible head.

Over the centuries, the Bishop of Rome became the leading authority in both civil and religious matters and assumed the title *Pope* from the Latin *papa* and the Greek *pappas*, meaning father. The Pope acted as the supreme teacher and could not err; he was infallible. However, the Second Vatican Council created the doctrine of infallibility, which caused major problems and was the subject of controversy among Roman Catholic theologians. Nevertheless, the Pope is recognized as having supreme religious authority.

The hierarchy of the Roman Catholic Church is a structure of authority that weaves its way from the parish priest all the way up to the Pope.

Priests

Each local church is attached to a district called a parish. A priest runs the parish and is a liturgical leader and a pastor. He is responsible for the administration of the sacraments, including the Mass. A priest hears confessions and assigns penance.

Bishops

A group of parishes in a region are called a diocese and are presided over by a bishop. Bishops are priests nominated by other bishops and appointed to their office by the Pope. Traditionally, a bishop was a teacher and leader of worship, but today, a bishop is more of a manager and administrator.

Cardinals

Cardinals are bishops who have been chosen and elevated to this position by the Pope. They join the College of Cardinals, which is a group of approximately 120 bishops who have also been elevated to cardinal. Membership of the college is divided among those who hold office in the Vatican and those who are bishops in major cities in the world. The United States has eight cardinals.

The Pope

The Pope leads the bishops and is the ultimate authority in the Roman Catholic Church. The College of Cardinals elects a new Pope when the one in office dies.

The Virgin Mary

The Virgin Mary is revered as the mother of God and holds a unique devotional position in the Catholic Church. Catholics gave her the title "Queen of Heaven." They believe that she rules over death in that capacity.

Based on the gospels of St. Matthew and St. Luke, Jesus Christ, who had no natural father, was conceived by Mary through the power of the Holy Spirit. Most Christian churches and Islam accept the virgin birth of Jesus.

Prayers to the Virgin Mary include the Ave Maria Prayer, which praises God and asks for intercession:

Hail Mary, full of grace!
The Lord is with thee.
Blessed are thou among women,
And blessed is the fruit of thy womb, Jesus.
Holy Mary, mother of God.
Pray for us sinners
Now and at the hour of our death.
Amen

Sin, Confession, and Penitence

The Catholic Church teaches that penance is a sacrament instituted by Jesus Christ. The church recognizes two kinds of sin: venial and mortal.

Venial sins concern lesser offenses and carry lesser consequences. Mortal sins are obviously more dire, as are their consequences.

It used to be that Catholics were instructed to observe a weekly rite of confession; however, this sacrament has declined in ritual observance, although it does remain an important part of a Catholic's spiritual life. To make an act of confession, the penitent has to enter the confessional box. This is typically a boxlike structure with a division creating two halves. There is a small, screened sliding door in the division. The penitent sits in one half, the priest in the other. However, today many Catholics have the option of a face-to-face confession in a reconciliation room. The principle remains the same; only the form has changed.

The penitent says to the priest, "Bless me father for I have sinned. It has been (however long) since my last confession." Then the penitents say what they consider to be their sins. The priest will ask if the penitent is sorry. The answer to this question is important because if the penitent isn't genuinely sorry and does not make a firm commitment to change his or her ways, he or she won't be forgiven. After the sins have been confessed, the penitent then finishes by saying an Act of Contrition. The following is an example of an Act of Contrition prayer:

My God, I am sorry for my sins with all my heart. In choosing to do wrong and failing to do good, I have sinned against you whom I should love above all things. I firmly intend, with your help, to do penance, to sin no more, and to avoid whatever leads me to sin. Our Savior Jesus Christ suffered and died for us. In his name, my God, have mercy.

The priest will then give an admonition. Depending on the severity of the sins confessed, the penitent's penance might consist of several prayers such as Hail Marys, Our Fathers, and such. Then the priest will release the person, guilt-free, with the directive, "Sin no more."

Holy Writings

The Roman Catholic Church bases its teachings on the Holy Bible. However, the Catholic canon differs from the Protestant version of the

Bible. The Roman Catholic canon has forty-six books in the Old Testament; the Protestant version has thirty-nine. Both Bibles include twenty-seven books in the New Testament. This happened because of the questionable nature of certain texts. According to the Protestants, books of Tobit, Judith, and a few others were not inspired by God and therefore did not belong to the Scriptures.

The Ten Commandments hold an important place in Catholic teachings. Young Catholics are expected to memorize and understand them. They differ slightly from the Commandments as given in Exodus 20 in the Holy Bible because they have been simplified.

The Ten Commandments as they are taught to Catholics are:

1. I am the Lord your God. You shall not have strange gods before me.
2. You shall not take the name of the Lord thy God in vain.
3. Keep holy the Sabbath.
4. Honor your father and your mother.
5. You shall not kill.
6. You shall not commit adultery.
7. You shall not steal.
8. You shall not bear false witness against your neighbor.
9. You shall not covet your neighbor's spouse.
10. You shall not covet your neighbor's goods.

Beliefs and Rituals

The Catholic Church has extensive rules; one such set of rules is called Precepts of the Catholic Church. While different sources may express them in varying ways, they essentially all come down to the same thing. Here is an example:

1. You shall attend Mass on Sundays and Holy Days of Obligation.
2. You shall confess your sins at least once a year.
3. You shall humbly receive the Lord Jesus in Holy Communion at least during the Easter season.
4. You shall observe the Holy Days of Obligation.

5. You shall observe the prescribed days of fasting and abstinence.
6. The faithful have the obligation of supporting the Church.

Another, even more extensive listing of rules is the Canons. Canon Law is a complex system of rules totaling, at the moment, 1,752. They are regularly reviewed and updated. They define the internal structure and describe the rights and obligations of a Catholic religious life. The Canon Laws affect everything from how and when marriages take place to the way in which church teachers are chosen.

The Seven Sacraments

The Catholic use of the word sacrament often causes confusion in the church. The accepted meaning is a religious ceremony or an outward and visible sign of inward and spiritual grace. The seven major sacraments of the Catholic Church are: **Baptism**, **Confirmation**, **Holy Eucharist**, **Holy Orders**, **Matrimony**, **Reconciliation**, and **Anointing of the Sick**. Of these seven, probably only two need further explanation—Holy Orders and Anointing of the Sick.

Holy Orders is a sacrament reserved for the three separate levels of ordination—deacon, priest, and bishop. It is a sacrament whereby a person commits to serve the faith for life. When that commitment is made, the church grants the recipient the responsibility and power to offer Mass, forgive sins, give blessings, administer other sacraments, and attend to the spiritual life of the people served.

Historically, Anointing of the Sick was called the Last Rites or Extreme Unction. The old rules reserved this sacrament for those about to die; today it can also be used as a healing aid for the very ill, the elderly, and the frail. Timing is of the essence. Having a "good death" is important, particularly to devout Catholics who wish to make their last confession to a priest and receive absolution. Once that's done, the dying person is anointed with consecrated oil.

Death

The Irish Wake is an example of a death ritual. This tradition crossed the Atlantic, from the old country to the new predominately Irish communities on the East Coast. What generally happens is that the body is properly prepared and neighbors come to the house to join in the ceremonies and offer their condolences. There will be a crucifix on the breast of the corpse and rosary beads (used for praying the Rosary in devotion to the Virgin Mary) entwined in its fingers.

Sometimes the toes are tied together to ward off the myth that the person may otherwise come back as a ghost. A pair of boots is placed at the feet so that the person may walk through purgatory; that's if they're up to it. In a traditional wake, the corpse is laid out on a wooden slab that rests on four kitchen chairs, and a linen cloth covers the body; the face, hands, and toes are left bare. Once the neighbors have arrived, there will be much dramatic sobbing and candles will be lighted.

While all this is going on the men will be organizing the food and drink. The clocks will be stopped, all mirrors will be turned to the wall, and salt will be sprinkled around the room to ward off evil spirits. If the family can afford it, the bed of the deceased will be taken out and burned.

FACTS

Purgatory is thought of as a place. The Pope has said that the soul of a dead person goes to purgatory if he or she has not completely repented for any wrongdoing. That is why people pray for the dead person; they believe their prayers will shorten the time the soul spends in purgatory.

Once the sobbing and condolences are over, the stories about the deceased will start, relating good times and bad and accomplishments and failures. As the evening wears on the tales become more exaggerated and boisterous. The next morning's routine will roughly follow the traditional type of service, one to which most of us are more accustomed.

Views on Controversial Topics

The Catholic Church opposes unrestricted abortion. The view of the Vatican is that as God is the originator of life; the conception of a child is a gift from him. The stand taken is that life begins at the moment of conception. The Vatican conceives life as sacred and the fundamental value of life must be awarded to the soul in the womb. The church allows abortion only if it is necessary to preserve the mother's life. Pregnancy resulting from rape, coercion, or ignorance has not been addressed. The church approves of birth control only if it is accomplished by natural means. The church opposes artificial means, such as pills, condoms, IUDs, foams, jellies, sterilization, and the noncompletion of the act of sexual union (coitus interruptus or the withdrawal method).

The Roman Catholic opinion on capital punishment has not yet received an absolute official directive, except that the Pope has certainly made strong statements against it. The Vatican proposes that life can be taken in cases of self-defense and a just war. (The definition of a just war has yet to be clarified.)

CHAPTER 4

Prevalent Christian Faiths

The majority of the Christian denominations follow the established forms, beliefs, rituals, and customs of traditional Christianity. Of course, there are exceptions to be noted. This chapter will concentrate on those Christian faiths that are well known throughout the world.

Amish

The Amish, also called the Amish Mennonites, originated in Europe as followers of Jakob Ammann, a seventeenth-century elder whose teachings caused a schism among members in many parts of Europe. Ammann was not an easygoing man because of his strictures and orders. He introduced the washing of feet into services and taught the plainness of dress and habit that became part of the Amish way of life.

The Amish began migrating to North America from Europe in the early eighteenth century and settled first in eastern Pennsylvania. A settlement is still in that part of the country. Schisms again occurred after 1859 between the old and the new orders, resulting in the formation of smaller churches or amalgamations within the Mennonite Church.

FACTS

Amish children attend public elementary schools, but are not sent to high schools. This practice has caused problems because of school attendance laws. Some Amish have gone to jail rather than allow their children to go to high school.

Each Amish settlement is generally made up of about seventy-five baptized members. If a group becomes any larger, a new group is formed because members meet for services in each other's homes. They have no church buildings. Each district has a bishop, two to four preachers, and an elder. Holy Communion is celebrated twice each year. Services are conducted in a mixture of English and palatine German, known as Pennsylvania Dutch. Adults are baptized when they are admitted to formal membership, generally when seventeen to twenty years of age. The Amish believe in the Trinity and affirm the scriptures, particularly the New Testament.

The Amish are famous for their way of life, which even today includes homemade plain clothing without buttons; hooks and eyes are used instead. The men wear broad-brimmed black hats and beards without moustaches. The women wear bonnets, long dresses with capes over the shoulders, shawls, and black shoes and stockings. No jewelry of any kind is ever worn. The mode of dress is said to be a following of the early traditions established in Europe.

They live without telephones or electric lights. The Amish drive horses and buggies rather than automobiles, and they shun modern farm machinery, although they have a reputation for being excellent farmers.

Their children attend school only through the eighth grade. After that, they work on their family's farm or business until they marry. The Amish feel that their children do not need more formal education than this. Although they pay school taxes, the Amish have fought to keep their children out of public schools. In 1972, the Supreme Court handed down a landmark unanimous decision that exempted the Old Order Amish and related groups from state compulsory attendance laws beyond the eighth grade. However, Amish students do have access to higher education by enrolling in their own colleges, seminaries, and Bible schools.

Anglicans

The Church of England is the mother church of the Anglican Communion; it has a long history. The Anglican Church was created in the sixteenth century by King Henry VIII who wished to get an annulment from his first wife, the aging Catherine of Aragon, so that he could marry Anne Boleyn in an effort to produce a son for the throne of England. However, Pope Clement VII refused to grant the annulment. In short, King Henry took over the English church, broke with Rome, and created the Anglican Church. He was then able to have the Archbishop of Canterbury, Thomas Cranmer, pronounce the marriage to Catherine null and void, which left him free to marry Anne Boleyn.

FACTS

Though King Henry had established this new church in order to wed Anne Boleyn, he had actually already done so in secret. Incidentally, Anne Boleyn gave birth to a daughter, the future Queen of England, Elizabeth I.

The Church of England spread throughout the British Empire spawning sister churches throughout the world; part of this colonial expansion and influence spread into India and North America. All together this activity made up the Anglican Communion as it is today, a body headed spiritually by the Archbishop of Canterbury, which has about 80 million adherents, making it the second largest Christian body in the Western World.

The Episcopal Church in the United States came into existence as an independent denomination following the American Revolution. It now has about two or three million members in the United States. Isaac Newton was an Anglican clergyman and theologian, as were some of the founders of the Royal Society. The Episcopal Church continues this tradition. The church routinely requires its clergy to hold university as well as seminary degrees. For more than twenty years, the American Episcopal Church has ordained women to the priesthood. In 1988, it elected the first Anglican woman bishop, Barbara Harris.

Central Beliefs and Holy Writings

The Anglicans include features from both Protestantism and Catholicism; they prize traditional worship and structure and operate autonomously. They have few firm rules and great latitude in the interpretation of doctrine. They consider the Bible to be divinely inspired, and hold the Eucharist, or the Lord's Supper, to be the central act of Christian worship. They recognize both the Nicene and Apostles' Creeds. Anglicans have a reputation for respecting the authority of the state without submitting to it; likewise, they respect the freedom of the individual. The following is the Nicene Creed, which will help the reader to understand the Anglican beliefs.

We believe in one God,
The Father, the Almighty,
Maker of Heaven and earth,
Of all that is, seen and unseen.

We believe in one Lord, Jesus Christ,
The only Son of God,
Eternally begotten of the Father,
God from God, light from light,
True God from true God,
Begotten, not made,
Of one being with the Father.
Through him all things were made.

For us and for our salvation
He came down from Heaven:
By the power of the Holy Spirit
He became incarnate from the Virgin Mary,
And was made man.

For our sake he was crucified under Pontius Pilate;
He suffered death and was buried.
On the third day he rose again
In accordance with the scriptures;
He ascended into Heaven
And is seated on the right hand of the Father.

He will come again in glory to judge the living and the dead,
And his kingdom will have no end.

We believe in the Holy Spirit, the Lord, the Giver of Life,
Who proceeds from the Father and the Son.
With the Father and the Son he is worshipped and glorified.
He has spoken through the prophets.
We believe in One, Holy Catholic, and Apostolic Church.

We acknowledge one baptism for the forgiveness of sins.
We look for the resurrection of the dead,
And the life of the world to come.

The Book of Common Prayer is a major influence not only on the faith but also on English society in general. It is used by churches of the Anglican Communion. Since its publication in the sixteenth century, it continues in various editions as the standard liturgy of most Anglican churches of the British Commonwealth. Most churches outside the Commonwealth have their own variants of the prayer book.

Expansion

The expansion of Anglicanism was directly related to British colonization. The Church of England's great missionary societies went out into all the English colonies and promoted Christian knowledge. They were instrumental in creating a decentralized body of national churches that were loyal to one another and to the forms of faith inherited from the Church of England.

The scope of the missionary work was immense, and Anglicanism spread from Nigeria to Kenya, South Africa, India, and Australia. It also traveled east to China and Japan. As was stated earlier, in America, the Revolution was the force behind the organization of the Episcopal Church, which was completed in 1789. The first American bishop, Samuel Seabury, was consecrated in Scotland in 1784. The Anglican Church of Canada had its own organization in 1893.

Baptists

The first Baptist church in the United States had an independent origin. It was established by Roger Williams in the 1600s. Williams was a minister of the Church of England who, because of his separatist views, fled to America in search of religious freedom. He became a minister in Salem, Massachusetts, where he upset the civil authorities who subsequently banished him. Williams then bought land from the

Narragansett Indians. Other colonists joined him, and together they set up one of the first settlements in the country established on the principle of complete religious freedom. Eventually, through extensive missionary work, the Baptist church spread throughout the world.

FACTS

In the twentieth century, Archbishop William Temple of the Church of England stated that the church was a community of worship in step with modern life.

Baptists are well known as evangelists. The Association of Baptists for World Evangelism (ABWE) was founded in August 1927 in the home of Marguerite Doane in Rhode Island. In keeping with the Baptist philosophy of independence, the ABWE states that it is an independent Baptist mission agency with a missionary presence in over forty-five countries.

The Baptist churches operate, as they say, democratically because they believe every other form of church government infringes on their beliefs. Individual members have an equal right to voice their convictions and to vote according to their consciences when the congregation makes decisions.

In America there are many sects; they are particularly prevalent in the American South.

Baptists have six convictions that bind them together:

1. The supreme authority is the Bible. They are noncreedal people who look to the scriptures rather than to any confession of faith.
2. Baptists hold very strongly to what is called Believer's Baptism as the badge of a Christian. Only to those whose faith has been awakened can baptism be rightly administered.
3. Membership of a Baptist church is restricted to believers only. Members must exhibit clear evidence of their Christian faith and experience.
4. Each church member has equal rights and privileges in determining the affairs of the church. Pastors have special responsibilities by consent of the church, which only they can discharge, but they have no unique priestly status.
5. The supreme authority of the church is Christ. While individual

church independence is stressed, individual churches affirm their unity in Christ by forming associations and conventions.

6. Baptists insist that a church be free to be Christ's church, determining its own life and charting its own course in obedience to Christ without outside interference—a separation of church and state that leaves Christian religion free to every man's conscience.

FACTS

Baptists were instrumental in the fight for religious freedom in England and the United States. Their convictions about the liberty of the individual played an important role in securing the adoption of the "no religious test" clause in the U.S. Constitution and the guarantees embodied in the First Amendment.

Baptists see the Old and New Testaments as their final authority; the Bible is, they say, to be interpreted responsibly. Of the edicts they embrace, pluralism of race, ethnicity, and gender, and the acknowledgment that there are individual differences of conviction and theology are featured strongly.

However, they are opposed to homosexuality and are firmly anti-abortion. They are also on record as believing that the *Harry Potter* books are truly satanic.

Christian Scientists

Mary Baker Eddy founded the Church of Christ, Scientist in nineteenth-century America. She had a stern Calvinist upbringing, which she rebelled against. In her search for good health, she experimented with alternative healing methods: homeopathy and suggestive, charismatic therapeutics as practiced by Phineas Parkhurst Quimby. Following Quimby's death, she increased her studies toward finding a universal spiritual principle of healing in the New Testament. It was during that period that she reportedly experienced a sudden recovery from what was thought to have been a severe accident.

In 1875, Eddy published *Science and Health*, which was repeatedly revised over the following thirty-five years. It was meant as a textbook for the study and practice of Christian Science. In 1879, Eddy and a group of followers founded the Church of Christ, Scientist based on the belief that the spiritual world is the true reality.

A Christian Scientist does not have to employ spiritual means for healing. The church encourages its members to be scrupulous in obeying public health laws, quarantine regulations, the reporting of contagious diseases, and immunization requirements where religious exemptions are not provided by law. The services of dentists, optometrists, and physicians for the setting of bones and doctor or midwife for delivery of a child are also sanctioned.

Study and prayer are basic requirements of the denomination, as is the readiness of members to meet the challenges of Christian healing. All Christian Science churches maintain Reading Rooms for this purpose.

QUESTIONS?

Can Christian Scientists go to their own doctor or a hospital for medical care?
Christian Scientists say that they always have freedom of choice in caring for themselves and their families. If an individual departs from the use of Christian Science by choosing some other kind of treatment, he or she is neither condemned by the church nor dropped from membership.

Apparently, spiritual healing does not depend on age or experience. Children are said to respond naturally to God's love and to the mental environment surrounding them. Infants, it is claimed, often heal more readily than adults.

Christian Scientists say that healing comes through scientific prayer or spiritual communion with God. It is specific treatment. Prayer recognizes a patient's direct access to God's love and discovers more of the consistent operation of God's law of health and wholeness on his behalf. They know God, or Divine Mind, as the only healer. A transformation or spiritualization of a patient's thought changes his or her condition.

Those members who indulge in a full-time healing ministry are called Christian Science practitioners and are listed in a monthly directory. They usually charge their patients a nominal amount.

The spiritual aspect of healing has come under direct criticism by the medical profession. There have been cases in which the law has stepped in to force conventional medical treatment, particularly when a child is involved.

However, Christian Scientists point out that what they do has been practiced effectively for more than 100 years and that during the past 112 years, more than 50,000 testimonies of healing have been authenticated. Many of these, it is said, have medical verification. In addition, thousands of accounts of healing are given each week at Wednesday testimony meetings in Christian Science churches around the world.

FACTS

The church is known worldwide and has a well-earned reputation of excellence for its international daily newspaper, *The Christian Science Monitor*, which is published in Boston, Massachusetts.

Three books—*Healing Spiritually* and *A Century of Christian Science Healing*, both published by The Christian Science Publishing Society, and *Spiritual Healing in a Scientific Age* by Robert Peel (San Francisco: Harper & Row, 1987)—give detailed accounts of verified healings.

Congregationalists

Congregationalism came to America with the Pilgrims in 1620 and blossomed in New England. As the country grew, Congregational churches were established in newly opened frontier regions. The movement originated in England in the late sixteenth and seventeenth centuries. Theologically they fall somewhere between Presbyterianism and the more radical Protestants. The denomination maintains the right of each individual church to self-government and to its own statement of doctrine. In its home country, England, Congregationalism has declined, but not as markedly in the United States. Even so, they have not expanded at the same rate as other religions. In 1931, Congregational churches were united with the Christian Church under the name General Council of the Congregational and Christian Churches of the United

States. In 1957, many Congregational churches united with the Evangelical and Reformed Church to form the United Church of Christ.

Congregational philosophy, ideas, and practices have influenced many other churches and have been a major factor in shaping the institutions and general culture of the United States.

There has always been a strong bent to preaching in the faith because the Word of God, as declared in the scriptures, has great importance to Congregationalists.

Baptism and the Lord's Supper are considered to be the only sacraments instituted by Christ. Infants are baptized generally by sprinkling, not immersion. The Lord's Supper is usually celebrated once or twice a month. Interestingly, and a clue perhaps to the continued independence of the faith, if the sermon is preached after the interval that generally follows the celebration, many of the congregation have the option to leave.

FACTS

The works of the great Congregationalist hymn writer Isaac Watts are featured prominently in Congregational worship. The English compilation, *Congregational Praise* (1951), maintains the tradition.

Jehovah's Witnesses

The Witnesses have little or no association with other denominations, nor with secular governments. They hold that world powers and political parties are the unwitting allies of Satan. They refuse to salute the flags of nations and to perform military service; they almost never vote.

The belief grew from the International Bible Students Association founded in Pittsburgh, Pennsylvania, in 1872 by Charles Taze Russell. A successor to Russell, Joseph Franklin Rutherford, aimed to have Jehovah (Yahweh) reaffirmed as the true God and to identify those who witness in his name as God's specially accredited followers. It was Rutherford's successor, Nathan Homer Knorr, who directed a group of Witnesses to produce a new translation of the Bible.

They are a high intensity faith group that expects a dedicated commitment from its members. Jehovah's Witnesses are in over 200 countries.

 Publishing activities have formed a major part of the belief's work, including books, tracts, recordings, and the successful semimonthly magazines *Watchtower* and its companion publication *Awake!*, which are claimed to have a circulation of over 10 million distributed in eighty languages.

Beliefs

The goal of their belief is the establishment of God's Kingdom, the Theocracy (a form of government by God). They believe that this will come about after Armageddon, based on their interpretation of the Biblical books of Daniel and Revelation, which they used to make apocalyptic calculations. Pastor Russell determined that 1874 would be the year of Christ's invisible return. He also figured that 1914 would be the year of Christ's Second Coming and the end of the Gentiles. Apparently, making prophecies is not done in this way anymore, which isn't surprising considering the track record. Nowadays, analysis is based on modern life and current events.

Jehovah's Witnesses insist that Jesus Christ is God's agent and that through him man will be reconciled to Jehovah. The Bible is considered to be infallible and the revealed word of God. Their own version of the Bible is called *New World Translation of the Holy Scriptures.* It is available in many languages. Biblical scholars have disagreed sharply with what they claim are distortions in the translations.

As far as hell and the inevitability of eternal life are concerned, Jehovah's Witnesses dismiss both. Many of them believe that death is the end; total extinction.

Witnesses meet in churches called Kingdom Halls. There are appointed members called Overseers or Elders. There are also Presiding Overseers and Service Overseers. From here on it can get complicated because of the administrative structure, which includes Districts, a number of which form a Branch, Branches form a Zone, and so on.

Members are baptized by immersion and must adhere to a strong moral code. Divorce is not approved of except on the grounds of adultery.

A major and much criticized condition of membership is the prohibition against blood transfusions. Even the storing of one's own blood for auto transfusion, generally done prior to major elective surgery, is not permitted.

Witnesses believe that any blood that leaves the body must be destroyed. In 1967, they stated that organ transplants are a form of cannibalism and are to be shunned. This directive was reversed in 1980 and left up to personal conscience, which wasn't of much value to those members who needed transplants to save their lives during the thirteen years of prohibition. There have been many court cases over the claims of the deaths of children, mothers, and other adults who might possibly still be alive had a transfusion been given.

Rituals and Customs

Only one day of celebration is acknowledged: Memorial of Christ's Death at the time of Passover. They believe that Jesus was born on October 2. Neither that date nor any so-called pagan holidays—Christmas, Thanksgiving, Independence Day, Halloween, birthdays—are celebrated. There is no Sabbath; all days are regarded as holy.

All positions of authority are reserved for men.

As most people know, doorstep preaching is a very visual part of Jehovah's Witness practices. In addition to those activities, members are expected to spend five hours a week at meetings in Kingdom Hall.

If members decide to leave the Witnesses or are disfellowshipped, life may become very difficult for them. In many cases entire families have shunned their relative completely. If a person has been a devout member, the effect of being excommunicated, as it were, can be devastating. Some former members have set up groups to help other former members deal with the psychological fallout.

FACTS

Three groups direct Jehovah's Witnesses: Watch Tower Bible and Tract Society of Pennsylvania; The Watch Tower Bible and Tracts, Inc., of New York; and the International Bible Students Association.

Mennonites

Members of the Protestant church with roots in the Anabaptists, Mennonites were named after a Dutch priest, Menno Simonz, in the sixteenth century. They have been categorized as a group that withdrew from society. However, they became deeply involved in sectarian virtues—frugality, hard work, and piety. Around 1663, Mennonites moved virtually en masse to America.

Interestingly, some Mennonites also settled in Russia, arriving in the Volga region at the end of the eighteenth century. All Mennonite communities in Russia were either destroyed during World War II or dissolved by the Soviets after 1945. Today, they live scattered among the Russian population.

Today, Mennonites worship in over sixty countries with an estimated membership of more than a million. Twenty formally organized Mennonite groups are in America; all of which have their origins in the Anabaptist movement. Mennonites retained much of their Anabaptist philosophy, particularly the rejection of infant baptism. Adult baptism is carried out when an adult declares faith in the church.

While there is no single defining set of beliefs, Mennonites affirm both the Trinity and the scriptures. The New Testament and the teachings of Jesus are the bedrock of their faith. Their services tend to be plain. Sermons are common and frequently address problems in the community and elsewhere. Independence has always been the thrust of their faith. Basically, they became known for wanting to be left alone to worship God in their own way. Similarities can be seen in the Amish, who also had Anabaptist roots. Until the nineteenth century, Mennonites retained their German language, which tended to ensure their isolation in the community.

A Mennonite statement to the Pennsylvania Assembly in 1775 said, "It is our principle to feed the hungry and give the thirsty drink; we have dedicated ourselves to serve all men in everything that can be helpful to the preservation of men's lives, but we find no freedom in giving, or doing, or assisting in anything by which men's lives are destroyed or hurt."

Mennonites are well known for their stand for peace. Many choose not to participate in military service. Some even object to government military spending, and a few withhold a percentage of their annual income taxes that would go for military spending. During the American Civil War, Mennonites hired substitutes or paid exemption fees of three or five hundred dollars to either side to avoid fighting in the war. Those who did decide to fight were excommunicated.

In North America, the Mennonites support their own colleges and seminaries. Similarly, they maintain secondary and Bible schools. New interest in their faith and history has fostered a reawakening, and they became more involved in society with an emphasis on witness, service, and evangelism. Instead of withdrawal, they found new ways of relating to the world.

A deeply felt commitment to social concerns, both nationally and internationally, combined with their nonresistance ethic, has motivated the Mennonites to create various worldwide aid relief committees. Their missionaries have established churches in Latin America, Africa, India, and in many other parts of the world.

Investigation into any religion will inevitably reveal strife, dissension, and schisms as the followers traversed their long historical development. It would seem that as faith is such a deep, personal emotion, it is self-evident that strong feelings are evoked.

Mormons

The Church of Jesus Christ of Latter Day Saints is the principal formal body embracing Mormonism. It had well over nine million members by the late twentieth century. It is headquartered in Salt Lake City, Utah. The next largest Mormon denomination is the Reorganized Church of Jesus Christ of Latter Day Saints, which is headquartered in Independence, Missouri. It has membership of more than a quarter of a million.

Joseph Smith founded Mormonism in upstate New York after he translated his revelation of *The Book of Mormon*, which recounts the history of certain tribes of Israel that migrated to America before Christ was born. They apparently underwent experiences similar to those written in the Old Testament. Mormons accept the Bible only "as far as it is translated correctly," because Joseph Smith did not finish his translation. However, he did produce another scripture called *The Pearl of Great Price.*

A major difference between the two sects is that the Reorganized Church, while holding to *The Book of Mormon*, rejects certain parts of it, in particular the evolutionary concepts of deity and polytheism, the new covenant of celestial marriage, baptism on behalf of the dead, polygamy, and tithing. They also reject *The Book of Abraham* because they do not believe it is of divine origin.

Way of Life

The Mormon way of life is distinguished by order and respect for authority, church activism, strong conformity with the group, and vigorous proselytizing and missionary activities. As an example of the strictness of the faith, the official pamphlet on *Dating and Courtship* calls passionate kissing prior to marriage a sin. The church advises young people not to engage in any behavior with anyone that they would not do with a brother or sister while in the presence of their parents. The church also discourages interracial dating.

As for military service, the church considers it a duty of its members. However, any member can opt for conscientious objection, but not by giving the church as a reason for it. The church discourages conscientious objection, and, in fact, endorses a corps of chaplains who serve in the United States armed services.

Mormons believe that faithful members of the church will inherit eternal life as gods, and even those who had rejected God's law would live in glory.

FACTS

There have been Mormon splinter groups that adopted polygamist marriage practices in spite of the church's renunciation of them in 1890. Some of those groups in Utah and northern Arizona continued the practice in secret.

Divisions and Teachings

Basically, the Mormons are divided into what are called stakes, which usually have about 5,000 members and are run by a stake president. Within each stake are wards, comprised of a few hundred members, under a lay clergyman. It is through this structured administration that the church regulates the lives of its members. At the high end, presiding over the entire church, is a supreme council of three high priests, called the First Presidency or the president and his counselors. Next are twelve apostles, who are equal in authority to the First Presidency. Essentially, those officers run the show.

In addition to the semiannual general conferences, stake and ward conferences are held; included in these are, of course, the usual Sabbath meetings. It is at these meetings that the consent of the people has to be obtained before any important actions are taken.

The Mormon Church is supported by tithes and offerings from its members. The money is used to support the church and its missionaries in the field.

QUESTIONS?

Can a young man or woman marry outside the temple?
The edict is that unless the young people who do marry outside the temple repent in a hurry, they cut themselves off from exaltation in the celestial Kingdom of God.

There is an accent on teaching the philosophy of the faith in Sabbath schools and young ladies' mutual improvement associations, which are primarily religious in nature and offer support for the unfortunate. A group called The Relief Society is a women's organization that has a special mission for the relief of the destitute and the care of the sick.

The Church of Latter Day Saints is world-famous for its genealogy repository, the Family History Library in Salt Lake City. It boasts more than two billion names and is considered the finest such repository in the world. The church has made available, free to church members and nonmembers alike, over 600 million names for research purposes on its

Family Search Web site on the Internet. It encourages its members to trace their ancestors as a religious obligation. This service is now available to anyone.

Presbyterians

In 1876, the Presbyterian Church of England was formed by a merger. Various factions from English and Scottish congregations came together and adopted the Presbyterian system of church government. Its history is a rocky one, and didn't come close to real stability until 1972 when it merged into the United Reformed Church in England and Wales.

Similarly, in 1983 the American Presbyterian Churches' headquarters in New York City and Atlanta, Georgia, merged to end a North-South split that had dated from the Civil War.

Merger seems to have been the historical norm in the Presbyterian Church because it didn't consist of just those mentioned above, but was present through the years with the North America Church, the Southern Church, the Cumberland Church, the Secession Church, and the Synod of Ulster. Perhaps this isn't surprising considering the church was a blend of New England Puritans—the Scottish, Irish, English, and Welsh. Actually, the Cumberland Presbyterian Churches, which were founded on the American Frontier in the early 1800s, have two heritages, one from the 1800s and a new version that came about in 1906. It has survived all the upsets, and today is centered in Memphis, Tennessee.

It should come as no surprise to learn that the church avoids highly centralized authority in the government.

FACTS

During the English Civil War (1642–1651), Oliver Cromwell, a Congregationalist, and his army became supreme in England. In 1648, the army purged Parliament of all Presbyterians. The military dictatorship under Cromwell terminated the Presbyterian establishment and granted freedom to all religious groups while giving special privileges to Congregationalists.

Foundations of Faith

Presbyterians believe in the Trinity: God the Father and Creator, Jesus Christ his Son, and the Holy Spirit. The Bible is considered the

foundation of their faith, and they acknowledge the common creeds of the church (Apostles' and Nicene Creeds). They hold that they are saved "by faith alone, by God's grace only, through scripture only."

The sacraments are two: baptism for infants and adults and the Lord's Supper, open to all baptized Christians.

The churches are governed by elders who are elected by their congregations. Similarly, the congregation elects and ordains pastors. Elders and pastors from all the churches are gathered to form presbyteries for mutual support and cooperative governance. It is a policy of the church that they seek community with all Christian churches.

Stands on Controversial Issues

The Special Committee on Problem Pregnancies and Abortion recommended in 1992 that the General Assembly approve a paper and adopt it as policy. The report stated that it affirmed the ability and responsibility of women, guided by the scriptures and the Holy Spirit, in the context of their communities to make good moral choices in regard to problem pregnancies. There were strong recommendations that all Presbyterians work for a decrease in the number of problem pregnancies, thereby decreasing the number of abortions.

It considered the decision of a woman to terminate a pregnancy morally acceptable, though certainly not the only or required decision.

Further, the report stated that there may be possible justifying circumstances including medical indications of severe physical or mental deformity, conception as a result of rape or incest, or conditions under which the physical or mental health of either woman or child would be gravely threatened.

The report went on to say that it did not wish to see laws enacted that would attach criminal penalties to those who seek abortions or to appropriately qualified and licensed persons who perform them in medically approved facilities.

It was stated that it was the Christian community's presumption that since all life is precious to God, members are to preserve and protect it. Abortion ought to be an option of last resort. The large number of abortions in society was a grave concern to the church.

This was followed by pointing out that it must be clearly stated to the individual who has undergone an abortion and who believes the abortion to be sinful that there is no biblical evidence to support the idea that abortion is an unpardonable sin.

FACTS

As do many other religions and denominations, Presbyterians have an extensive infrastructure of missionary and social-work programs in many parts of the world, particularly in Africa.

In 1997, all members voted on the issue of ordination of homosexuals. The result was to bar any members who were sexually active outside marriage from the office of clergy, elder, or deacon. The church's Book of Order was specifically amended to address the church's deep division over homosexuality.

In June 2001, a move forward took place that was intended to include lesbians, homosexuals, bisexuals, and transgender people as candidates for ordained ministers, elders, or deacons. A decision was made to change the language in the Book of Order that would do away with any prohibition of sexual minorities. That decision has to be ratified by the majority of the denomination's local governing bodies, the presbyteries.

CHAPTER 5

Other Christian Faiths

Christianity has several branches. In the previous chapters, you were introduced to the more common ones. However, those certainly aren't the only ones. In this chapter, you will explore the lesser known, though no less important, Christian faiths.

Adventists

A group of Protestant Christian churches with a belief in the Second Coming—the visible return to earth of Christ in glory—Adventism has roots in the Hebrew and Christian prophetic tradition. They believe that when Christ returns he will separate the saints from the wicked.

The founder of the faith, William Miller, was a Baptist preacher. He came to the conclusion that Christ would arrive sometime between March 21, 1843, and March 21, 1844. Although he was encouraged in this view by some other clergymen and followers, Miller was also accused of being a fanatic because he insisted that Christ would arrive on schedule with a fiery conflagration.

As is well known, Christ did not appear as predicted. So, Miller set a second date: October 22, 1844. That day passed quietly, too, and was called the "Great Disappointment" by Adventists. Nevertheless, members called Millerites did persist; they believed Miller had set the right date, but it had been interpreted incorrectly.

Some members of the faith independently believed that Christ's advent was still imminent, although they didn't set a new date, which was probably a wise move. They also believed that worshipping on the seventh day, Saturday, rather than Sunday, would help bring about the Second Coming. Thus, they came up with a new name: the Seventh-Day Adventists. That was in 1863.

Back in 1844, Ellen Gould Harmon experienced the first of 2,000 visions. In 1846, she married the Reverend James S. White, an Adventist minister. They spread the word together, beginning in New England. In 1855, the Whites moved to Michigan and set up an Adventist center. During the 1860s and 1870s, Mrs. White was a temperance advocate. In 1880, she and her husband published *Life Sketches of Elder James White and His Wife, Mrs. Ellen G. White.* The following year, Mrs. White's husband died. After that she became an Adventist missionary in other parts of the world, including Europe and Australia.

Once the Seventh-Day Adventists were formed, their General Conference, the church's governing body, decided to meet every five years. The General Conference oversees evangelism in more than 500 languages, a large parochial school system, publishing houses in several countries, and a number of hospitals. Volunteers distribute Adventist literature from door to door.

Members avoid eating meat and the use of narcotics and stimulants, which they consider harmful. This belief is based on the Biblical consideration that the body is the temple of the Holy Spirit.

Adventists observe Saturday as the Sabbath, not Sunday. Saturday, according to the creation story in the Bible, was instituted by God as the day of rest, and the commandment concerning Sabbath rest is part of God's eternal law.

Deists

Deism is an unorthodox religion, so unorthodox that many wouldn't call it a religion at all; nonetheless it is a belief. Lord Herbert of Cherbury (Edward Herbert) and a group of writers and intellectuals introduced deism in seventeenth-century England. It has had a rocky history.

Even the derivation of its name is controversial. According to the *Concise Oxford Dictionary, deism* is derived from the Latin *Deus* (God, Deity) and means "belief in the existence of a supreme being arising from reason rather than revelation." Then there is the word *theism,* which is said to be a Greek translation from the Latin *deism*. The dictionary says theism means "belief in the existence of gods or a god, especially a God supernaturally revealed to man."

It is the translations and interpretations of those two words that symbolically draw the lines between the established religions, particularly Roman Catholicism, and Deism.

At first the concept of deism was met with tremendous enthusiasm, followed by equally enthusiastic condemnation; over time the belief waxed and waned. Discussion about it grew stridently acrimonious at times, on both sides, with each party throwing virtual insults at the other's doctrines.

Deists consider that the following quote from Albert Einstein offers a good Deistic description of God: "My religion consists of a humble admiration of the illimitable superior spirit who reveals himself in the slight details we are able to perceive with our frail and feeble minds. That deeply emotional conviction of the presence of a superior reasoning power, which is revealed in the incomprehensible universe, forms my idea of God."

Central Beliefs

The expressed beliefs of deism are based on reason and nature. Deists believe that God exists, is good, and gave people free will. They do not believe the edicts that a person must believe and have faith in order to be saved or go to heaven. For deists the best approximation of the will of God is using the combination of reason and free will in the decision-making process. To act rationally is considered to act divinely. This common sense approach to God and a spiritual philosophy gives deists a profound sense of peace and happiness and a way of eradicating religious fear, superstition, and violence.

Deists readily accept the moral teachings of the Bible, but not the historical reports of miracles. They take exception to those who insist on literal interpretation of the scriptures as divinely revealed. Religious fanaticism and overabundant enthusiasm are not their bag.

The *Catholic Encyclopedia* states that "Deism, in its every manifestation was opposed to the current and traditional teaching of revealed religion." In another part it says: "They [the deists] never tired of inveighing against priestcraft in every shape or form, finding as they went so far as to assert that revealed religion was an imposture, an invention of the priestly caste to subdue, and so the more easily govern and exploit the ignorant."

Those two comments, which are relatively mild when compared with others in the literature, indicate the relationship, or lack thereof, between the two beliefs.

Instead of adhering to the general concept that God shaped and sustained human history, the deists believe that after God created the world, that was it. He left humanity to itself to operate according to rational natural rules. The majority of members came to the conclusion that the liturgical practices and trappings of Roman Catholicism were analogous to ancient pagan superstitions and rejected them. To them, the order of nature was evidence of God's design. That led them to postulate moral striving and tolerance of religious reason.

"Some books against Deism fell into my hands; they were said to be the substance of sermons preached at Boyle's lectures. It happened that they wrought an effect on me quite contrary to what was intended by them; for arguments of the Deists, which were quoted to be refuted, appeared to me much stronger than the refutations; in short, I soon became a thorough Deist."
—Benjamin Franklin

Perhaps the most interesting fact about the early acceptance of deism in America is that the first three Presidents of America, the Founding Fathers—George Washington, John Adams, and Thomas Jefferson—were all deists.

Holy Writings

It might be thought that the deists wouldn't have any holy writings, but this is not quite the case. They did have two early secular books, one by Herbert called *Of Truth* (1624) and another by John Toland entitled *Christianity Not Mysterious* (1696). Both books cracked the taboo of challenging Christian dogma, which was a courageous undertaking for both authors because others who had questioned the established religions were subject to persecution.

As for holy writings, one must turn to Thomas Jefferson and his *Jefferson Bible* (1816). He wrote in a letter to a William Canby: "Of all the systems of morality, ancient or modern, which have come under my observation, none appear to me so pure as that of Jesus. A more beautiful or precious morsel of ethics I have never seen."

He told John Adams that he was rescuing the philosophy of Jesus and the "pure principles which he taught," from the "artificial vestments in which they have been muffled by priests, who have travestied them into various forms as instruments of riches and power for themselves." After having selected from the evangelists "the very words only of Jesus," he believed "there will be found remaining the most sublime and benevolent code of morals which has ever been offered to man."

He proceeded to gather together sections of the Bible and arrange them in a certain order by time or subject. He literally did a cut and paste job on the then existing Bible by removing items such as the virgin birth and the resurrection, which he felt were supernatural. The result was *The Life and Morals of Jesus of Nazareth.* It is available in paperback.

Other more modern books were produced, this time by Thomas Paine and Ethan Allen. Both not only spoke openly about deism but also expressed their views without hesitation. Paine's *The Age of Reason* (1793) was attacked by both preachers and politicians. In England, a bookseller who sold copies was arrested for blasphemy. Ethan Allen was equally outspoken about his deist beliefs. His book *The Only Oracle of Man* (1785) provides an in-depth view of deism. Apparently, when Ethan Allen said he did not believe in the Christian doctrine of original sin, he was told that without original sin there is no need for Christianity. It's said that he agreed.

QUESTIONS?

Is deism a form of atheism?
No. Atheism teaches that there is no god. Deism teaches there is a god. While it rejects the revelations of religions, deism does not reject God.

Diversification into Modern Society

While it is claimed that deism is growing rapidly throughout the world because of people's disillusionment with the established religions, the numbers of adherents do not appear to be available, and if they were, would probably be difficult to substantiate. However, the World Union of Deists, founded in 1993 by Robert L. Johnson, has offices in various parts of the United States, England, and Ireland.

Lutherans

Lutheranism, a major Protestant denomination, originated in the sixteenth century and was founded by a German Augustinian monk—Martin Luther. He was also a professor of theology at the University of Wittenberg in Saxony. He wanted to reform the Western Christian Church. But, because he criticized what he saw as immorality and corruption in the Roman Catholic Church, he was excommunicated by the Pope. So, Lutheranism went its separate way, which essentially broke up the organizational unity of Western Christendom.

Martin Luther's teachings spread through Germany and Scandinavia and, in the eighteenth century, to America, then to the rest of the world. Lutheranism is the state religion of many north European countries. Lutherans claim to see their movement centered in the understanding that, thanks to the saving activity of God in Jesus Christ, they are themselves "justified by grace through faith." Lutherans, like most Protestants, base their teachings not on churchly authority but on the divinely inspired Bible.

Central Beliefs

Lutherans believe that all human beings are sinners, and because of original sin, are in bondage to the power of Satan. Their faith, therefore, is the only way out.

Worship is firmly based on the teachings of the Bible, which Luther insisted was the only way to know God and his will. The Bible was the divine word, brought to man through the apostles and prophets.

 In America, the churches linked together for common purposes and formed groups. In 1987, the Association of Evangelical Lutheran Churches united to form the Evangelical Lutheran Church of America.

Unlike the practice of the Roman Catholic Church, Luther conducted worship not in Latin, but in the language of the people. Apparently, the use of the vernacular enhanced the delivery and acceptance of the sermons, to say nothing of the rest of service. Because of this serious change, access was given, not only to the highly educated members but also to the general population. Luther also reduced the established seven sacraments to two: baptism and the Lord's Supper. Infant baptism was considered to be God's grace reaching out to the newborn, and as such, a symbol of unconditional love. Congregational participation in worship was encouraged, particularly through the singing of the liturgy and of hymns, many of which Luther himself wrote. One of them was a hit: "A Mighty Fortress Is Our God."

Lutheranism Today

Lutheranism, like many religions, went through various phases. One such movement—Pietism—which was of German origin, emphasized personal faith in protest against secularization in the church. It spread quickly and expanded to include social and educational aspects.

QUESTIONS?

Are Lutheran priests allowed to marry?
Yes, unlike in the Roman Catholic Church, Lutheran priests do marry.

It is estimated that Lutheranism throughout the world constitutes the largest of the churches that have come out of the Reformation. Lutherans number about seventy million worldwide, with approximately 10 million in the United States and Canada.

Methodists

Methodism came to America from Ireland, brought by immigrants who had been converted by Charles and John Wesley. John Wesley also sent preachers with them, the most successful of whom was Francis Asbury, who arrived in 1771. He preached far and wide from settlements to the frontiers. During the Revolution, Wesley took the side of the English, and Asbury took the side of the new American republic.

The church grew very rapidly, but schisms developed. The slavery problem split the Methodist Church into two. In 1845, the Methodist Episcopal Church and the Methodist Episcopal Church, South were organized. The church in the South lost its black members during the Civil War. After the Civil War, both churches grew rapidly.

In 1939, the Methodist Church was formed, and the Methodist Protestant Church joined in the same union. At that time the Central

Jurisdiction was formed for all the black members wherever they lived. It existed alongside other jurisdictions. Then, in 1968, it was abolished and black Methodists were integrated into the church.

In 1924, Methodist women were given limited clergy rights. In 1956, they were accepted for full ordination.

The United Methodist Church was created on April 23, 1968, when Bishop Reuben H. Muller of the Evangelical United Brethren Church and Bishop Lloyd C. Wicke of the Methodist Church merged at the General Conference in Dallas, Texas, to form the United Methodist Church. The combined church then had eleven million members, which made it one of the largest Protestant churches in the world.

An increasing number of women have been admitted to the ordained ministry and to denominational leadership as consecrated bishops. In 1980, Marjorie Matthews was the first woman elected to the church's episcopacy.

The United Methodist Church has published their Social Creed to be distributed, read, and continually available in every congregation. It reads:

We believe in God, Creator of the world; and in Jesus Christ, the Redeemer of creation. We believe in the Holy Spirit, through whom we acknowledge God's gifts, and we repent of our sin in misusing these gifts to idolatrous ends.

We affirm the natural world as God's handiwork and dedicate ourselves to its preservation, enhancement, and faithful use by humankind.

We joyfully receive for ourselves and others the blessings of community, sexuality, marriage, and the family.

We commit ourselves to the rights of men, women, children, youth, young adults, the aging, and people with disabilities; to the improvement of the quality of life; and to the rights and dignity of racial, ethnic, and religious minorities.

We believe in the right and duty of persons to work for the glory of God and the good of themselves and others and in the protection of their welfare in so doing; in the rights to property as a trust from God, collective bargaining, and responsible consumption; and in the elimination of economic and social distress.

We dedicate ourselves to peace throughout the world, to the rule of justice law among nations, and to individual freedom for all people of the world.

We believe in the present and final triumph of God's Word in human affairs and gladly accept our commission to manifest the life of the gospel in the world. Amen.

As with many Protestant denominations, the Methodist Church recognizes and practices two sacraments: baptism and the Supper of the Lord. The UMC looks upon us all as sinful creatures who have become estranged from God and who have wounded ourselves and others. As we have wreaked havoc throughout the natural order, we stand in need of redemption.

The Methodist Church has an extensive, worldwide missionary organization. Missionaries are trained to carry their religion and philosophy throughout the world using a global communications network. They also explore and sustain ecumenical cooperation with other missionaries.

The equality of the sexes within the church is established. The church affirms the right of women to equal treatment in employment, responsibility, promotion, and compensation. An official statement reads: "We affirm the importance of women in decision-making positions at all levels of Church life."

Orthodoxy

Orthodoxy is the third great branch of Christianity. (It is also called the Orthodox Eastern Church and the Greek Orthodox Church.) It evolved in 1054 following the climax of the major cultural, intellectual, and theosophical differences between the Roman Catholic Church and the Orthodox Church, called the Great Schism. At that time the membership of the Eastern Orthodox Church was spread throughout the Middle East, the Balkans, and Russia, with its center in Constantinople, now called Istanbul. Today, the church has spread from those original countries throughout the world and numbers about 300 million adherents.

Central Beliefs

Members believe that the Orthodox Church was founded by Jesus Christ and that it is the living manifestation of his presence. Orthodoxy further believes that the Christian faith and the church are inseparable, that it is impossible to know Jesus Christ, to share in the life of the Holy Trinity, or to be considered a Christian apart from the church, and that it is through the church that an individual is nurtured in the faith.

Orthodoxy means "the state of being orthodox, what is authorized or accepted as right and true." The Orthodox church stresses "right belief and right glory." It also means holding the correct or currently accepted opinions, especially on religious doctrine. The word is used in Judaism where it means the orthodox or right practice of that faith.

Essentially, Orthodox adherents' beliefs are very similar to those of other Christian traditions. For instance, they recognize seven sacraments, but express them slightly differently from other faiths: Baptism, Confirmation, Holy Eucharist, Confession, Ordination, Marriage, and Holy Unction.

When death occurs, they believe that the person's soul, being immortal, goes to God, who created it. Immediately after death the soul is judged, which is called the Particular Judgment. The final reward is believed to take place later at the time of the General Judgment. During the time between the Particular and the General Judgment, which is called the Intermediate State, a soul has a foretaste of the blessings or punishments accorded.

The church today is an invaluable treasury of rich liturgical tradition that has been handed down from early Christianity. There is grandeur in the works of art and music and mystery in the Orthodox icons. Many of the churches are rich in history (the Church of Constantinople). Others are relatively young (the Church of Finland). Some are large (the Church of Russia); some are small (the Church of Sinai).

The international organization of the Orthodox churches is one of autocephalous (self-governing) branches. The churches hold the same dogmas and faiths, although the principle of "authority with freedom" prevails. Each church is independent in internal organization and follows its own particular customs. The Orthodox Church acknowledges that unity does not mean uniformity. In America, where Orthodoxy is relatively young, there are a number of dioceses and archdioceses that are linked directly to one of the autocephalous churches.

FACTS

Each Orthodox Church is led by a synod of bishops. The president of the synod is known as the Patriarch, Archbishop, or Metropolitan. Among the various bishops, the ecumenical Patriarch of Constantinople is accorded a "place of honor" and is regarded as the "first among equals."

The administration of the church is spiritual and civil in character. The laymen in the church are prominent not only in the election of candidates to the priesthood but also in the sharing of the spiritual and administrative affairs of the church. Laymen share these duties with the clergy and have a responsibility for the discipline of the membership of the church. They also have the right to participate in the tasks of the church in teaching, mission, and charitable obligations.

There is no one person who leads or speaks for the church, nor do all its members act separately. They are seen as a whole, the one "Mystical Body of Christ."

Holy Writings

Scriptural authority is stressed and there is an insistence upon the gospel, which is considered the foundation of the faith. It has been quoted that "scripture is fixed, it is the ground and pillar of our faith."

The Bible, therefore, is highly regarded by the church; a portion of it is read at every service. The church sees itself as the guardian and interpreter of the scriptures. The content of the Old Testament is seen as preparation for the coming of Jesus. The New Testament with its four gospels, twenty-one epistles, the Acts of the Apostles, and the Book of Revelation are all accepted and are part of the church. (As you will see, this is not always the case with other religions.)

The Major Feast Days

Like the Roman Church, the Eastern Orthodox Church has an active religious calendar. What follows is a listing of the most important feast days observed by the Orthodox Church. Unfortunately, a comprehensive explanation of the meanings and origins of each feast day is beyond the scope of this text.

Nativity of the *Theotokos**, September 8
Exaltation of the Holy Cross, September 14
Presentation of the *Theotokos** in the Temple, November 21
Christmas (Nativity of Jesus Christ), December 25
Epiphany (Baptism of Christ), January 6
Presentation of Christ in the Temple, February 2
Annunciation (*Evangelismos*), March 25
Easter (*Pascha*), dates vary year to year

Ascension, forty days after Easter

Pentecost, fifty days after Easter

Transfiguration of Christ, August 6

Dormition of the *Theotokos**, August 15

* *Theotokos* (Greek: "God-Bearer") in Eastern Orthodoxy is the designation of the Virgin Mary as mother of God. The term has great historical importance.

Protestants

The key to Protestantism, if there is one, is its amazing diversity. The catalyst that gave birth to such diversity was the Reformation in the sixteenth century. While there was deep dissension within the Roman Catholic Church, which led to liberal Catholic reform earlier in the century, the traditional beginning of the Reformation occurred when Martin Luther, a German Roman Catholic priest, posted his Ninety-five Theses for debate on the door of the Castle Church in Wittenberg, Germany, on October 31, 1517, the eve of All Saints' Day.

Luther was a pastor and professor at the University of Wittenberg. In his theses he attacked what he saw as the theological root of corruption in the life of the church. He insisted that the Pope had no authority over purgatory and that only the scripture was authoritative. His critique was against the doctrine of the church. In essence he said that the church was acting as a mediator or filter between the individual and God. To the Reformers the church seemed to be a transaction in place: The people would attend Mass, make confessions, do penance, and so on, and the church would give approval and access to God's pleasure.

Another part of the argument was that because Catholics lived in fear of failing to provide what the church said God required and their only dispensation was via the church, church leaders had both political leverage and the ability to exert terror and compliance over the general populace.

Understandably, this attack didn't sit too well with the Roman Catholic establishment and Pope Leo X excommunicated Luther in 1521.

It might be said that Luther and the Reformers sought to cut out the middleman—the Roman Catholic Church as the institution responsible for mediation between God and man—and go straight to the source.

John Calvin was the leading French Protestant reformer and the most important second-generation figure of the Reformation. He was a highly educated man who studied Greek, Hebrew, and Latin in order to further improve his studies of the Scriptures. Because of internal religious strife in France, he went to Basel in Switzerland. The same thing eventually happened in Switzerland as happened in France, and he was expelled from the country. Years later he returned to establish the Geneva Academy for the training of ministry students. In the mid-1560s, he produced what became his masterpiece, "Institutes of the Christian Religion," which became the single most important statement of Protestant belief.

Central Beliefs and Holy Writings

Jesus Christ and the Bible formed the authoritative base of the faith. The Protestant churches were organized with biblical supremacy. They believed in what might be called a democracy of believers—every Christian could communicate directly with God without having to go through the intermediary of a priest or saint. Thus, the Protestant principle, you might say, is that the church is not God, neither are priests, pastors, nor ministers; only God is God and he alone should be worshipped.

The Reformation rebelled against what was called "fixed prayer," that is prayers that had been composed by others to be remembered by rote and later regurgitated at the appropriate time and place. Freedom from the strictures of the Roman Catholic Church was emphasized and people were encouraged to pray frequently and directly from the heart and not the head. Protestants recognize two sacraments: Baptism and Holy Communion (the Eucharist). There have been variations in sacramental doctrine among Protestants over the years, but these two have become virtually universal.

The New Testament, especially the letters and writings of Paul, captured the Protestant sense of having discovered a religious hero, a mentor who exemplified their philosophy. He was brought up in one strict faith, in which he was striving to please God, but he had failed and then went through a period of self-doubt and problems with his worthiness—what today would be called self-esteem. His conversion through the epiphany with Jesus and his acceptance of Christ as a savior were seen in the light of a sinner who had been looked on by God who was blind to his sins because of faith. Thus, Paul was the perfect example of the Protestant theology of justification by grace through faith. In other words, God didn't have to be satisfied to forgive and accept.

The literature of the Reformers shows that they did not believe that good works by themselves produced God's appeasement or salvation. Rather, good works inevitably flowed from the forgiven heart and were the consequence of the justified person's life. The law of God measured human frailties and judged them.

The other side of this belief presented Protestant leaders with a dilemma: When people were saved it was to God's credit; when they were not it was their own fault. It couldn't be both ways. Some leaders saw themselves solving the problem in Biblical terms by stressing God's loving relationship to humanity in sending his own Son, Jesus Christ, to suffer on their behalf.

One might say that the Protestant ethic formed what was later referred to, particularly in the United States, as the work ethic. High value was given to honesty, hard work, and thrift. In the Calvinist view, these attributes were seen as the underpinnings of eternal salvation. Sociologists have argued that the Protestant ethic contributed significantly to the beginning and later development of capitalism.

Diversification into Modern Society

Protestantism increased the importance of the laity. In most denominations they exercise more control over the hiring and firing, if necessary, of their pastor. They have a hand in church policy and offer advice on secular concerns. They also help in leading worship and they get involved in many other activities of the church. Some of the laity even participate in various church conferences, in which they help to set policy.

Protestantism has led the way in providing women with the ability to become ministers. Today, in many of the denominations, there are even female bishops.

Protestantism became strong in northwestern Europe, England, and English-speaking America. Through the missionary movement, it was taken to all parts of the world and joined Roman Catholicism as a minority presence in Asia and Africa. Protestantism became part of the history of the North Atlantic nations. While there are more Protestants than Catholics in the United States, Catholicism is the single largest church.

The Protestant heritage of separation led to diversity, which in turn contributed to the vast array of denominations within it.

Quakers

Quakers, a Christian group, are also known as the Society of Friends; members are called Friends. It is said that the name Quaker came about through Justice Bennet of Derby, England, who called them that because they bid him tremble at the word of God. George Fox, a nonconformist religious reformer, founded the movement in the seventeenth century in England. He had a vision and heard a voice that told him, "There is one, even Jesus Christ, who can speak to thy condition," which motivated him to become a preacher. He believed in an "Inner Light"—the presence of God's spirit within each individual.

The existence of the "Inner Light" means that everyone has direct access to God. Fox reasoned that there was no need to have a church or a priest to act as a go-between. Nor did people need elaborate rituals, creeds, dogmas, or even to dress up in church garments.

None of this sat well with the infamous Cromwell and his Puritan government. As a result, Fox and his followers had to face persecution.

The philosophy of intense concern for others was developing; it has continued to the present day and is a bulwark of the movement. The early

Quakers were agitating for an end to slavery and improvement in the treatment and conditions in mental health institutions and penitentiaries.

When the Quakers came to the United States, they didn't fare any better than they had at home. They were looked at as witches, and many were hanged. They eventually settled in Rhode Island, known for its religious tolerance. As time went by they became accepted as a denomination. Nevertheless, they distanced themselves from society in general, which was evidenced by their simple clothing and their way of speaking—they used *thee* and *thou* instead of *you*.

QUESTIONS?

Do Quakers go to wars and fight?
Quaker pacifists make an absolute personal stand against war. They refuse to register for selective service and thus forfeit conscientious objectors' status. (You may find it enjoyable and instructive to rent the film *Friendly Persuasion*, which deals with that question.)

The Revolutionary War sparked resentment against the Quakers again because they refused to pay military taxes or to join in the fighting. Some of them were even exiled. After the war their attitudes toward helping improve society and the people in it gained ground. Quaker organizations sprang up in opposition to slavery and poverty, and they formed the "Underground Railroad," which was specifically set up to help runaway slaves escape to the northern states and Canada.

It almost goes without saying that disagreements developed and schisms, two of them actually, eventually resulted in the formation of four groups: the Hicksites, a liberal group mainly in the eastern states; Gurneyites, an evangelical group that had pastors; Wilburites, a more traditional sect; and Orthodox, a Christ-centered group.

Central Beliefs

The beliefs of the various groups and even the members within them were diverse. Quakers are one of the least ritualized religions. Spiritual soul-searching is a common element with them all, culminating in a mutual closeness with God. Much stress is made on the "Inner Light," which has mystical aspects to it in that members receive an immediate sense of God's presence.

Meetings are held to worship God and wait for his word. Generally, members will sit in a circle or a square, facing each other. In some American meetings there may be a pastor to lead it. Sometimes the meetings are silent. At others, members express a new understanding that has come to them. Incidentally, men and women are equal in the faith. Whenever a "message" comes out of these meditations that might require action, it is put to the group, considered, and if there is consensus, then they act on it. The action to be taken generally has a strong social bias to it; something has to be put right irrespective of the consequences to the group or individual members. Thus, courage and conviction are paramount.

FACTS

In business, Friends/Members were trusted as reliable partners, a reputation that allowed them to flourish. There are many successful Quaker firms and banks; Barclay's is a well-known example.

Quakers have no stated creed or ritual, but they do have an agreement, regarding the philosophy and beliefs of the faith. These include: worship is an act of seeking, not asking; the virtues of moral purity, integrity, honesty, simplicity, and humility are to be sought after; there shall be concern for the suffering and unfortunate; and true religion is a personal encounter with God. Quakers refuse to take oaths. They believe that one should tell the truth at all times, therefore an oath is irrelevant. They feel that taking an oath implies that there are two types of truthfulness: one for ordinary life and another for special occasions.

The individuality of the Quakers is embodied in the belief, or not, of life after death. Very few believe there is eternal punishment in hell. They see all life as sacramental with no difference between the secular and the religious. No one thing or activity is any more spiritual than any other. Baptism, in the accepted sense, is not a practiced sacrament; Quakers believe in the "inward baptism of the Holy Spirit" (Ephesians 4: 4–5).

In short, seeking the guidance of the Holy Spirit and reading from the Bible are stressed. Outward rites are rejected as is an ordained ministry. The Society is grounded in the experience of God and the philosophy that God is in everyone, which they believe informs conscience and redirects reason. While the experience of this inner guide is mystical, it is also practical. Meetings to worship God and await his word are essential to Quaker faith and practice. Anyone can go to a Quaker meeting.

Quakerism in Today's World

Meetings are held all year in North America. These include: Friends United Meeting, about fourteen meetings each year; Friends General Conference, some 500 meetings; and Evangelical Friends International and the Friends World Committee for Consultation, which is an international group in London, England.

Today, Quakerism has spread in Africa and Europe.

FACTS

Most of the early suffragist leaders in America were Quakers. In the nineteenth century, American Friends founded colleges such as Earlham, Haverford, and Swarthmore. Individual Friends founded Bryn Mawr College, Cornell University, and Johns Hopkins University. Friends' schools tend to emphasize science.

Quakers have practically and visually contributed to the promotion of tolerance, peace, and justice more than most any other Christian denomination. In 1947, the Society of Friends was awarded the Nobel Peace Prize. It was awarded to the American Friends Service Committee and the (British) Friends Service Council for their active work in ministering to refugees and victims of famine.

Unitarian Universalist Association

Unitarians and Universalists have often been considered heretics because they want to choose their faith, not because they are rebellious.

The roots of the Unitarianism beliefs were formed in Transylvania, which is now the border area of Hungary and Romania. The church was influenced by an important man of the times named Ferenc David who was a convicted heretic. He taught that prayers could not be addressed to Jesus, since Jesus was only a human and not divine. David died in prison. However, the church he founded is the world's oldest surviving Unitarian body.

A similar Unitarian movement developed in England in the seventeenth century with a number of dissenter churches. The early history of the movement is full of dissension. Some of the members wanted to change the name to "Free Christian"; which suggests the way those members approached their vision and version of religious thought. The movement prospered and eventually became the British Unitarian Association.

FACTS

In 1791, the laboratory of an English scientist and Unitarian minister, Joseph Priestly, was burned and he was hounded out of England. He fled to America and established American Unitarian churches in the Philadelphia area.

The origins of the movement in the United States developed slowly in New England out of Congregational autonomy, which stressed moderation, reason, and morals over spiritual revivalism. In 1825, following yet another schism between various sects of the movement, the American Unitarian Association was formed. The church was still not a cohesive unit though, and in many ways was experimenting in its beliefs and the way they would be incorporated into the movement or movements. One might say there was religious diversity. By then the church had expanded its presence to Canada and to the Midwest and the South.

The movement stressed free use of reason in religion and believed that God existed in one person only; they did not believe in the Trinity, and, as did Ferenc David, they also denied the divinity of Jesus Christ. They had no creed and individual congregations varied widely in religious beliefs and practices. For instance, a man named Thomas Starr King is credited with coming up with a definition that endeavored to show the difference between Unitarians and Universalists: "Universalists believe that

God is too good to damn people, and the Unitarians believe that people are too good to be damned by God."

Right from the early days, the movement embraced the marginalized elements of society, and that included the Universalists becoming, in 1863, the first denomination to ordain a woman to the ministry: Olympia Brown. They affirmed that God embraced everyone and that dignity and worth are innate to all people regardless of sex, color, race, or class.

It took until 1961 for a new organization to be formed, this time through a merger of the Universalist Church of America and the American Unitarian Association; there had been other mergers earlier between American and British groups. The new group was called the Unitarian Universalist Association. This association is also a member of the International Association for Religious Freedom. The National Headquarters are in Boston, Massachusetts, with departments dealing with the ministry, religious education, adult education, world service, world churches, and publications. The General Assembly of delegates from churches and fellowships meets annually.

In the Unitarian Universalist Association today, the ethic of embracing all has been extended to include the rights of homosexuals, lesbians, bisexuals, and transgendered persons. Homosexuals and lesbians may be ordained as clergy. In 1996, same-sex marriages were accepted.

While the denomination does not require its members to subscribe to a statement of beliefs or religious doctrine, it has adopted a list of basic principles. These are:

The inherent worth and dignity of every person.
Justice, equity, and compassion in human relations.
Acceptance of one another and encouragement to spiritual growth in congregations.
A free and responsible search for truth and meaning.
The right of conscience and the use of democratic process within our congregations and in society at large.
The goal of world community with peace, liberty, and justice for all.
Respect for the interdependent web of all existence of which we are a part.

CHAPTER 6

Islam and Islamic Sects

Islam is a major world religion that originated in the Middle East after Judaism and Christianity. While the distribution of Islam throughout the world generally covers Africa, the Middle East, and sections of Asia and Europe, it is becoming a growing religious factor in the United States. More than six million Muslims are United States residents and that number increases every year.

Muhammad

The founder and prophet of Islam, Muhammad was born in Arabia in 570 C.E. He belonged to the Quraysh tribe, whose members served as custodians of the sacred places in Mecca.

As an adult he became a respected and successful trader. On a trading journey to Syria he was put in charge of the merchandise of a rich middle-aged woman. She was so taken with him that she offered herself in marriage. She eventually bore him six children, two sons and four daughters. The best known of these children was Fatima who became the wife of Muhammad's cousin Ali, who was regarded as Muhammad's divinely ordained successor.

Muhammad was known for his charm, courage, impartiality, and resoluteness. He was considered a man of virtuous character who epitomized what would later become the Islamic ideal. His personal revelation came when he was meditating in a cave outside the city of Makkah when he was forty years old. He had a vision of the angel Gabriel who said to him, "Recite." Muhammad refused three times until the angel said, "Recite in the name of thy Lord who created." The words that were given to Muhammad declared the oneness and power of God, to whom worship should be made.

Following his revelation, Muhammad began preaching. It was a turbulent time of military conquest and political expansion throughout the area, and Muhammad met with opposition. He and his followers fled the persecution and migrated to Medina, where his teachings began to be accepted and the first Islamic community was founded.

FACTS

Arabia in the seventh century C.E. was host to many religions, including Christianity, Buddhism, Judaism, and Zoroastrianism. Geographically, it covered an area that bordered on the Byzantine Christian Empire, Yemen, and the boarders of the Zoroastrian Persian Empire. Muhammad traveled widely and studied with followers of other tribes and religions, among them Syrian Christians and many Jews.

The major achievements of Muhammad were the founding of a state and a religion. He was politically successful, created a federation of Arab tribes, and made the religion of Islam the basis of Arab unity. He died in 632 C.E. in Medina.

What followed was an amazing expansion of the Muslim faith throughout a large part of the world from Spain to Central Asia to India, Turkey, Africa, Indonesia, Malaya, and China—the same areas where the Muslims were very active traders. But, the expansion was also due to suppression of alternate religious faiths. Jews and Christians were given a special status; they had to pay a tax to maintain their religious autonomy. Other religions were given a different choice: Accept Islam or die.

In the early days of the faith, Islam became a part of both the spiritual and temporal aspects of Muslim life. There was not only an Islamic religious institution but also Islamic law, state, and other government institutions. It wasn't until the twentieth century that the religious and secular were formally separated. Even so, Islam actually draws no absolute distinction between the religious and temporal parts of life; the Muslim state is by definition religious.

Central Beliefs

Islam is a monotheistic religion—Allah is the sole god, the creator, sustainer, and restorer of the world. The overall purpose of humanity is to serve Allah, to worship him alone, and to construct a moral lifestyle.

The Five Pillars of Islam were set down as the anchor for life as a Muslim. A Muslim should express belief in them and uphold them in his or her daily life. They are:

1. **Profession of faith.** There is no God, but God; Muhammad is the prophet of God. Sometimes a variation is used: There is no God, but God and Muhammad is his prophet.
2. **Prayer.** A Muslim must pray five times a day facing Mecca: before sunrise, just after noon, later in the afternoon, immediately before sunset, and after dark.

3. **The *Zakat.*** Each Muslim must pay a *zakat* to the state government. (A *zakat* is an obligatory tax paid once a year.)

4. **Fasting.** A Muslim must fast for the month of Ramadan (the ninth Muslim month). Fasting begins at daybreak and ends at sunset. During the fasting day eating, drinking, smoking, and sexual intercourse are forbidden.

5. **Hajj.** Hajj means pilgrimage. A Muslim must make a pilgrimage to Mecca at least once in his or her lifetime provided they are physically and financially able.

FACTS

A person who practices Islam is called a Muslim. The Arabic term *Islam* means "surrender," which provides a strong indication of the fundamental underpinning of the faith. A believer, a Muslim, surrenders to the will of Allah (Arabic for God).

Holy Writings

The Qur'an (also known as the Koran) is the holy book of Islam. According to one Muslim tradition, it was written by God and revealed to Muhammad by the angel Gabriel over the period of his life from his first revelation when he was forty until his death at sixty-two. In another of the many traditions regarding the writing of the Qur'an Muhammad had the revelations written down on pieces of paper, stones, palm leaves, or whatever writing materials were available. It is believed that he indicated to the scribes the context in which the passages should be placed.

After the prophet's death, it was decided to find people who had learned the words by heart and to locate written excerpts from all parts of the Muslim Empire. The resulting information was edited to complete a correct edition of the work.

Thus, an authoritative text of the Qur'an was eventually produced. It is held in very high regard. Its Arabic language is considered to be unsurpassed in beauty and purity. To imitate the style of the Qur'an is a sacrilege.

The Qur'an is the primary source of every Muslim's faith and practice. It deals with the subjects that concern all human beings: wisdom, beliefs, worship, and law. However, it focuses on the relationship between God and his creatures. It also provides guidelines for a just society, proper human relationships, and equal division of power. The Qur'an also posits that life is a test and that everyone will be rewarded or punished for their actions in the life after this one. For example, on the last day, when the world will come to an end, the dead will be resurrected, and a judgment will be pronounced on every person in accordance with his or her deeds.

FACTS

Mecca is the birthplace of Muhammad and is the most sacred city in Islam. According to tradition, Muslims around the world must face Mecca during their daily prayers. Every year, during the last month of the Islamic calendar, more than one million Muslims make a pilgrimage, or hajj, to Mecca.

Another source of Islamic doctrine is the Hadith (a report or collection of sayings attributed to the prophet and members of the early Muslim community). The Hadith is second only to the authority of the Qur'an. It has been thought of as the biography of Muhammad made from the long memory of the members of his community. Hadith was a vital element during the first three centuries of Islamic history, and its study gives a broad index into the philosophy of Islam.

To the non-Muslim, the Hadith is virtually an introduction to the world of Islam with almost encyclopedic inclusiveness. Provisions of law are the primary element, dealing with the moral, social, commercial, and personal aspects of life and the theological aspects of death and final destiny. The content of the Hadith has the kind of minutia found in the Talmud, the body of Jewish civil and ceremonial law and legend.

There is evidence of the impact on Islam of Jewish and Christian philosophies and theology, particularly as they relate to the last judgment.

The Qur'an and the Hadith form the basis of Islamic law.

Worship and Practices

The Qur'an forbids the worshiping of idols, which means that Muslims are not permitted to make images either of Allah or of the prophet. Some Muslims object to any form of representational art because of the inherent danger of idolatry. For this reason, mosques are often decorated with geometric patterns.

A great sin in Islam is something called shirk, or blasphemy. The Qur'an stresses that God does not share his powers with any partner. It warns that those who believe their idols will intercede for them will find that they and the idols will become fuel for hellfire on the Day of Judgment.

Many of Muhammad's restrictions in the Qur'an were explicit in establishing distinctions between Arabs and Jews as shown, for example, in his dietary rules, which borrowed heavily from the Mosaic Law. The most radical difference between the Qur'an and Mosaic laws has to do with intoxicating beverages. Jews frown on alcoholic beverages, but they do not forbid them entirely; wine is an important element in many Jewish rituals and feasts. However, Muhammad absolutely forbade the use of such beverages.

FACTS

Different grades of shirk have been identified in Islamic law. The shirk of custom includes all superstitions, such as the belief in omens. The shirk of knowledge, for instance, is to credit anyone, such as astrologers, with knowledge of the future.

Prayer and Mosques

Prayer has been described as the act of communication by humans with the sacred or holy. The Islamic Qur'an is regarded as a book of prayers as is the book of Psalms in the Bible, which is considered to be a meditation on Biblical history turned into prayer. Prayer obviously takes as many forms as there are religions.

The act of prayer in Islam, as we know, is prescribed: Muslims are expected to pray five times a day at definite times wherever they happen to be. In addition to that practice, on Fridays all Muslim men are also expected to attend the mosque for the after-midday prayer. Friday is not an identifiable holy day in the manner that Christians and Jews, for instance, consider the Sabbath. In Islam, business may go on as usual either before or after the midday prayers.

A mosque is actually defined in Islam as any house or open area of prayer.

QUESTIONS?

What's the purpose of mosques?
The first mosques were modeled on Muhammad's place of worship, which was the courtyard of his house in Medina. The first mosques were just plots of earth marked out as sacred.

Islam teaches that the whole world is a mosque because a person can pray to God anywhere. Islam makes no distinction between what is sacred and the everyday. However, every mosque has an area with a water supply so that the devout may wash their hands, feet, and face before prayer; Muslims may use sand for washing if water isn't available.

There is no prescribed architectural design for mosques. They generally have a minaret in an elevated place, usually a tower, for the crier or muezzin to proclaim the call to worship.

The muezzin's call to worship is followed by the imam, who leads the community prayers, and then the *khatib*, who often preaches the Friday sermon. Sometimes the imam performs all three functions. The imam is not a priest. Although he can't perform any rites, he usually conducts marriages and funerals. The imam generally acts as a leader of the local Muslim community and gives advice about Islamic law and customs. He's picked for his wisdom.

The muezzin who proclaims the call to prayer stands at either the door or side of a small mosque or on the minaret of a large mosque. He faces each of the four directions in turn: east, west, north, and south. To each direction he cries:

Allah is most great.
I testify that there is no God but Allah.
I testify that Muhammad is the
prophet of Allah.
Come to prayer.
Come to salvation.
Allah is most great.
There is no God but Allah.

Many mosques have installed loudspeaker recordings to be used at the call to prayer. There may also be slight variations in the call.

Islam does not use liturgical vestments in the way many religions do, instead it has universal regulations governing dress. For example, all who enter a mosque must remove their footwear; and all individuals on a pilgrimage must wear the same habit, the *hiram*, and thus appear in holy places as a beggar.

Inside a mosque no representations of Allah, or of any humans, plants, or animals are allowed. Women who attend, particularly in America, should wear a head scarf, and avoid wearing jewelry, particularly any that might depict people or animals or Jewish or Christian religious imagery. Modesty should be the guiding factor. Muslim girls and women cover their hair completely.

While women may attend prayers in a mosque, they are seated in a separate area, often upstairs, if there is one, in a gallery, so that neither sex is distracted.

On Fridays, the imam often gives a sermon that addresses both political and religious problems or points of interest.

All Muslim prayer is made facing Makkah (Mecca). When prayers are held congregationally, people stand in rows shoulder to shoulder with no gaps or reserved spaces. All are considered equal when standing before God. Muslim prayers are memorized; new members of the faith generally have someone to guide them until they commit the prayers to memory.

Rituals and Customs

Birth is not observed in any established routine manner; local traditions vary greatly. Many Muslims wish that the first sounds a baby hears is the call to prayer whispered in each ear. Boys must be circumcised between the ages of seven days and twelve years.

Marriage in Islam is considered God's provision for humanity. No value is given to celibacy. Parents are responsible for choosing marriage partners for their children. Marriage is considered to be a joining of two families, not just two people. However, the Qur'an says that the girl must give her consent and not be forced into marriage.

Marriage is a contract between a man and a woman, not a religious rite. Although it does not have to be performed in a mosque with an imam in attendance, it must be conducted according to Islamic law with two male Muslim witnesses. Nevertheless, marriage is seen as a state blessed by God.

Divorce is allowed, but it is certainly discouraged. Islamic law allows a man to have more than one wife; in traditional Islamic societies, this is one way of trying to make sure that women can have the protection of family life. However, the Prophet Muhammad advised that unless a man feels able to treat the wives equally he should marry only one.

Observant Muslims believe that their deaths are predetermined by Allah as part of his design. Therefore, death should not be feared for the deceased will go to Paradise. To overdo mourning would show a mistrust of God's love and mercy.

In Islam, on the Day of Judgment Allah will raise all the dead and judge them. The good will go to Paradise, the others to the fire.

After death, the body is ritually washed and wrapped in a linen shroud. All Muslims regardless of sect are dressed in the standard grave clothes, which number three: an upper shroud, a lower garment, and an overall shroud. Only martyrs are buried in the clothes in which they die, without their bodies or garments being washed. As evidence of their state of glory, the blood and dirt are on view.

Festivals and Celebrations

There are few major Islamic festivals in the year. However, local Muslim communities have their own traditions, which add to the year's festivities.

QUESTIONS?

Do Muslims follow a different calendar from the western world?
Yes, they do. The Islamic calendar is lunar, and unlike most other lunar calendars, is not adjusted to keep in step with the solar year. Thus, Muslim dates tend to change constantly in relation to the western solar calendar. Years are counted from the prophet Muhammad's move to Medina in 622 C.E. The year 2000 C.E. was 1420/21 A.H. (in the year of Hegira).

Muharram is the first month of the year in Islam. New Year's Day is not a major holiday. Ramadan is the ninth month of the Muslim year. Ramadan is a month of fasting. Adult Muslims do not eat, drink, smoke, or have conjugal relations from dawn to sunset. Children under the age of puberty are exempt, although they make a limited fast.

Lailat ul-Qadr, also known as The Night of Determination, is believed to have occurred around the twenty-seventh, but is now considered one of the last ten nights of Ramadan. Many Muslims spend these days and nights in the mosque, so as to be in prayer on The Night of Determination when Allah makes decisions about the destiny of individuals and the world as a whole.

Eid ul-Fitr celebrates the end of the month of fasting and lasts for three days. Prayers are offered, special foods prepared, and gifts are exchanged.

Eid ul-Adha, known as the Feast of Sacrifice, celebrates the willingness of Abraham to sacrifice his son Isaac when God asked him to. God commanded a lamb be sacrificed instead of Ishmael. The sacrifice of a lamb is an important part of the festival.

Al-Isra Wal Miraj is the night of the ascension of Muhammad to Heaven to meet with Allah. It is celebrated on the twenty-seventh day of the seventh month. It is said the prophet set out the disciplines of the daily prayers.

Muhammad-Maulid al-Nabi celebrates the birth of the prophet Muhammad. It is held on the twelfth day of the third month and is a highly popular festival that draws thousands of visitors who join in processions and prayers.

The purpose of the Muslim ceremony called the *dhikr* is to glorify Allah and seek spiritual perfection. In the performance part of this ceremony, participants dress in conical hats and black mantles, and they dance in a building where their members sit in a circle and listen to music. Then, slowly standing to greet the master, they take off their black coats to show white shirts and waistcoats. Beginning to revolve rhythmically, they then throw back their heads and raise the palms of their right hands—keeping their left hands down. The rhythm accelerates, they whirl faster and faster and faster until they are in a trance in which they lose themselves trying to seek union with Allah. These participants are called the whirling dervishes.

Developments of Modern Islam

To be a Muslim, or at least a reasonably devout one, is a way of life. Whereas other religions usually have a division, if not marked then implied, between the secular and the religious, that is not the case with Muslims. Daily life is where Islam resides—the religion is about a way of living. The Qur'an and the Hadith provide the guidance to carry that out.

Islamic Law

Islamic law is founded on the *shari'ah* that is based on the Qur'an, the Hadith, and the advice and wisdom of scholars. Allah is seen as the supreme lawgiver. The integration of this philosophy is directly related to the demographics of the country where Islam is being practiced. In countries where Muslims are in the minority, the integration of religion and secular activities will be less than where Muslims are in the majority. Money comes under the guidance of the Qur'an, which forbids usury and the charging of interest, but it approves making a fair profit. Naturally, this can be difficult to implement in a world market. In the Qur'an, business dealings and their outcome are described as "seeking the bounty of God." Wealth made should be used first for the support of family, then given to those in need. The Qur'an also forbids gambling.

FACTS

Because of Western influence in the Middle East generally and the operation and economics of interest-based banks, many Muslims have abandoned the ban on usury. But many countries have Islamic, non–interest-bearing banks in Muslim communities.

Jihad

Jihad in Arabic means fighting or striving. In Islam, it is a doctrine that calls upon believers to devote themselves to combating the enemies of their religion. The term has been used to describe a "holy war," even though this is not its literal meaning. Historically, the term was applied in wars both between various Muslim sects and non-Muslim ones.

Family Life

Family life is an essential part of the Muslim way of living. All family members should care for one another. The Prophet Muhammad made particular reference about a man taking care of his mother. Animals, too, are to be respected and treated in ways that do not violate their lives in the family or community. Animals that are being used for food must be slaughtered in the correct way. Pig meat is strictly forbidden. The Qur'an outlaws alcohol.

Sunnis and Shiites

Of the two main groups within Islam, the Sunni compose about 90 percent of all adherents and the Shiites about 10 percent. Sunni Muslims look at themselves as the traditional, mainstream, pragmatic branch of Islam; in fact, they became known as the orthodox element in Islam. This claim, however, is in dispute as it is considered that all orientations in Islam are a result of the common Islamic origin.

Religious and Political Differences

In early Islamic history, the Shiites were the more political of the two groups. When problems arose over the rightful successors to Muhammad, the Sunni said the first four caliphs were Muhammad's rightful successors, whereas the opposing minority, the Shiites, believed that Muslim leadership belonged to Muhammad's son-in-law, Ali, and then to his descendants. This disagreement led to continuous internal wars that proved to be, from Ali's point of view, largely unsuccessful. However, Ali's status was eventually recognized, and he was made a major hero of Sunni Islam.

In contrast to the Shiites, who believed that the leadership of Islam was determined by divine order or inspiration, the Sunni regarded leadership as the result of the prevailing Muslim political realities. Historically, the leadership was in the hands of the foremost families of Mecca. For the Sunni, balance between spiritual and political authority afforded both the correct exercise of religious order and practical maintenance of the Muslim world.

In the late twentieth century, the Sunni made up the majority of Muslims in all nations except Iran, Iraq, Bahrain, and perhaps Yemen. All in all, they numbered nearly one billion.

Sunni orthodoxy placed strong emphasis on the majority view of the community. Over the years this perspective provided them the opportunity to include matters that were outside the root teaching of the Qur'an. Thus, the Sunni have earned the reputation of being religiously and culturally diverse.

The religious and political differences between the Sunni and the Shiite have been fraught with enmity and dissension throughout history. Today, Iran is the bastion of Shiite Islam—its state religion—and the majority of Iranians are Shiites. Even so, people in Iran do practice other religions, such as Judaism, Christianity, and even Zoroastrianism, an ancient faith that predates Judaism. Shiite adherents also live in Syria, East Africa, India, and Pakistan. Overall, Shiites comprise somewhere in the region of eighty million people, or a tenth of all Moslems. For instance, the Kurdish, who live in northern Iran, Iraq, and eastern Turkey, are Sunni Muslims.

The Shiites maintain that only those in the bloodline of Muhammad are the legitimate heirs of Islam. Shiitism is often called "twelver" because Iranians generally recognized only twelve imams, or supreme religious leaders, following the death of Muhammad. The twelfth of these is Mardi, the so-called hidden imam, who is believed to still be alive in some celestial state. The ayatollahs, highly respected scholars and teachers of Islam, are thought to be standing in for Mardi as they interpret the words of Muhammad.

Religious Practices

The religious practices of the Shiites are different from those of the Sunni. For devout Shiites, a pilgrimage to Mecca is the most important religious practice, but they also visit the tombs of the eleven earthly imams, and Iranians frequently cross the boarder into Iraq to visit the tomb of Ali.

In the twentieth century, Shiites became a major political force in Iran, where they deposed a secularist monarchy, and in Lebanon, where they led resistance to Israeli occupation in the south during the 1980s and 1990s.

The Shiites, from a western point of view, would probably be considered the most conservative of the two main factions in Islam. Their doctrine has always firmly revolved around the Qur'an, and in modern times, they have become the chief voice of militant Islamic fundamentalism.

Sufism

Sufism—a mystical sect—arose in Islam around 661 C.E. as an apparent reaction against the worldliness of the Muslim community of the time. Sufism sought the truth of divine love and knowledge through direct personal experience with Allah.

FACTS

The meaning of the word *jihad* in most Muslim sects is "fighting or striving" to fulfill a duty in one of four ways—the heart, the tongue, the hand, and the sword. The Sufis chose the first of the four, "the greater jihad," which is by the heart.

Sufism has influenced parts of Muslim society. The orthodox Muslims, of course, disagreed with Sufi beliefs and actions—saint worship, musical performance, visiting tombs, and miracle mongering, to name a few. They thought that the Sufi leaders could gain dangerous authority and political influence over illiterate villagers in backward areas.

However, by educating the masses and deepening the spiritual side of their lives, Sufism made an important contribution to those members of Muslim society. For all the criticism they created for themselves, the Sufis scrupulously observed the commands of the divine law.

Probably the greatest contribution they made to the Islamic community flowed from their love of Persian poetry. The mystics also contributed to national and regional literature where they provided artistic works in not only their own language but also the languages of the local adherents, for instance, Punjabi and Urdu-speaking areas of South Asia and in Turkey. The literature produced during this highly creative time of the Sufis is considered to be the golden age among Arabic, Persian, and Turkish languages.

The Sufis were responsible for tremendous missionary activity throughout the world, which continues today.

Over the years Sufism has declined in many countries. But, in the West, Sufism has been popularized recently. Whether or not this is a fad or is a devout attempt can't be said. What is known is that Sufism requires strict discipline before its goal of divine love is achieved.

CHAPTER 7

Hinduism and Hindu Sects

Hindus see their religion as a continuous, seemingly eternal, existence—not just a religion but a way of life. Its collection of customs, obligations, traditions, and ideals far exceed the recent Christian and Western secularist tendency to think of religion primarily as a system of beliefs.

Origins and Development

Although the English coined the word Hinduism sometime around the beginning of the nineteenth century, the name Hindu has been in the language ever since Greek times. Some Hindus did not take to the word Hinduism, preferring the ancient name: Vedic. The Vedic texts are known as the Vedas and they provide the only textual source for understanding the religious life of ancient India. Veda means "sacred knowledge" or "learning" in Sanskrit, the oldest written language of India.

The Vedas were not an easy read. In the beginning they were comprised of 1,000 hymns, which served the priestly families; these were followed by the Veda of Chants with musical notations for the performance of sacred songs. Prose works were added to explain the ceremonial aspects of the text.

Over the years Vedic rites became so complicated and had so many rules that only highly trained priests could read the texts explaining them. It was from this background and legacy that the practice and belief in Hinduism evolved. The textbooks on Hinduism, composed in the early twentieth century, were written by Hindus to explain the faith so that it could be taught to their young.

More than any other major religions, Hinduism celebrates the breadth and depth of its complex, multileveled spectrum of beliefs. Hinduism encompasses all forms of belief and worship. It has been said that no religious idea in India ever dies; it merely combines with the new ideas that arise in response to it. There is a Hindu prayer: "May good thoughts come to us from all sides."

Hindus see the divine in everything and are tolerant of all doctrines. A Hindu may embrace another religion without giving up being a Hindu because he or she is disposed to regard other forms of worship and divergent doctrines as inadequate rather than wrong.

Hinduism has more than 650 million adherents in India and at least 100 million in the rest of the world. Of these, 700,000 are in South Africa, nearly 600,000 in North America, and 500,000 in the United Kingdom. Its wide variety of beliefs has evolved in many different ways. Hinduism is an intrinsic part of the cultural fabric of India.

Hinduism has neither a single prophet nor one god to worship. Rather it offers a plethora of ideas—a metaphor for the gods. It has been called a civilization and congregation of religions. Hinduism has no beginning, no founder, no central authority, no hierarchy, and no organization. Every attempt to classify or define Hinduism has proved to be unsatisfactory in one way or another. These efforts have been compounded because the scholars of the faith have emphasized different aspects of the whole.

Hindu Deities

While they do not worship one single ultimate god, Hindus do believe in a supreme being who has unlimited forms. This is not a contradiction in terms, because of the many forms these deities take. For instance, Vishnu and Lakshmi have the full powers of a god, but Brahm and Sarasvati have only partial godlike aspects. The Hindu approach to all this has their philosophy of nonspecific inclusion at its core.

The search for the worship of the "One that is All" is made through a favorite divinity, of which there are many. However there is no exclusivity in the choice of the divinity to worship during the search. Imagine that the search for the "One that is All" is like a revolving glass mirrored ball in a dance hall. The observer meditates on the search and a beam of light goes on illuminating one side of the glass ball, which is slowly turning in the light. As it turns, mirrored facets are visible and the observer selects one on which to concentrate. The ball is the "One that is All," its mirrored facets are its deities.

Hindu teachings revolve around what, to western eyes, might seem to be a vast series of interlocking narratives, rather like the actions in a play. In fact, that is exactly how some of them are presented. Their purpose is to draw the Hindu audience into a discourse. For several years people have responded to prominent stories of a divine play and interactions between gods and humans. In watching the narratives being played out, Hindus have often experienced themselves as members of a single imagined family. To play out the narratives, a deity enters this world as an *avatar*—a deity who descends and is manifest in a bodily form.

Among the most popular and best-known avatars are some of the ten incarnations of Vishnu, which include Krishna and Rama. Krishna is probably number one in popularity.

The plot of such a presentation follows. Women performers sometimes act out the story of a popular narrative called *ramayana*. The cast is comprised of Rama, Sita, and the wicked Havana. It is a tragic story, one of love, honor, and courage. Havana kidnaps Sita. Rama rescues Sita and kills Havana, but the lovers are forced to separate. The story represents the tragedy of life in the real world where love of the soul for god is constantly being tested.

Central Beliefs

In an effort to tie down the belief in a way that is palatable to western thought, maybe it's not a bad idea to start with what is concrete, or appears so, or is at least explainable, or partially so. In Hinduism, the law of karma states that all actions produce effects in the future. A concept that is linked to karma is that of dharma, one's duty or station in this life. The relationship between dharma and karma is discussed at length in Bhagavad-Gita, a major text within the Hindu tradition.

Reincarnation

Indigenous to this belief is the idea of reincarnation. In more technical terms, Hindus accept the doctrine of transmigration and rebirth, and believe that previous acts are the factors that determine the condition into which a being is reborn in one form or another. The idea of reincarnation is virtually universal in India.

According to a basic Hindu concept, people are born over and over again into a state of suffering. Deeply involved in this transformation is a Sanskrit word, *atman*—the self, the eternal core of the personality that survives after death that is headed to a new life or is released from the bonds of existence. The atman is inextricably joined with brahman, the Being itself, a concept that may also be thought of as high god. To be released from the cycle of rebirth, one must attain the atman/brahman identity. That is, one must become one with Being.

One reason people keep getting born over and over into suffering is that they do not understand this connection. As long as people think atman is separate from braham, or world-soul, the cycle will continue forever.

The philosophy of the doctrine of karma and reincarnation came to the Hindus from the Vedic Faiths.

Spiritual Goal

Another Sanskrit word, *moksha,* reflects the ultimate spiritual goal—the individual soul's release from the bonds of transmigration—to get out of the endless cycle of reincarnation. Now, if the individual is hampered by bad karma, moksha will not occur. But, if the individual has achieved moksha, then the atman is free to reunite with brahman, thus concluding the cycle of suffering. Those who do not accept that his or her being is identical with brahman are thought to be deluded—in such cases, you might say that the atman is clouded by maya, illusion. The only possible solution is to come to the realization that the core of human personality (atman) really is brahman. What is believed to block this understanding is the attachment to worldly goods, an obsession that prevents people from reaching salvation and eternal peace. (Hindus sometimes use the largely Buddhist term *nirvana* to describe this state.)

To add to the difficulties in understanding this process it should be noted that meanings and interpretations differ from one Hindu school to another. In spite of that, most of them agree that *moksha* is the highest purpose in life.

Brahman is a word meaning spirit. It is considered to be the energy that keeps the universe going and is present in all things. It is said that it is impossible to describe, and they are probably right. It has been said to mean world-soul or world-spirit.

The Caste System

To some, Plato's *Republic* might have a relevance to the early Hindu doctrine of dividing society into groups, each of which had a role and a place. Brahmins were the priests; Kshatriyas were the warriors; Vaishyas were the merchants; and Shudras were the craftspeople.

This division was the beginning of the Indian caste system. As it progressed into Indian society, the castes multiplied, encompassing a vast range of occupations, rules, and traditions. The *Laws of Manu* (circa 100 C.E.) provide the text that explains all the complexities of this system. One's caste and one's station in life determines one's dharma. Members of one caste would not socialize or trade with another. Certain professions were limited to certain castes. Intermarriage between members of different castes was not permitted.

Eventually, a group (caste) who called themselves Dalit (downtrodden) formed. Members of this caste did what we might call the dirty grunt work, the menial work, such as street cleaning and clearing away dead bodies, either human or animal. They became known at the "untouchables."

In 1950, a law was passed outlawing the practice of "untouchability"; nevertheless, this group remains socially and economically the dregs of the caste system. It is said that some members of the caste deny that they are Hindus in an effort to overcome the stigma of Dalit.

There are arguments made that the caste system offers a strong sense of belonging and identity.

Holy Writings

The sacred scriptures of the Hindus are the Veda (knowledge). They were written in the ancient language of India, Sanskrit, and were considered to be the creation of neither human nor god. They were believed to be the eternal truth that was revealed or heard by gifted seers. Most of the Veda has been superceded by other Hindu doctrines. Nevertheless, their influence has been pervasive and long lasting.

In the western world, two publications stand out in the vast collection of Hindu scriptures and texts—The Upanishads and The Bhagavad-Gita.

The Upanishads

The Upanishads record the wisdom of Hindu teachers and sages who were active as far back as 1000 B.C.E. The texts form the basis of Indian philosophy. As they represent the final stage in the tradition of the Vedas, the teaching based on them is known as the Vedanta (Conclusion of the Veda).

The philosophical thrust of the Upanishads is discerning the nature of reality. Other concepts dealt with include equating atman (the self) with Brahman (ultimate reality), which is fundamental to all Hindu thought; the nature of morality and eternal life; and the themes of transmigration of souls and causality in creation.

Various translations of the Upanishads were published in Europe during the nineteenth century. Though they were not the best of translations, they had a profound effect on many philosophical academics, including Arthur Schopenhauer.

The Bhagavad-Gita

The Bhagavad-Gita has been the exemplary text of Hindu culture for centuries. The Sanskrit title has been interpreted as "Song of the Lord," which is a philosophical poem in the form of a dialogue. Although it is an independent sacred text, it is also considered to be the sixth book in the Mahabharata.

The Mahabharata—the longest great Indian war epic poem—contains mythological stories and philosophical discussions. One of the main story lines is the conflict between Yudhishthira, the hero of the poem, and his duty or dharma. The Bhagavad-Gita's structure is in the form of a dialogue between two characters—Arjuna, the hero preparing to go into battle, and Krishna, his charioteer. But, Krishna is not quite what he seems. Arjuna is characterized by not only his physical prowess but also his spiritual prowess, which involves a mystical friendship with Krishna. From the start, Arjuna knows that his charioteer is no ordinary mortal. The power of Krishna's divinity gradually unfolds in all of its terrible glory, and Arjuna sees himself mirrored in the divine.

Such is the power of the Bhagavad-Gita that Henry David Thoreau took a copy with him to Walden Pond and made subsequent mention of it in his own works. The Bhagavad-Gita is a complex piece of philosophical writing, and it has influenced almost all later developments in Hindu thought. The present text is thought to be around 2,000 years old.

The following example from The Bhagavad-Gita, Krishna's Counsel in Time of War (translated by Barbara Stoler Miller, Bantam Books), is taken from The Tenth Teaching, Fragments of Divine Power, 18–24. Remember, it is a dialogue between two people.

Arjuna

Recount in full extent
The discipline and power of your self
Krishna, I can never hear enough
Of your immortal speech.

Lord Krishna

Listen, Arjuna, as I recount
For you in essence
The divine powers of my self;
Endless is my extent.

I am the self abiding
In the heart of all creatures;
I am their beginning,
Their middle, and their end.

I am Vishnu striding among the sun gods,
The radiant sun among lights;
I am lightning among wind gods,
The moon among the stars.

I am the song in sacred lore;
I am Indra, king of the gods;
I am the mind of the senses,
The consciousness of creatures.

I am gracious Shiva among howling storm gods,
The lord of wealth among demigods and demons,
Fire blazing among the bright gods;
I am gold Meru towering over the mountains.

Arjuna, know me as the god's teacher,
Chief of the household priests;
I am the god of war among generals;
I am the ocean of lakes. . . .

Worship and Practices

Hindu worship is called *puja* and encompasses the ceremonial practices that take place in the home or in the temple. The majority of the worship is carried out in the home because Hinduism is part of life, so there are no special days for worship. Any time is a time for worship. *Puja* is the daily expression of devotion. Virtually every home has a shrine with images of the gods and goddesses.

The ceremonial practices vary considerably according to sect, community, location, time of day, and requirements of the worshiper. An image of the worshiper's chosen deity is displayed in the home and accorded the honor that would be given to a royal guest. The worship can be modest or elaborate depending on the circumstances. A daily *puja* might involve offerings of flowers, fruit, rice, incense, sandalwood paste, and milk water. If a *puja* is performed at a mealtime, food will be placed at the shrine blessing it before it is consumed. Also included might be a circumambulation of the shrine in the home. The temple would probably have a path circling the shrine. In either case the worshipers chant their prayers as they walk.

An important type of *puja*, in both the temple or at home, is waving a lighted lamp before the image of a deity or person to be honored. The worshiper circles the image with the lamp three or more times in a clockwise direction while chanting prayers or singing hymns.

Hindu temples range from buildings that can accommodate hundreds of worshipers to simple village shrines. However, the layout, both inside and out, is nearly universal. Most temples will have a ceremonial chariot called a rath, which is like a miniature temple on wheels. A small version of the main deity is placed on it. It is used in processions at festivals. The temple will have a shrine room for one or more deities in which only a Brahmin priest may perform the *puja*.

The variations among temples will, of course, be considerable ranging from the elaborate to the simple. But, the mode and philosophy of worship will follow the same principles; devotees will endeavor to create a constant exchange of love and commitment between themselves and the deities.

Rituals and Customs

Hindu domestic life cycle rites are called *samskara*. The sacraments are designed to make a person fit for the next phase of his or her life by removing sins. Historically, there was a lengthy array of sacraments; which have been reduced to sixteen, many of which are bundled in the childhood phase.

Birth

Traditionally, birth rites included a prenatal rite for the prospective father to affect the child to be fair or dark, a learned son or daughter, and so on. This was called the impregnation rite. During pregnancy there were other rites, but, of course, the most important one was at the birth.

There are mixed opinions about the Hindu name-giving ceremony, which culminates in the father whispering the child's name into his or her ear. In modern times, many of the rites have fallen into disuse.

Marriage

Marriage is the most important rite. Once a suitable spouse has been found for the son or daughter, the match must be approved by both sets of parents. The approval process may include hiring the local astrologer to draw up the couple's horoscopes. Once mutual approval is achieved and the bride's family pays a dowry to the groom, the ceremony can proceed. As with most marriage ceremonies, the rite includes prayers, and songs of blessing.

At the conclusion of the ceremony, the bride and groom offer their right hands, which are symbolically bound together with cotton thread that has been dyed with yellow turmeric. Water is then sprinkled over them. Then, they walk around a prepared sacred fire three times. The final ritual is for the bride and groom to take seven steps and make a vow at each step. The steps represent food, strength, prosperity, well-being, children, happy seasons, and harmony in their marriage. That's it; the couple is now married and after the typical prayers, the wedding feast begins.

Death

When a Hindu dies the body is usually cremated. Cremation is chosen because of the Hindu belief in reincarnation, thus the body is not required after death, only the atman (soul). The body is bathed, wrapped in a new cloth, and laid on a stretcher. Depending on whether the cremation is to take place on a river with the body laid on a pyre or put into a coffin and taken to the crematorium, appropriate scriptures are recited. After the cremation, and if practical, the ashes, flowers, and bones are collected and scattered on a body of water.

Calendar of Religious Festivals

The Republic of India uses the Gregorian calendar for its secular life. For its Hindu religious life, it uses the traditional Hindu calendar, which is based on a year of lunar months. The discrepancy between the years—365 days (solar) and 354 days (lunar)—is resolved by intercalation of an extra month every thirty months. Each month is divided into a bright fortnight (two weeks) when the moon is waxing and a dark fortnight when it is waning.

It may come as no surprise that Hinduism has an extensive range of festivals both in India and throughout the rest of the world. Many of them are accompanied by chanting, music, dancing, singing, and even the use of stains using watercolors and powder. Following are the nine major traditional religious festivals that are, generally, universally celebrated:

- Mahashivaratri celebrates the new moon night of every month, honoring the image of Shiva.
- Sarasvati Puja honors the goddess Sarasvati who is the patron of the arts and learning.
- Holi celebrates the grain harvest in India and also recalls the pranks Krishna played as a young man.
- Rama Naumi celebrates the birthday of the god Rama.
- On Rata Yatra a huge image of the god Vishnu is placed on an enormous chariot and pulled through the streets.
- The Raksha Bandhan is a ceremony of tying a rakhi (a thread or band, made of silk or decorated with flowers).
- Janmashtami celebrates the birth of Krishna and his delivery from the demon Kansa.
- Navaratri honors the most important female deity, Durga, consort of Shiva.
- Divali—the most widely celebrated festival—celebrates the return from exile of Rama and Sita.

Vishnu

Vishnu is a principal Hindu deity. According to ancient Hindu literature there were 33,333 deities; the figure was amended upwards, then downwards until it came to what are called "The Thirty-Three." The worship of Vishnu and his many incarnations, which came to be known as Vaishnavism, gave rise to diverse groups that had slightly different beliefs, which were practiced in different parts of India. As in many beliefs, the followers tended to adapt from the original core of the belief to add or subtract something of their own.

Some believers feared that if Vishnu, often referred to as "the Preserver," departed the whole world, it would be destroyed. Vishnu blesses his devotees with freedom from material desires, thus releasing them from the cycle of reincarnation.

A key to understanding Hinduism is grasping the meaning of the word *avatar*. In Sanskrit it means "descent." As interpreted, it means an incarnation of a deity in either human or animal form to carry out a particular purpose. Vishnu is known as the protector, the binding force that holds the universe together. His job is to restore dharma or moral order. To do this he manifests part of himself anytime he is needed to fight some evil. One translation from the Bhagavad-Gita expresses the Lord Krishna telling Arjuna, "Whenever there is a decline of righteousness and rise of unrighteousness then I send forth Myself. For the protection of the good, for the destruction of the wicked, and for the establishment of righteousness, I come into being from age to age."

It is generally accepted that Vishnu has ten versions of himself to utilize in his manifestations. Just to complicate matters, depending on local customs, the number, names, and identities of Vishnu's avatars are sometimes changed.

The ten avatars of Vishnu:

1. Matsya (the fish)
2. Kurma (the tortoise)
3. Varaha (the boar)
4. Narasimha (the lion-man)
5. Vamana (the dwarf)
6. Parashurama (Rama with an axe)

7. Rama (the Prince of Ayodhya)
8. Krishna (the black tribal)
9. Buddha (the completely enlightened one)
10. Kalki (the incarnation to come)

In some places, Krishna is considered a deity and thus elevated. If that happens then his half-brother Balarama takes his place in the list of ten as an avatar.

Each one of the avatars has a mythical story. Sculptures or paintings of avatars and reproductions of them can be seen throughout India, in the streets, offices, and, of course, in homes. They frequently take human-animal form. For instance, in the case of Matsya the fish, the man is shown as the upper half, the fish as the lower half.

Krishna is a good example of the mythology that swirls around the various divinities. Krishna—the most revered and popular of divinities—is worshiped as the eighth incarnation (avatar) of Vishnu. He is also a supreme god in his own right. Over the years, believers have produced a vast array of poetry, music, and paintings in his honor. So much so that there are cults devoted to him.

As a child Krishna was loved for his mischievousness, his miracles, and his slaying of demons. In his youth, he herded cows. He gained a reputation as a great lover, and the wives and daughters of other cow herders would leave their homes and go into the forests—where Krishna played the flute—to dance with him. They were called *gopis*. As a man Krishna served as a charioteer to Arjuna and taught him the Bhagavad-Gita.

Krishna's favorite *gopi* was the beautiful Radha. Radha inspired poets, musicians, and artists. Much love poetry have been written about Krishna and Radha's mythical union.

Brahma

Brahma shouldn't be confused with Brahman who is the supreme existence, the absolute, the font of all things. Brahma, in fact, has lost status over the years. In the Vedic period he was one of the major gods of Hinduism and was known as the creator. Accounts of how he came to be differ. According to mythology, he was born from a seed that had become a golden egg; on birth, he split into two to make the heaven and the earth and everything in it. A later account said that he was born from a lotus that came from the navel of Vishnu. At that time, Brahma was the ultimate reality, the unknowable force, the origin of all creation; he was pure intelligence.

Originally, Brahma was on a par with Vishnu and Shiva, but over the centuries his power waned; he lost his claim as a supreme deity and sank to the level of a lesser god. Today, there are no cults or temples dedicated to him, except for one place of pilgrimage in Pushkar. However, all temples that are dedicated to Vishnu and Shiva must have an image of Brahma in them.

In artwork Brahma has four faces, symbolic of the four Vedas: Rig, Yajur, Sama, and Atharva. He has four arms that hold a string of beads and a book. He is either seated on his mount or a swan or standing on a lotus throne.

Shiva

In Sanskrit, Shiva means the "auspicious one." He is known as the destroyer and the restorer. He takes life away so it can be recreated. He is a god of contradictory opposites, a paradox in that he is both terrible and mild, one of eternal rest and ceaseless activity.

Shiva is the god of asceticism, art, and dancing. In statues and paintings he is usually depicted as ash-colored with a blue neck wearing a necklace of skulls. His neck is blue, said to be from holding in his throat the poison thrown up at the churning of the cosmic ocean, which threatened to destroy humankind. He has three eyes; the third one, the inner eye, is capable of destruction when focused outwards. His hair is arranged in a coil of matted locks. In some representations he is sitting in the lotus position, which gives rise to a claim that he is the god of Yoga; he has also said to have been a cosmic dancer.

Some Hindus worship Shiva as the supreme deity and think of him as a benevolent god of salvation as well as a god of destruction. As the supreme ascetic, Shiva is the destroyer of maya, illusion, which opens the way to moksha.

CHAPTER 8
Buddhism

The absolute aim of Buddhist worship and its practice is following and preserving the teaching of the Buddha. Now, this doesn't mean just following, it means living and doing. It means that Buddhists live their beliefs in everyday life.

Origins and Development

Scholars disagree about the date, but not the place, of the Buddha's birth. The place was in the kingdom of Sakyas, on the border of present-day Nepal and India. The date was either around 448–368 or 563–483 B.C.E. Regardless of the date, an amazing number of religions were active in the area. So, it should come as no surprise to learn that religious upheaval and turmoil were rampant.

Buddhism and Hinduism, although separate religions, share some basic beliefs while rejecting others. For example, Buddhism did not accept the Vedic literature and rites or the caste system, though it did retain the concept of reincarnation. They also use many of the same words: atman (self or soul), yoga (union), karma (deed or task), and dharma (rule or law), to name a few.

Buddha means "Awakened" or "Enlightened One." It was the title given to Siddhartha Gautama, the founder of Buddhism. The majority of Buddhists believe that there have been, and will be in the future, many other Buddhas. Some even claim that Jesus Christ was a Buddha.

FACTS

Buddha is not a proper noun, it is a title. Therefore, it should always have an article before it: the Buddha, a Buddha. In Buddhist tradition, there have been many Buddhas in the past, as there will be many in the future. When the term "the Buddha" is used today, it's assumed to mean Buddha Gautama, the Buddha of the present era.

Buddhism has expanded into many parts of the world. Nevertheless, during the twentieth century it has been subjected to great suppression by the Chinese, more than at any other time in its history. During the Vietnam War many of its monasteries and temples were closed. As we enter the twenty-first century, there are positive signs that Buddhism is entering a stage of revitalization.

As the Buddhists use it, karma applies to the many worlds that have passed away and the many more that are yet to come. They believe in the law of cause and effect: Positive actions build up merit, negative ones, detract. Buddhists try to live the good life and believe that good karma causes a person to be reborn in a form that is more enlightened and, therefore, allows for greater progress toward the ultimate goal. According to Buddhism the ultimate goal is to be released from the law of karma altogether—to attain Nirvana.

Nirvana is the aim of a Buddhist's religious practice; it is said to be ridding oneself of the delusion of ego or freeing oneself from the claims of the mundane world. Compare this to the approach of Hinduism. Whereas the Hindu goal is to achieve the atman/brahman identity, Buddhists teach the concept of anatman, no self. For them, all that exists is the brahman, the universal soul, and understanding the brahman brings enlightenment. Those who successfully achieve enlightenment overcome the round of rebirths, thus achieving the final goal.

The Buddha

The search for a historical Buddha by Buddhists is remarkably similar to the search by Christians for the historical Jesus. Both religious heads have been accepted on faith by their disciples based on scriptures that were communicated orally, then set down in writing, together with the input of legends that developed about their teachings and works.

There are many recorded utterances from the Buddha that seemed to have been mirrored some 500 years or so later by Jesus. For example, The Buddha said, "Everybody fears being struck by a rod. Everybody fears death. Therefore, knowing this, feeling for others as for yourself, do not kill others or cause others to kill" (from *The Dhammapada* 10:1). Jesus said, "And as ye would that men should do to you, do ye also to them likewise" (from the Bible, Luke 6:31).

In another example, the Buddha said, "Of what avail is thy matted hair? Of what avail is thy antelope hide? Within you there is a forest of defilements. You deal only with outside" (from The Dhammapada 26:12). And Jesus said, "Beware of false prophets, which come to you in sheep's clothing, but inwardly they are ravening wolves" (from the Bible, Matthew 7:15).

The Life of Siddhartha

The parallels between the two great spiritual leaders continues with the story of the Buddha's birth. His mother Mahamaya, the queen of the kingdom of Sakyas, had a dream. In it a beautiful silver elephant entered her womb through her side. Priests interpreted the dream and predicted the birth of a son who would be a Buddha. Ten lunar months later the queen had to take a journey, and she gave birth in an enclosed park.

Immediately following the announcement of the birth, a wise man, who was her husband's teacher, went to see the child. He predicted that based on the signs he saw on the child's body that one day the child would become a Buddha. Shortly thereafter, the boy was given the name Siddhartha, which means "one whose aim is accomplished."

FACTS

On the seventh day after her son's birth, Siddhartha's mother died, and he was brought up by her sister. At the age of sixteen, Siddhartha married his cousin, the princess Yasodhara, and became a father.

His father, the king, tried in every way to make Siddhartha's life easy. He lived with his family in the seclusion and luxury of the palace and was provided with riches and comfort. His father had his son's life mapped out for him: He'd become a warrior and a great king. But, this young man had thoughts of his own.

The turning point came when he went outside the palace with his charioteer. On the first trip he saw an elderly, ill man tottering along. The next day he repeated the trip; this time saw a sick man who was on the ground suffering and obviously very ill. When he went out on the third day he saw a corpse. He was shocked by what he saw because until then he had lived a very sheltered life. He asked his charioteer to explain what had gone on with each of the men. The charioteer told him that was what life was all about. Siddhartha started to change dramatically. Each time after the trip he'd gone back the palace and started to meditate about it all because he was bothered by what he had seen in the outside world.

He continued to search for some kind of meaning. On the fourth trip with his charioteer, he saw an old man with a shaven head wearing a yellow robe. The man had a calm, serene appearance. Siddhartha asked the charioteer who he was. The charioteer told him he was a holy man, an ascetic who had attained complete enlightenment and thus freedom. Siddhartha was so impressed that he started a pattern of fasting and self-mortification as if, he thought, that would show him the way to enlightenment. It was at this time that his son was born. He named him Rahula, which means Fetter or Bond.

The Great Renunciation

Siddhartha then made what is known as the Great Renunciation, which is as important as it sounds. He decided to give up being a prince to become a wandering ascetic. He was twenty-nine years old when he saddled his horse and left in the middle of the night. He didn't want to wake his wife or son. He figured he would one day return to them. He rode south to a place called Gotama where there were centers of spiritual learning.

One day Siddhartha went to meditate beneath a pipal tree, now known as a bondhi tree in a place called Bodh Gaya. He sat cross-legged and went into a trance in which he was tempted by Mara, the evil one (the Lord of the Senses), but he resisted. It was then that the Four Noble Truths came to him.

Following his enlightenment, the Buddha gathered five of his companions and delivered his first sermon. He preached that those searching for enlightenment should not look to find the two extremes of self-indulgence and self-mortification, but should avoid them. He taught instead that they should discover the middle path that leads to vision, to knowledge, to calmness, to awakening, and to nirvana.

What does "nirvana" mean? Does it have any connection with the music group?
Nirvana means perfect bliss. In itself, it does not have a connection with the music group, although perhaps they took it because of what it means.

The Buddha was a charismatic young man. It was said that he was very handsome, charming, of perfect stature, and noble of presence. He quickly built a reputation as a great teacher and a master of debate. Many a person went to him with the idea of trying to change his mind, but each ended up being converted to the Buddha's way of thinking instead.

He also seems to have had a liberal attitude towards society because he refused to recognize the long-established caste system and said that it was the religious potential of men and women from all social ranks that counted most. He preached that trying to suppress crime by punishment was futile. Poverty, he asserted, was a cause of immorality and crime.

Central Beliefs

The central beliefs of Buddhism stem directly from the mind, life, and personality of its founder, the Buddha. The teachings of his first sermon were not empty words; they needed attention and it says a lot for the power of the Buddha's personality that he was able to communicate such serious ideas with such positive results.

Individuals need to be aware of fundamental realities in order to find the path to enlightenment. These fundamental realities are the Four Noble Truths:

1. All life is suffering.
2. Suffering stems from desire.
3. There can be an end to desire.
4. The way is the Eightfold Path.

The basic underpinning of the Buddha's work recognizes that suffering is a universal feeling in people and offers a way to end suffering. But, the process requires discipline, both in thought and action, because there is no value in thoughts alone unless they are carried through into positive actions. To obtain liberation from the misery in life, the Buddha said, requires purification that can be achieved by following the Eightfold Path. But the way is not easy; many Buddhists seek a learned teacher to help them.

The Eightfold Path:

1. Right views—knowledge and understanding of the Four Noble Truths
2. Right aspirations—discarding desire and avoiding hurting others
3. Right speech—telling the truth
4. Right conduct—not stealing or cheating
5. Right livelihood—earning a living in a way that does not harm or cause bloodshed to others
6. Right effort—thinking positively in order to follow the path
7. Right mindfulness—being aware of the effects of thoughts and actions
8. Right meditation—attaining a peaceful state of mind

Literature

The teachings of the Buddha were first transmitted orally from one monk or nun to another and eventually written down on palm leaf manuscripts in Sri Lanka to create the Dhammapada. Written in Pali, the Indian dialect that the Buddha spoke, and known as the Pali canon, it records the conversations of the Buddha. The book is acknowledged as a wonderful spiritual testimony, one of the very few religious masterpieces in the world.

If you think that asking for a copy of Dhammapada isn't going to get you very far in your local bookstore, think again. A number of English translations are available, and many of them are in paperback editions. A translation of the subtitle would be, "Words of Doctrine," "Way of Truth," or "The Path of Truth."

Here is the way the Buddhist philosophy is expressed in the Dhammapada, Chapter 20, 1–3: The Way (translation by Ananda Maitreya).

The eightfold path is the best of ways.
The four noble truths are the best truths.
Freedom from desire is the best of states.
Whoever is clear-eyed and wise is the best of men.

This is the one and only way.
There is no other leading to the purity of vision.
Follow this path;
This bewilders Mara, the tempter.

Following this path, you shall put an end to suffering.
Having myself realized the way that can lead to removal
Of the thorns of defilements,
I have shown it to you.

The Dhammapada has been used in Sri Lanka for centuries as a manual for novices; it is said that every monk can recite it from memory. It is also popular in both Theravada and Mahayana traditions, which will be discussed later.

Other written works also contain records of conversations the Buddha had when he was teaching. Three such works were gathered into a Tripitaka or "Three Baskets," so called because the palm leaf manuscripts were kept in three woven baskets. Incidentally, sometimes they are called the "Triple Baskets."

The Three Baskets are: Sutta Pitaka, the basket of discourse, attributed to the Buddha; Vinaya Pitaka, the basket of discipline, the oldest and smallest of the three sections, that contains the regulations for monastic life; and Abhidhamma Pitaka, the basket of special doctrine, the latest of the three, that contains what might be called further knowledge (not entirely attributed to the Buddha, but highly venerated).

Worship and Practices

In countries where Buddhism is the majority religion, devotion to the Buddhist life is a natural part of it, including diet; the job, trade, or profession chosen; daily meditation; and giving offerings at shrines, temples, and/or monasteries.

Like other religions, Buddhism has a collection of its own practices; two of these are deeply rooted in the Buddhist history. The first one is the veneration of the Buddha. Most Buddhists recognize the existence of many Buddhas, depending upon which Buddhist sect they belong to, the part of the country they live in, and maybe even how their family was brought up. When they go to the temple they will make their devotions to any number of Buddhas. The devotions will be carried out in the shrine room; many adherents also have a shrine room of their own in their homes. In carrying out a devotion the person stands before a holy image—art that shows, perhaps, the Buddha sitting in the lotus position (a yoga meditation position with the legs crossed) with his outstretched arm touching the earth, signifying his enlightenment—then the adherent would recite the three refuges:

I take refuge in the Buddha.
I take refuge in the Dharma.
I take refuge in the Sangha.

After saying the devotions, the adherent usually bows three times before the holy image in respect to the three refuges, which are also known as the Three Jewels. Chanting may be done and offerings may be made.

The second basic practice is the exchange that takes place between monks and the laity. Buddhists have always stressed involvement in the community, and throughout Buddhist history an understanding of the relationship between the monks and nuns and the lay segments of the community has developed.

FACTS

Meditation and chanting form an important part of Buddhist devotional practices. Meditation is used to free the swirling mind from the everyday emotions. Meditation should be done daily. Chanting is another part of Buddhist practice, both at the temple or monastery and in the home. Phrases, verses, or passages from Buddhist scriptures are chanted. Chanting is also an important part of the various festivals and ceremonies.

Sangha

An assembly of monks, say in a monastery, is called by a generic name, Sangha, which dates to the origins of Buddhism. Ordination as a Buddhist monk requires accepting and keeping certain monastic rules, including the Three Jewels and the Five Precepts that prohibit drinking, lying, stealing, harming a living being, and what some call misuse of the senses.

Most people know the common image of a Buddhist monk—the shaven head, the robe, and a look of serenity and pleasure. A monk will own nothing except the robe on his back and his alms-bowl. Originally, the life of a monk was one of poverty and begging. Today, most of these practices have become symbolic. Nevertheless, the life of a monk is still one of strict adherence to the monastic rules.

A new monk has to accept the Five Precepts as absolute rules. Other rules are contained in the Vinaya Texts, and depending on the school, number between 227 and 253 rules. The first part of the texts has the four gravest rules—the prohibition of sexual intercourse, theft, murder, and exaggeration of one's miraculous powers. A monk who breaks one of these rules may be expelled from the monastery.

Every fortnight (two weeks) the monks assemble and recite all the rules. They pause after each one so that any monk who has transgressed may confess and receive his punishment. Other rules deal with transgressions of a lesser nature.

QUESTIONS?

Must all monks still remain celibate, or has that rule been relaxed in modern times?
Most Buddhist schools still stress celibacy, although some groups, particularly in Tibet and Japan, have relaxed this discipline. In other areas, young men can join a monastery for a short time, but do not have to vow to remain celibate for the rest of their lives.

Meditation

Meditation, which has made a secular place for itself in the Western world, has been part of the practice of many Eastern religions, including Buddhism and Hinduism, for centuries. Meditation can open the door to subtle perceptions, which can change conviction and character, and the daily practice of meditation nourishes the roots of a person's personality.

According to medical literature, meditation calms the emotions, strengthens the nerves, and even lowers blood pressure. However, wonderful though that might be for a person's health, it is not the prime reason a Buddhist practices meditation.

Because the Buddha reached his enlightenment through meditation, the practice is the most important aspect of Buddhism. The Sanskrit word, *samadhi*, recognized in both Hinduism and Buddhism, means total self-collectedness. It is the highest state of mental concentration that a person can achieve while still bound to the body. It is a state of profound, utter absorption, undisturbed by desire, anger, or any ego-generated emotion. *Samadhi* is an absolute necessity for attaining release from the cycle of rebirth.

Meditation is not easy because of how difficult it is to still the mind. Meditation can be done sitting, standing, or walking. Many illustrations of the Buddha show him sitting in the yoga lotus position. The techniques that can be used to attain a meditative state are endless, but most of them include instruction in breathing. The goal of meditation is always enlightenment.

Zen

Zen is one of the oldest traditional schools of Buddhism in Japan. Originated in China, where it's referred to as Ch'an Buddhism, Zen teaches that the potential to achieve enlightenment is in everyone but lies dormant because of ignorance. This potential can be awakened by a sudden breaking through of the boundaries of logical thought. A person must try to understand that words are only the surface of things and they have to learn to get beyond words alone in order to understand the meaning of existence.

Zen monks spend endless time, more than most people could handle, meditating on a phrase called a *koan*. A koan is a paradoxical statement used as a meditation discipline. The effort to solve a koan is intended to exhaust the analytic intellect and the egotistic will.

The most famous koan is the question: "What is the sound of one hand clapping?" Think about it.

Rituals and Customs

Of the major rites—birth, marriage, and death—Buddhist monks and nuns generally get involved only marginally, except for death. A monk would attend celebrations of birth and weddings or the bride and groom might visit the monastery, present gifts to the monk, and in turn the monk might offer a sermon. Today, in the west, marriage rituals are sometimes performed, but this is a new development.

Death in the Buddhist community, and in the Tibetan Buddhist community in particular, has been described as the science of dying—the rituals and beliefs around death are important and complex. A full account of these rituals and beliefs is available in the *Tibetan Book of the Dead*. Buddhist temples are very popular for funerals and anniversaries.

The death of the Buddha took place in Mallas in Kusinara in the north of India where he was later cremated. His age is disputed, just as his birth date is. Some say he died when he was seventy years old, others say eighty years. His last words delivered to a group of monks are reported to have been: "Transient are all conditioned things. Try to accomplish your aim with diligence."

Pilgrimages form an important part of Buddhist ritual. Hundreds of sites have drawn pilgrims who often come a very long way to reach a specific destination. While some of the sites might seem to be esoteric, many are shared by other religions, such as Hindus, Muslims, and Christian. Some locations are obvious, for instance, the Buddha's birthplace at Lumbini Grove; Bodh Gaya, where he found enlightenment; Sarnath, where he preached his first sermon on the Four Noble Truths; and Kusinara, where he died.

The places, dates, and nature of Buddhist festivals are many and various. The important times in the life of the Buddha are obvious events to be celebrated. It's probably sufficient to say that a Buddhist festival is a colorful event with temple fairs and visits, alms-giving and offerings at shrines, puppet shows, and theatrical and musical events; in short, they are lively.

Theravada and Mahayana

There are two major forms of Buddhism: Theravada and Mahayana. What has been written in this book so far has basically been taken from the Theravada school. The exceptions are Ch'an and Zen Buddhism, which come under the umbrella of Mahayana. Essentially, Theravada and Mahayana both practice the same core teachings of the Buddha. The schism that occurred after the first council on the death of the Buddha resulted from a political and administrative disagreement, not a theological one. But, once the division occurred, the followers of each part went their separate ways. The Theravada school was referred to as the Lesser Vehicle, and the Mahayanist school was referred to as the Greater Vehicle. Right from the beginning, the Mahayanaists distanced themselves from the more conservative Theravada in their view of the nature of the Buddha and the goal of a Buddhist. The Theravada monks interpret the sacred texts literally, but the Mahayanist scholars have a more liberal interpretation. This difference led to the Mahayanist view of a Bodhisattva, or teacher, a soul who has already reached enlightenment. But, because of compassion he decides to postpone ascension into nirvana in order to work toward the salvation of others who are trapped in the cycle of rebirth, which is seen as an incredible act of wisdom. Compassion, the chief virtue associated with the Bodhisattva, is accorded an equal place with wisdom.

FACTS

The first Mahayanist scriptures were written in Sanskrit in the first century C.E. Like the Pali canon, many of them contain the Buddha's words, although new texts were also written. With the spread of Mahayanist Buddhism to China, Japan, and Tibet, translations were made and added to by scholars.

The Theravada Buddha is supramundane—above or superior to the world—to whom individuals work on their own to eventually attain enlightenment, but without thought for the progress of others. The Theravada ideal is the *arhat*, or perfected saint, who attains enlightenment as a result of his own efforts. The Mahayanists consider this to be a selfish goal and view the supramundane as connected only externally with the worldly life. Their idea of the Buddha contributed to the growth of the Mahayanist movement.

A Mahayanist Buddhist philosopher, Nagarjuna, said that the idea of the world being made up of building blocks called *dharmas* was not correct. He argued that if *dharmas* existed they were impermanent. He even went further and said that nothing is permanent or solid, including the self or the Buddha. This kind of teaching is called the Way of Emptiness.

Allied to this way is the principle of duality—the theory that in any domain of reality there are two independent underlying principles: mind and matter, form and content. In this kind of thinking the use of language has little value because there are no words in which to express itself at all. Words, therefore, give way to intuition.

The Mahayanist version of Buddhism has now spread to Central Asia, China, Japan, mainland Southeast Asia, Java, Sumatra, and parts of Sri Lanka. There are also outposts, as it were, in the United States and other Western countries.

CHAPTER 9
Judaism

Although numerically a modest-sized religion (about twenty million adherents), Judaism has provided the historical foundation for two of the world's largest religions: Christianity and Islam. The main belief of Judaism is that there is an all-powerful God with whom Jews have a personal relationship.

Origins and Development

To understand modern day Judaism one has to be relatively well informed about its long history. It might be said to have started when God made the Jews his "chosen people." He promised Abraham that his descendants—his son Isaac and grandsons Jacob and Esau—would become a great nation. The promise or Covenant is recorded in Jewish scriptures. Here is the Covenant as taken from the Authorized King James Version of the Bible, Genesis 12:1–3:

> *Now the Lord had said unto Abram, Get thee out of thy country, and from thy kindred, and from thy father's house, unto a land that I will shew thee:*
> *And I will make of thee a great nation, and I will bless thee, and make thy name great; and thou shalt be a blessing.*

Abraham followed God's instructions in his search for the promised land, and after many years of wandering around ended up in a place called Canaan. Along the way, God tested his faith by asking him to sacrifice his son Isaac. But, at the last minute God intervened and stopped the sacrifice. He then repeated his promise to Abraham about becoming the father of a great nation. Abraham and his descendants settled in Canaan. When the famine came, Abraham's son Jacob took his family to the land of Egypt.

They settled in and Jacob fathered many sons and the family prospered. The descendants of Jacob's sons would later become the twelve tribes of Israel. The new pharaoh of Egypt became worried that Jacob's family might become mightier than the Egyptians. He was already rigorously treating the Israelites as slaves, but, that wasn't enough so he came up with an idea on how to restrict their proliferation: Kill every newborn male child at birth. The account of this, which is recorded in the Bible in Exodus, has within its horror a wonderful story.

The midwives tried to get around Pharaoh's edict and had some success, so the Pharaoh stepped up the campaign and ordered that every newborn son be cast into the river. The Israelites' daughters were spared.

Moses

A couple conceived and had a son. When the mother saw that the boy was fit, what was called a goodly child, she decided to hide him. She made an ark from bulrushes and daubed it with slime and pitch, put the boy in it, and laid it by the riverbank.

One day the daughter of Pharaoh came to the river to wash herself and when she walked along the bank she saw the ark and told one of her maids to fetch it. The Pharaoh's daughter opened the ark and saw a baby boy; it was crying and she had compassion. She said to the maids that the child was one of the Hebrews' children.

The sister of the child then came to the Pharaoh's daughter and suggested that she call a Hebrew woman to nurse the child. The Pharaoh's daughter agreed, and the sister went to get her mother. The Pharaoh's daughter told the woman when she came to take the child and nurse it that she would pay her wages. When the child grew, he was brought to Pharaoh's daughter and became her son; she named him Moses.

When Moses was fully grown he saw an Egyptian slave master beating an Israelite. Moses killed the slave master, so he had to flee from Egypt. He settled in a rural farming area called Midian where he eventually had a son, whom he named Gershom, by one of the shepherd's daughters. Around the same time Pharaoh died, and the Israelites were suffering. God remembered his covenant with Abraham and looked on the people and had respect for them.

Moses was tending to his work in the desert, when he came to a mountain. An angel appeared to him from a flame of fire out of a bush that was not being consumed by the flame. A voice came from the bush and told Moses that he had been chosen to deliver the people from the Egyptians and take them to another land flowing with milk and honey. God commanded Moses to return to Pharaoh. Moses wasn't too sure about any of that, and started to argue with God. Because Moses stammered, God told him to take his brother Aaron with him to act as spokesman. That settled, God didn't waste any more time; he told Moses what he had to do and what miracles he might have to present to get his way.

There is a famous answer to the question from Moses, "Who do I say sent me?" God said, "I am that I am . . . Thus shalt thou say unto the children of Israel I am hath sent me unto you . . . This is my name for ever, and this is my memorial unto all generations."

Pharaoh, as expected, refused the demands from Moses. As punishment, God sent ten plagues to the Egyptians. Among them were plagues of boils, hail, and locusts; none of these had any effect. The final one did, though, for it brought death in one night to the firstborn son of every Egyptian family. This might seem to be God's revenge for what the Pharaoh had done to the Jews. God had warned Moses and told him that all Israelite families should smear lamb's blood on their doorposts so their sons would not be killed on that night when he would pass through the land of Egypt to smite all the firstborn of Egypt. The lamb's blood would be a token, and when God saw the blood he would pass over the house. God said this sacrifice should be observed forever. And it has been as the eighth day of the Jewish festival of Passover (Pesach), which is generally celebrated in April.

This final plague worked and Pharaoh let the Israelites go. Then, he had second thoughts and sent his army after them. They caught up with the Israelites at the banks of the Red Sea. The army prepared to destroy them, but God parted the Red Sea so the Israelites could get safely across. Once they were on the other side and the army gave pursuit, God made the Red Sea close in on them and they were all drowned. Actually, there is another account which says that, in fact, it was not the Red Sea, but the Sea of Reeds which was a papyrus lake that the Israelites crossed safely, but in which the Egyptians were engulfed. Regardless, the Israelites escaped from the Egyptians.

The Ten Commandments

Moses was now the leader of a large number of contentious people on the move and he had some administrative problems. Being pursued was one of them; the others were hunger, thirst, and rebellion. Fortunately, God was still communicating with him and issuing instructions.

About three months after leaving Egypt, the Israelites were camping in the wilderness of Sinai. God told Moses to go up to the top of the mountain for a meeting. At the meeting, God revealed to him the Ten Commandments, which were written on two tablets of stone. They dealt with the people's relationship with God and each other. God also gave Moses hundreds more detailed rules and laws.

The Ten Commandments, also called the Decalogue (from the Greek word for ten words), form the basis of all the Jewish laws. They have had, and continue to have, immense influence on many other religions throughout the world. Actually, the Commandments didn't have any special importance in the Christian religion until the thirteenth century when they were included with the instructions for those who came to confess their sins, and later were incorporated into catechisms of religious training.

FACTS

The Commandments can be read in the Hebrew Bible or the Old Testament of the Christian Bible in Exodus 20:2–17 and in Deuteronomy 5:6–21. Different traditions provide slightly different versions and different numbering of the Commandments.

Pursuing the Promised Land

While Moses went up to Mount Sinai, where he received the Law from God, the Israelites became impatient. They made an image of a golden calf and proclaimed it to be their god, bowing down to it and offering it sacrifices. God saw this and told Moses to return to his people. When Moses returned to the camp and saw what his people were doing, he became very angry and threw down the stone tablets God had inscribed His laws upon, breaking them into many pieces. (This story is recounted in Exodus 32:1–19.)

In Deuteronomy 31, we are told that when Moses was 120 years old, the Lord came to him and told him he was about to die, and that he would not reach the "promised land." God commanded Moses to write down the law and gave it to the Levites who carried the "Ark of the Covenant." Moses' brother Joshua was appointed by God to succeed as leader of the Israelites. Moses then climbed up Mount Pisgah, which overlooked Canaan, the Promised Land that he would never enter. He was never seen again and how he died remains a mystery. It is written that he did formulate the Decalogue and work on the first five books of the Hebrew Bible. While he certainly may have done that, there is no question that without Moses there would have been no Israel and no Torah.

The two tablets containing the Laws that God gave to Moses were housed in a gold-plated chest called The Ark of the Covenant. The Israelites carried the Ark with them before they settled in the Promised Land, and from time to time took it into battle. It was taken to Jerusalem by King David and was eventually placed in the Temple by King Solomon. Placed inside the Tabernacle within the Temple of Jerusalem, the Ark was seen only by the high priest of the Israelites on Yom Kippur, the Day of Atonement. The final fate of the Ark is unknown.

As time went on, the Israelites were ruled by a series of kings: Saul, David (who wrote many of the psalms in the Bible), and David's son,

Solomon. After Solomon's death, the kingdom of Israel split in two and formed Judah and Israel. Throughout the centuries that followed, the Israelites were exiled to Babylon, although some came back. Then, the Romans in 63 B.C.E. conquered the land and gave it a new name: Palestine. Three years later, the Jews revolted against Rome, but were defeated. The Temple in Jerusalem, which was rebuilt after the Israelites returned from exile in Babylon, was finally destroyed in 70 C.E.

FACTS

All that remains of the Temple is the western wall, called the Wailing Wall. It is now a center of pilgrimage and prayer for Jews from all over the world. This site, Judaism's holiest place on earth, is used for private prayer (performed while facing the Wall), and for public services and bar mitzvahs.

Central Beliefs

Judaism is a religion of ethical monotheism. God is unique and the ultimate authority, but the utter and essential backbone of the entire religion is the Torah, comprised of the first five books of the Bible, which are attributed to Moses.

In addition to the Torah, the Hebrew canon includes the Nevi'im, or the books of the prophets. Nevi'im are generally divided into two sections: the former prophets (comprised of twenty-two books) and the latter prophets, of which there are twelve. The writings of the twelve minor prophets are copied onto one scroll, so that they can be counted as one entry, so to speak. The total number of books in the Hebrew canon, the Christian Old Testament, is thirty-nine, which was the number of scrolls on which they were originally written.

The Torah

The Torah is the most important section of the Jewish Bible. It is a series of narratives and laws that chronicle, in historical order, the beginning of the world all the way through to the death of Moses.

Jewish people and Christians agree that Moses was the author of the five books. For those who may be interested in creative writing, it might be useful to note that the books are written in the third person. This gave, and gives, some scholars difficulty.

The study of the Torah is considered an act of worship for the Jews. It should be read religiously each Sabbath. Over the course of a year, the entire Torah will be read on Sabbath and festival days. There are daily and weekly classes and groups for those who wish to study the Torah.

The Talmud, which means study or learning, is a reference to the interpretations of the Torah. It is the supreme sourcebook of law as it takes the rules listed in the Torah and describes how to apply them to different circumstances. It's not actually a legal code, there are other works that do that, but it is the ultimate source material used to decide all matters of the Jewish law. The Mishnah is the first part of the Talmud.

It should be apparent that Judaism, like all other religions, is a disparate one, in that while its members are deeply involved and certainly members of the same group, they sometimes give the appearance of being at odds with their faith and each other. This is the nature of religion that accommodates diversity, but with the Jews, the thread that binds them is the law.

There is a confession of faith called a Shema made up of three scriptural texts from Deuteronomy and Numbers that demonstrates the power and demands emanating from the Jewish God. Because the original requirement to study the Torah night and day was sensibly understood to be a tough duty, the Shema became a substitute as a minimum requirement. It is said that pious Jews hope to die with the words of the Shema on their lips. Here is a short extract:

And ye shall teach them (these words) to your children, talking of them, when thou sittest in thy home, and when thou walkest by the way, and when thou liest down, and when thou risest up . . . remember and do all My commandments, and be holy unto your God. I am the Lord your God, who brought you out of the land of Egypt, to be your God: I am the Lord your God.

The fifth of the Ten Commandments says that nobody shall work on the Sabbath. (Remember that the Jewish Sabbath, Shabbat, starts at dusk on Fridays and ends at dusk on Saturdays.) The synagogue has services Friday night and Saturday morning.

Jews start the Sabbath by dressing up for a good meal, with maybe some singing and celebration. Saturdays they go visiting friends and family and sit around reading the Torah.

At the end of the Sabbath, on Saturday evening, a ceremony called Havdalah marks the end of it. The family gathers and a candle is lit and a box of sweet-smelling spices is passed around. If dinner is served after Havdalah it must have been prepared earlier because cooking is not permitted on the Sabbath.

ESSENTIALS

The Torah, also know as the Pentateuch, is the collection of the five books of Moses—Genesis, Exodus, Leviticus, Numbers, and Deuteronomy. Some consider the entire Jewish Bible as the Torah, or the entire body of religious law and learning.

Synagogues

The synagogue is the center of Jewish community life. It has three traditional functions: House of Prayer where services are held on the Sabbaths and festival days, House of Assembly where Jewish people can meet for any purpose, and House of Study where the Torah and Talmud are studied. Children can also come to learn Hebrew and the Torah. A synagogue is the focal point of Jewish life. This developed after the destruction of the Temple in Jerusalem in 70 C.E., when the Jews scattered all over the Roman Empire.

Public congregational prayers are said at the synagogue every weekday. Prayers can only take place if there are at least ten men present in the synagogue, rather like the same principal as having a quorum at a board meeting. It is a Jewish man's duty to attend prayers as often as possible.

A rabbi (the word means teacher) has no more authority to perform rituals than any other member of the Jewish community. A synagogue can exist and operate quite well without one. However, there is usually a rabbi who is employed by the congregation to run things and settle disputes regarding Jewish law. Generally a rabbi has been formally educated in Halakhah (Jewish law). When a person has completed the necessary course of study, he or she is given a written document known as a *semikhah*, which confirms his or her authority. A rabbi's status does not give him or her the authority to conduct religious services. Any knowledgeable Jew can lead a religious service. However, rabbis are the spiritual leaders of the Jewish community. In many areas, particularly in the United States, rabbis carry out pastoral counseling, hospital and military chaplaincies, and teaching in Jewish schools.

A typical synagogue contains an ark—a special cupboard or alcove that faces Jerusalem—where the scrolls of the Law are kept; there will also be a perpetual lamp, or "eternal light," before the ark. The synagogue will have a *bimah*, which is a raised platform near the center of the room used for reading the Torah and for saying or singing prayers. Many Jewish prayers are sung; the singing may be led by a cantor or by a choir, or it can be congregational singing.

FACTS

Men and women are still segregated in Orthodox synagogues. Generally, the women's section was located in the balcony, while men sat in the main part of the synagogue. Now, the men and women may sit side by side, separated by a border that bisects the synagogue. The practice of segregation has been abandoned in Reform and Conservative congregations.

The Torah scrolls, which are handwritten on parchment, are protected by being "dressed" in velvet coverings and silver ornaments. The scrolls are valuable; the handwriting on them is carried out by a skilled expert and can take a year to complete.

In addition to the elaborate fastenings, there is a silver pointer used when reading the Torah to avoid finger contact with the parchment. It is the duty of every adult male to take a turn reading the Torah, which requires special training. When a boy does this for the first time, it is considered an important occasion in his life.

The public readings and worship of the Scriptures can be a complicated and elaborate ceremony depending on the time and day of the week and which kind of festival is being observed.

Rituals and Customs

Virtually everything a devout Jewish person does from the beginning to the end of life is regulated by an adherence to Jewish Law and obedience to the will of God. Perhaps nowhere is this more evident than in the various rites, rituals, and customs of the faith. Most Jews have a *mezuzah* on every doorpost in the home (excluding the bathroom and toilet) to remind everyone to keep God's laws.

A *mezuzah* is a parchment inscribed with religious texts attached in a case to a doorpost in a Jewish home as a sign of faith. When it comes to prescribed ritual, rites, and customs, Jewish people generally happily conform to their religious heritage.

Birth

Birth as far as Jewish boys are concerned means circumcision on the eighth day after the event. The Torah says it's the fulfillment of the Covenant between God and Abraham (Genesis 17:10–14). This procedure is performed by a specially trained person called a *mohel*. The mohel recalls the Covenant and recites a blessing while cutting off the foreskin. The baby's name is said at the same time.

Bar Mitzvah

Bar mitzvah is a ceremony held when a Jewish boy is thirteen and is therefore considered old enough to take responsibility for himself and his obedience of the Law. In Jewish religious terms he is considered an adult. The boy will be able to wear phylacteries (religious symbols worn on the forehead and left arm) during weekday and morning prayers. He may also be counted as an adult when ten males are needed to make a quorum for public prayers.

The public act of acknowledging religious maturity requires the boy to be called upon during the religious service to read from the Torah. Bar mitzvah generally takes place on a Sabbath. After the ceremony, there is frequently a festive Kiddush, or prayer, over a cup of wine and a family social dinner or even a banquet.

Marriage

Marriage and the raising of children is an important part of Jewish life just as it is in other religions. The role of matchmaker is still an important one in Jewish communities. Celibacy is not encouraged. The wedding ceremony can be held in a synagogue or in the open air. In the Jewish faith, though, it cannot take place on the Sabbath or on a festival. The bridegroom places a gold ring on the bride's forefinger, then the *kethubah*, marriage contract, is read and the rabbi recites the seven marriage blessings. At the end of the ceremony the bridegroom traditionally breaks a wineglass under his foot.

QUESTIONS?

What are the skull caps called that Jewish men wear?
They are called *yarmulkes* (Yiddish) or *kippahs* (Hebrew), and serve as physical symbols that demonstrate the wearers' submission to God. Most Jews, except the most liberal members of the Reform movement, wear yarmulkes during religious services. Some Jews wear yarmulkes any time they appear in public.

The Jewish marriage contract has, in some ways, similarities to a prenuptial agreement. Basically, it has conditions stipulated that guarantee the bride's right to property when her husband dies. In the Orthodox and

Conservative congregations it is a prerequisite for marriage. Originally, the contract was made to make divorce more costly for husbands as a deterrent against marriages that were made in a highly emotional state.

Death

Death in the Jewish faith goes along with the belief of other religions on the resurrection of the dead. Differences are evident when deciding on what happens to the body—burial or cremation—which depends on the sect to which the individual belonged. The body must be buried as soon as possible after death (within twenty-four hours is typical) and in Jewish consecrated ground. The body is washed, anointed with spices, and wrapped in a white sheet.

For a week after the death, close relatives sit at home observing *shivah,* wearing a torn or cut upper garment and taking no part in everyday life. Friends and relatives have a duty to visit and bring food and succor. For eleven months after death, a prayer known as the *kaddish* is recited every day at the synagogue, and thereafter every year the anniversary of the death is remembered.

Religious Festivals and Holy Holidays

Festivals are the backbone of the Jewish faith in that they reflect Jewish history and its teaching. They are commemorative, and it has been said that the festivals sanctified the Jews more than the Jews sanctified the festivals. Traditions are passed from one generation to another both orally and theatrically by the playing out of stories and singing, which can be joyful or sorrowful. They fulfill the purpose of festival remembrance by maintaining and passing on, one generation to the next, the emotions of a heritage carried forward into the present and therefore never lost. They nurture the sense of cohesiveness that has sustained the Jewish people throughout their long and often heartrending history.

In the Jewish calendar, the festivals are divided into two segments: major and minor. The five major ones are as laid down in the Torah: Rosh Hashanah, Yom Kippur, Pesach (Passover), Shavuot, and Sukkot (Feast of Tabernacles). All the rest are considered minor, although Hanukkah, officially a minor festival, has become so popular that it is often celebrated more than some of the major festivals.

The five major Jewish festivals are:

Rosh Hashanah: Rosh Hashanah, or the Jewish New Year, usually takes place sometime in September. This holiday is also known as the Day of Judgment or Day of Remembrance. Rosh Hashanah ushers in a ten-day period of self-examination and penitence.

Yom Kippur: The Day of Atonement, known in Hebrew as Yom Kippur, arrives ten days after Rosh Hashanah. Yom Kippur is the most solemn Jewish religious holiday. On this day, Jews seek purification by the forgiveness of others and through sincere repentance of their own sins. They abstain from food, drink, and sex.

Pesach: The days for the Festival of Pesach or Passover usually fall in March or April. Passover celebrates God's deliverance of the Israelites from captivity in Egypt. During this weeklong holiday, Jewish people eat unleavened bread, known as the *matzoh*, in commemoration of the quickly made unleavened bread the Israelites had to subsist on during their escape from Egypt.

Shavuot: Shavuot, translated into Greek as Pentecost by the early Christians, takes place seven weeks after Passover, and was originally an agricultural festival that marked the beginning of the wheat harvest. Additionally, this holiday also commemorates the anniversary of Moses receiving the Law of God on Mount Sinai.

Sukkot: This holiday is also known as the Feast of Tabernacles. It is an autumn festival that also celebrates the end of the harvest. During this holiday, which lasts a week, people build little huts, known as *sukkahs*, where they are required to spend some time in meditation.

The Jewish calendar is a lunar calendar. This produces the need to add a thirteenth month every now and then so that the major festivals fall in their proper season. It would take a Jewish mathematician to track what is called the lunisolar structure.

CHAPTER 10
Judaic Affiliations

Since the time of Jesus of Nazareth, when there were several Judaic affiliations, four main variations have been established. As you will see, these are Orthodox, Hasidic, Conservative, and Reform. Each has its own set of observations, many of which date back to ancient times.

Orthodox Judaism

Orthodoxy in Judaism came into existence around 1795 and supported a belief in the dual Torah. The dual Torah was revealed at Sinai and is

concerned with oral and written versions of the law. The argument was that the written law could never have stood alone and that it must have been accompanied by an oral tradition. For example, Exodus 12:15 says that the number of days during which unleavened bread must be eaten amounts to seven, whereas in Deuteronomy 16:8, it is six. Orthodox Jews rely on the oral Torah to account for the discrepancy.

Orthodox Judaism is not a unified movement; it is many different movements that adhere to a common principle. They believe the Torah—both written and oral—to be of divine origin and the exact work of God; the human element was not involved in its creation. So, the words are immutably fixed and remain the sole norm of religious observance. Most of the movements have similar observances and beliefs; it's the details that vary.

All Jewish groups consider themselves and each other firm adherents of the faith. However, this hasn't kept Orthodox rabbis from challenging the legitimacy of certain non-Orthodox marriages and divorces on the grounds that they violate Jewish Law.

Beliefs and Practices

While, as has been said, Orthodox Judaism adheres to the common Jewish principles, the following are some of the ways in which they are uncommon. In addition to the Sabbath, religious holidays include the three biblical pilgrimage festivals, Passover, Pentecost, Tabernacles, the New Year (Rosh Hashanah), and the Day of Atonement (Yom Kippur). All holidays except for the Day of Atonement are observed for two days. The first two and the last two days of Passover and Tabernacles are days on which work is forbidden, as it is on the Sabbath and other holidays. The preparation of food is prohibited only on the Sabbath and the Day of Atonement. Hanukkah and Purim are post-Biblical holidays, and do not include a prohibition against work.

Orthodox households have strict rules regarding the way foods and their utensils are used. Meat and dairy products may not be eaten together or at the same meal. A completely different set of utensils is used for the two types of food; there are different storage areas and the utensils should be washed separately. The law so affects Orthodox Jews that some find it virtually impossible to eat out, except in strict Kosher restaurants. This might be understandable when one considers that to eat eggs is fine if they are boiled or poached, but if they're fried in butter they can't be eaten with meat.

There are no restrictions about medical treatment. Orthodox Jews consider physicians instruments through whom God can effect a cure. When it comes to death, funeral, and burial requirements, the form is to follow the established way, but it prohibits cremation. Apart from very unusual circumstances, such as promoting justice, autopsies are not permitted because they break the prohibition against mutilation of the body and show disrespect for the dead. A rabbi should be consulted before an autopsy is considered.

Contraception is limited to women. A vasectomy or use of a condom by males is not permitted. Abortion is permitted if the continuation of the pregnancy presents grave physical or psychiatric dangers. Abortion on demand is not permitted.

Orthodox Judaism continues to insist on the segregation of the men and women in synagogues. Women are not permitted to attain the status of rabbi. The language used in formal worship is Hebrew.

Not surprisingly, because of their strong right-wing reputation, their attitude toward homosexuality is complete disapproval with frequent reference to Leviticus 20:13.

The Essential Element

The essential element of Orthodox Judaism is the complete and utter adherence to the established laws. Everything in the life of an Orthodox Jew is directly related to the affirmation of that ethic. There are even some communities of Orthodox belief who maintain that holy Israel should live wholly apart from gentiles. Other, more moderate members, agree that integration with Western culture while maintaining the law of the Torah together with secular politics and general social affairs is preferable.

FACTS

The home in a Jewish family is of great importance. It's where the Sabbath is usually celebrated and many details of the Law of Moses are observed. Private study time is also a feature of Jewish home living.

It is estimated that only about 10 percent of the total Jewish population in America is Orthodox. The Union of Orthodox Jewish Congregations, which represents about 1,000 member congregations, was founded in New York City in 1898.

Hasidic Judaism

Hasidic Jews are the most orthodox of the Orthodox movement even though, strictly speaking, both are distinct branches of Judaism. Hasidic Jews adhere absolutely to the teachings of the written law (the Torah) and the oral law (the Talmud). The sect began in Poland in 1760, led by a revivalist named Eliezer Ba'al Shem Tov (Master of the Good Name) who stressed the study of Jewish literature. In the Hasidic tradition, a Master is also known as a *Zaddik* or righteous man.

The Master was believed to have a direct line to God. After the founder's death Hasidism spread throughout Europe and diversified. The main body of the sect remained in Europe until the Holocaust when tremendous numbers of Hasidic Jews were slaughtered by the Nazis. Some escaped to the United States. In New York they settled predominantly in Brooklyn, where today around 100,000 followers live.

Customs

Hasidic Jews often get attention on the street because of their appearance. The men are usually dressed completely in black with wide-brimmed hats, long coats, beards, and extended, rope-like sideburns. Originally, their dress was the local custom in Poland; today, it symbolizes their religious fervor.

Jewish law says there should be a separation between the top and bottom halves of the body when praying. Most Hasidic men wear a *gartel*; others wear a regular belt.

Often a Hasidic man will be seen with a black box (*tefillin*) on his head or arm to follow the Torah commandant about having a box containing parchment verses from the Torah. During morning services the box is worn on the head ("between your eyes") or on the arm ("upon your hand"). In some congregations women also wear *tefillin*.

Another custom regards the hair, both on the head and on the face. As always, the law is open to interpretation. The most orthodox men who follow the law to the letter will not deviate from the commandment that a straight razor should not be used on one's temple or to shave one's beard. The sidelocks also are an answer to an interpretation of the law against shaving the temples. The long sideburns are called *peyot*.

Beliefs and Practices

Hasidic religious duties are carried out in a spirit of devotion. Prayer serves not to petition or supplicate God but as the way to ascend to a relationship of union with God.

While the Hasidic way of life may seem very restricted or even morose, it was the source of some profound music. In the 1700s, the Hasidic movement exerted a significant influence on what is called in Yiddish *klezmer*. The word is used to denote professional eastern European Jewish dance musicians. The term is a combination of two Hebrew words: *kle*, which means vessel or instrument, and *zemer*, which means song. In recent times, *klezmer* music has gained prominence. It was the Hasidic sect that made religion more accessible to the masses by emphasizing dancing and by singing with such intense urgency so as to "ascend" to higher realms through their music.

Conservative Judaism

Conservative Judaism is predominantly centered in the United States. Inspired by Zacharias Frankel in the 1800s, it was expanded in 1902 in New York by a Jewish Talmudic scholar, Solomon Schecter. In 1913, Schecter founded the United Synagogue of America, which eventually grew to over 800 Conservative congregations.

Central Beliefs

Conservative Judaism believes in observing traditional Jewish laws, sacred texts, and beliefs and being open to modern culture and critical secular scholarship, which allows for changes in practices.

The theology of the Conservative movement is midway between Orthodox Judaism and Reform Judaism, with Orthodox being the strict element and the Reform, the more liberal. For instance, in 1985 the Rabbinical Assembly, an organization of Conservative rabbis in the United States, Canada, Europe, and Israel founded in 1900, voted to allow the admittance of women as rabbis for the first time, something Orthodox Judaism has yet to do.

Many Conservatives stress Jewish nationalism, encourage the study of Hebrew, and support the secular Zionist movement, which emphasizes the importance of the Jewish national homeland and supports the development of Israel. In spite of the differences among the affiliations, the Conservatives have maintained continuity with tradition, which often makes it difficult to differentiate one theology from another. The Conservatives like diversity, which is why their views and practices range from Orthodoxy to Reform.

A Forward Movement

In 1960, the leadership of Conservative Jews agreed to allow the use of electricity on the Sabbath and a car to travel to the synagogue. This decision was a major step forward in the direction of modern thought for Conservative Jews.

The Conservative movement worries that having a modern attitude (though not as modern as Reform Judaism) may be misinterpreted by some to the point that they think Conservative Judaism is just like Reform Judaism, except there is more Hebrew in its services. They worry that future generations will not have the same commitment to Conservative Judaism as today's members do. The danger for this movement is that most of their followers will eventually gravitate to either Reform or Orthodox Judaism.

Conservative Jews maintain their links with the past by insisting on the sacredness of the Sabbath and respecting some dietary laws, like the prohibition against eating pork. However, they do not require a strict kosher kitchen. The rabbinical assembly, Conservative Judaism's official body, is located in New York City at the Jewish theological seminary, which educates future rabbis for the movement.

Reform Judaism

Reform Judaism is a movement that modified or abandoned many of the traditional Jewish beliefs, laws, and practices in order to bring Judaism into the modern world in all aspects of social, political, and cultural conditions. The movement began in Germany in the nineteenth century in response to appeals to update the Jewish liturgy and other rituals. The Jews were being liberated from their ghettos and many began to question Jewish tradition and its dietary laws, prayers said in Hebrew, and even the wearing of special outfits that set them apart as Jews.

The First Reform Services

A Jewish layman, Israel Jacobson, began a school in Seesen, Brunswick, Germany, in 1801. In 1809, he held the first Reform services. The liturgy was in German, not Hebrew, men and women were allowed to sit together, organ and choir music were added to the service, and Jacobson instituted confirmation for boys and girls to replace the traditional boys' Bar Mitzvah. The services also left out all references to a personal messiah who would restore Israel as a nation. The questions being asked were: "Who is Israel? What is its way of life? How does it account for its existence as a distinct and distinctive group?"

The Spreading Movement

The Reform movement was not a success in Europe. Many European governments that regulated religious communities didn't countenance more than one form of Judaism in any particular locale. It was in the United States, to which the movement was imported by the mass German-Jewish immigration in the 1840s, that it flourished. By 1880, almost all the 200 synagogues in the United States had become Reform.

In 1885 the Pittsburgh Platform, put together by Reform rabbis, declared that Judaism was an evolutionary faith and that it was to be de-orientalized. One conclusion was that the Talmud should be looked at as religious literature, not as legislation.

QUESTIONS?

What do Reform Jews believe?
One of the guiding principles of Reform Judaism is the autonomy of the individual. A Reform Jew has the right to decide whether to subscribe to each particular belief or practice.

Now movements are advocating a return to more traditional mores. In 1999, Leaders of Reform Judaism embraced keeping rituals that are associated more with Conservative and Orthodox Judaism than with the Reform movement, and are wearing yarmulkes and prayer shawls, observing dietary laws, and using Hebrew during prayer services.

CHAPTER 11
Confucianism

Confucianism is not officially considered a world religion because it is not organized as such. It is often grouped with religions, however, perhaps because it is a spiritual philosophy, a social ethic, a political ideology, and a scholarly tradition.

Origins and Development

The belief was started in China around the sixth to fifth century B.C.E. by Confucius. It has been followed by the Chinese people for over two millennia. A major part of the belief is its emphasis on learning and as a source of values. Its influence has spread to many other countries, including Korea, Japan, and Vietnam; it is also now being taken seriously in the United States where it has gone far beyond the derogatory stereotypical image of the Charlie Chan detective movies of the 1930s and 1940s and their fortune cookie sayings. Confucianism made its mark extensively in Chinese literature, education, culture, and both spiritual and political life.

Confucius lived in a time of political violence, so the stage was set for a teacher to emerge who had the ability to dispense a spiritual philosophy that would generate restorative thoughts of social and ethical calm, and who saw perfection in all people. It has been said that he initially attracted over 3,000 students, some of whom became close disciples.

FACTS

The Four Books—*The Analects, The Great Learning, The Mean*, and *The Book of Mencius*—refer to ancient Confucian texts that were used officially in civil service exams in China for over 500 years. They introduced Confucian literature to students who then progressed to the more difficult texts, the Five Classics: *The Book of History, The Book of Poems, The Book of Change (I Ching), The Spring and Autum Annals,* and *The Book of Rites*. Of the Four Books certainly one, *The Analects,* is reputed to have direct quotations from Confucius himself as told to his disciples and written down by them.

Confucius

Confucius was born in the small state of Lu in 551 B.C.E., in what is now Shantung Province. Confucius is a Latin version of K'ung Fu-tzu (K'ung the master). He was born into an aristocratic family that had seen much better times. His father died when he was only three years old.

His mother educated him at home. By the time he was a teenager, he inquired about everything and had set his heart on learning.

He started off as a keeper of stores and accounts, but moved on to other minor posts in government. However, he had difficulty in finding a good job even though he was ambitious and willing to do more or less anything. But, he never gave up his first love: learning. He found teachers who would school him in music, archery, calligraphy, and arithmetic. From his family he had learned the classics: poetry, literature, and history.

When he was nineteen years of age, he married a woman of a similar background to his own. Not much else is known about her. They apparently had a son and daughter.

The Teachings of Confucius

All the learning he had done qualified him to teach, which he started to do in his thirties. He was the first person to devote his whole life to learning and teaching for the sole purpose of trying to improve the lot of his fellow humans. He also became known as the first teacher in China whose concern was providing education for all. The rich had tutors for their children. He believed that everyone could benefit from self-education. During his life he worked to open the doors of education to everyone, and he defined learning as not only the acquisition of knowledge but also the building of character.

A major thrust in his teaching was filial piety, the virtue of devotion to one's parents. He considered it the foundation of virtue and the root of human character.

Interestingly, the male attitude toward sex was strict. The purpose of sex was to conceive children, in particular, sons. According to Dr. Mel

Thompson, an authority in eastern philosophy, there is a sense that male energy is dissipated through sexual union, and that men may be worn out both physically and morally by too much sex. Sexual excess on the part of a ruler was given as a valid reason to take from him the right to rule.

Proper social behavior and etiquette were considered essential to right living. A set of ethics is contained in the *Analects*, a collection of moral and social teachings, which amount to a code of human conduct. Many of the sayings were passed on orally. Here are some examples:

Clever words and a plausible appearance have seldom turned out to be humane.

Young men should be filial when at home and respectful to elders when away from home. They should be earnest and trustworthy. Although they should love the multitude far and wide, they should be intimate only with the humane. If they have any energy to spare after so doing, they should use it to study culture.

The gentleman is calm and peaceful; the small man is always emotional.

The gentleman is dignified but not arrogant. The small man is arrogant but not dignified.

In his attitude to the world the gentleman has no antagonisms and no favoritisms. What is right he sides with.

If one acts with a view to profit, there will be much resentment.

One who can bring about the practice of five things everywhere under Heaven has achieved humaneness. . . . Courtesy, tolerance, good faith, diligence, and kindness.

FACTS

Confucius concentrated his teachings on his vision, *Jen*, which has been translated in the most complete way as: love, goodness, and human-heartedness; moral achievement and excellence in character; loyalty to one's true nature; then righteousness; and, finally, filial piety. All this adds up to the principle of virtue within the person.

Confucian Literature

The most important Confucian literature comprises two sets of books. The major one is the Five Classics. While Confucius may not have personally written them, he certainly was associated with them. The Five Classics contain five visions: *I Ching* (Classic of Changes); *Shu Ching* (Classic of History); *Shih Ching* (Classic of Poetry); *LiChi* (Collection of Rituals); and *Ch'un-ch'iu* (Spring and Autumn-Annals). For 2,000 years, their influence has been without parallel in the history of China.

When Chinese students were studying for civil service examinations between 1313 and 1905, they were required to study the Five Classics. However, before they reached that level, they tackled the Four Books, which served as an introduction to the Five. The Four Books have commentaries by Chu Hsi, a great Neo-Confucian philosopher who helped revitalize Confucianism in China. Confucian Classics, as they were called, became the core curriculum for all levels of education.

FACTS

The *I Ching*, one of the Five Classics of Confucianism, combines divinatory art with numerological techniques and ethical insight. Accordingly, there are said to be two complementary and conflicting vital energies: yin and yang. Enthusiasts have claimed that this Classic of Changes is a means of understanding, and even controlling, future events.

The Reputation of Confucius

The edicts of Confucius did not go without criticism, much of it based on what was seen as his idealism and unrealistic attitudes. Confucius said that, unlike Buddhist belief, karma was not a force in the progress of man resulting from moral goodness or the lack of it, rather it was destiny. Confucianism taught that a person should choose what to do in a single-minded manner, without taking into consideration what the outcome may be.

Is human nature fundamentally good or bad? Confucius didn't have an answer. As time went by, the positive view became the orthodoxy.

Confucius developed his ambition to become active in the teaching of politicians. He wanted to put his humanist ideas into practice and saw government people as the best conduit. In his early forties and fifties he became a magistrate, then eventually a minister of justice in his home state of Lu.

It was probably around the age of fifty that the turning point in Confucius' life came. He was given an important job and was asked his advice about how to induce the people to be loyal. He answered, "Approach them with dignity, and they will respect you. Show piety towards your parents and kindness toward your children, and they will be loyal to you. Promote those who are worthy, train those who are incompetent; that is the best form of encouragement."

The reputation of Confucius grew, as did the number of his disciples. Trouble came, of course, because he generated the enmity of those who opposed his teachings and growing influence. His political career was short-lived, and at the age of fifty-six when he realized his influence had declined, he moved on and tried to find a feudal state in which he could teach and give service. He was more or less in exile, but his reputation as a man of virtue spread.

When he was sixty-seven years old he returned home to teach, write, and edit. He died in 479 B.C.E. at the age of seventy-two.

FACTS

Yin and Yang are thought to be the complementary forces that make up all aspects of life. Yin is considered as female, earth, dark, passive, and absorbing. Yang is male, heaven, light, active, and penetrating. In harmony the two are depicted as the light and dark halves of a circle.

Rituals and Customs

As Confucianism does not have all the elements of a religion, and is primarily an ethical movement, it lacks sacraments and liturgy. However, the rituals that occur at important times in a person's life became part of the movement. Confucianism recognizes and regulates four life passages—birth, reaching maturity, marriage, and death. At the root is the ritual of respect: A person must exhibit respect to gain respect.

Birth

The Tai-shen (spirit of the fetus) protects the expectant woman and deals harshly with anyone who harasses the mother-to-be. The mother is given a special diet and is allowed to rest for a month after delivery. The mother's family is responsible for coming up with all that is required by the baby on the first-, fourth-, and twelfth-month anniversaries of the birth.

Marriage

There are six stages the couple go through in the marriage process:

Proposal. The couple exchange the year, month, day, and hour of each of their births. If any unpropitious event happens within the bride-to-be's family during the following three days, then the woman is believed to have rejected the proposal.

Engagement. After the wedding day has been chosen, the bride announces the wedding with invitations and a gift of cookies made in the shape of the moon.

Dowry. This is carried to the groom's home in a solemn procession. Gifts by the groom to the bride, equal in value to the dowry, are sent to her.

Procession. The groom visits the bride's home and brings her back to his place, with much fanfare.

Marriage and reception. The couple recite their vows that bond them together for a lifetime, toast each other with wine, then take center stage at a banquet.

Morning after. The bride serves breakfast to the groom's parents, who then reciprocate.

Death

At death, the relatives cry aloud to inform the neighbors. The family starts mourning and puts on clothes made of coarse material. The corpse is washed and placed in a coffin. Mourners bring incense and money to offset the cost of the funeral. Food and significant objects of the deceased are placed into the coffin. A Buddhist or Taoist priest, or even a Christian minister, performs the burial ritual. Friends and family follow the coffin to the cemetery, bringing a willow branch, which symbolizes the soul of the person who has died. The branch is later carried back to the family altar where it is used to "install" the spirit of the deceased. Liturgies are performed on the seventh, ninth, and forty-ninth day after the burial, and on the first and third anniversaries of the death.

On Confucius' death his students compiled his thoughts in *Spring and Autumn Annals.* Mencius spread the values of Confucianism throughout the known world. With the increasing popularity in Confucius, his disciples and followers left sacrifices in temples dedicated to him. The People's Republic of China banned the ritual sacrifices in 1906.

Diversification into Modern Society

Not long after Confucius' death, his followers split into eight separate schools. All of them claimed to be the legitimate heir to the legacy. Many superior disciples surfaced, though, including Tseng-tzu, Tzu Kung, and Tzu-hsia. They were instrumental in continuing the teachings and legacy of Confucius. The man who had great influence on Confucianism and its continuance is Mencius; he was known as the Confucian intellectual. He sought social reform in a society that had become oriented almost totally for profit, self-interest, wealth, and power. It was the philosophy of Mencius that a true man could not be corrupted by wealth. Rather than challenging the power structure head-on, Mencius offered a compromise of right living and wealth. That way the wealthy could have their cake and eat it, and preserve protection for themselves and their families. Mencius' strategy was to make the urge for profit and self-interest part of a moral attitude that emphasized public-spiritedness, welfare, and rightness. This attitude of acknowledging human nature and its desire for success and self-improvement in shaping the human condition might, today, be thought of as surprisingly modern, particularly when one considers when it was said.

Mencius was followed by Hsun-tzu (300–230 B.C.E.), one of the most eminent of noble scholars. Unlike Mencius, Hsun-tzu taught that human nature is evil because he considered that it was natural for men to go after gratification of their passions. His attitude, as opposed to that of Mencius, was that learning produced a cultured person who, by definition, became a virtuous member of a community. Hsun-tzu's stance was a tough, moral reasoning, law-and-order one. He believed in progress, and his sophisticated understanding of the political mindset around him enriched the Confucian heritage. Confucians revered him as the finest of scholars for more than three centuries.

QUESTIONS?

Are there different schools of Confucianism?
There are six: Han Confucianism, Neo-Confucianism, Contemporary Neo-Confucianism, Korean Confucianism, Japanese Confucianism, and Singapore Confucianism.

The influence of Confucianism on China in particular was largely due to the power of its disciples and of the written works of not only Confucius but also his followers. The vitality of the Confucian ethic permeated much of the basic elements of societal thought and political action in the eastern hemisphere that was unprecedented. But, in modern times it began to wane due to the rise of Marxism-Leninism in 1949 as the official ideology of the People's Republic of China. Confucianism was pushed into the background. In spite of that, the upper crust of that society kept a publicly unacknowledged link that amazingly continued to influence aspects of behavior; it had an effect on the attitudes at every level of life; Confucian roots run extremely deep.

In other regions, especially Japan, Korea, Taiwan, Singapore, and North America, there has been a revival of Confucian studies. Thinkers in the West have been inspired by the philosophy and have begun to explore what it might mean today. Even in China, exploration is taking place between what might be a fruitful interaction between Confucian humanism and other kinds of political practices.

CHAPTER 12
Taoism

Taoism became evident in the first century C.E. The name came from the Chinese character that means path or way: Tao. In English it is pronounced "dow." The Tao is a natural force that makes the universe the way it is.

Origins and Development

The foundation of Taoism is attributed partially to Lao tzu and his written material called "Classic Way of Power" (Tao-Te Ching). It advocates the philosophy of disharmony or harmony of opposites, meaning there is no love without hate, no light without dark, no male without female—in other words, Yin and Yang. Collectively, the writings called Tao Tsang are concerned with the ritual meditations of the Tao. Adherents are called Taoists.

Taoist thought permeated the Chinese culture in the same way that Confucianism did, and the two are often linked. Taoism became more popular than Confucianism, even though Confucianism had state patronage. Taoism was based on the individual and tended to reject the organized society of Confucianism. The traditions became so well entrenched within China that many people accepted both of them, although they applied the concepts to their lives in different ways.

FACTS

The Taoist philosophy and religion have expanded beyond China into most of the Asian cultures, especially in Vietnam, Japan, Korea, and Taiwan. A western type of Taoism has developed in both Europe and the United States.

Taoism wasn't a religious faith when it was first started. It was conceived as a philosophy and evolved into a religion that has a number of deities. Lao tzu, whom many believed was the founder of Taoism, was so revered that he was thought of as a deity. On the other hand, there were some who thought of him as a mystical character.

Nonaction

A key Taoist concept is that of nonaction or the natural course of things. It is a direct link to yin and yang. Yin (dark/female) represents cold, feminine, evil, and negative principles. The yang (light/male) represents good, masculine, warmth, and positive principles. Yin (the dark side) is the breath that formed the earth. Yang (the light side) is the breath that formed the heavens. When civilization gets in the way, the balance of yin and yang is upset. A western person might say that one has to get out of one's own way to get anywhere. However, yin and yang are not polar opposites; they are values in people that depend on individual circumstances. So, what is cold for one person may be warm for another. Yin and yang are said to be identical aspects of the same reality.

The study, practice, and readings of yin and yang have become a school of philosophy in its own right. The idea is for the student to find balance in life where yin represents inactivity, rest, and reflection, while yang represents activity and creativity. The basic feature of Taoism is to restore balance. Extremes produce a swinging back to the opposite. Therefore, there is a constant movement from activity to inactivity and back again.

It's not easy to define Taoism in any formal way because its philosophy doesn't have a concrete system. While it shares many of the same ideas about man, society, and the universe as Confucianism, its attitude tends to be more personal and metaphysical. Taoism, it's said, has to be experienced and words like "power" and "energy" are frequently used to describe what actually can't be measured in any scientific form. In spite of that, it's interesting that Taoism had a bent toward science, especially medicine. Taoist faith healers contributed to medical knowledge and literature with the production of the medical book, *The Yellow Emperor's Esoteric Classic,* that included experiments with natural ingredients such as plants and minerals. Fifty-two chapters of pharmacopoeia called *Great Pharmacopoeia* came out in the sixteenth century.

The Tao is recognized to be fundamental, so much so that it's beyond description. It is said that the Tao that can be talked about is not the true Tao. The Tao is seen as the principle of creation and the source from which everything comes.

The interest in science was considered to reflect the Taoist emphasis on direct observation and experience of the nature of things. But, there is a sort of contradiction of terms because a tremendous amount of the work was based not on scientific discovery but intuitive thought and experience. It is said that much of the knowledge died with the men who discovered it, for they did not share it with the future generations.

The Competition among Religions

The other religion that was close to Taoism and shared influence with the people in the same way that Confucianism did was Buddhism. However, their ideas of the nonexistence of the individual ego and the illusory nature of the physical word didn't go down well with Taoism; in fact, they were opposed to them. But, there were borrowings between the two, for instance, with the practice of Zen.

Lao Tzu

The date of birth of Lao Tzu is unknown, but some scholars have put it between 600 and 300 B.C.E. The fact that an educated guess gives a 300-year window doesn't, perhaps, provide a student with too much in the way of confidence about the answer. But, it seems in line with the Taoist philosophy that the existence of its founder and his place of birth can't be verified; however, Lao Tzu's tremendous influence throughout the world is beyond question.

FACTS

The Taoist philosophy can perhaps be best summed up in a quote from Chuang Tzu:

"To regard the fundamental as the essence, to regard things as coarse, to regard accumulation as deficiency, and to dwell quietly alone with the spiritual and the intelligent—herein lie the techniques of Tao of the ancients."

In an effort to give some kind of answer for the reasons of Lao Tzu's obscurity, a scholar has said that he was a gentleman recluse whose doctrine consisted of nonaction. Perhaps a quote from Zen does something to substantiate this opinion: "Do Without Doing." It is noted in many historical reports that Lao Tzu was a contemporary of a younger Confucius. It goes without saying that there are many other legends concerning both great men, many of which, including this one, can't be substantiated.

The Tao-te Ching, which is purported to contain Lao Tzu's great teachings, is a compilation and not a single piece of authorship. Most scholars agree that the sayings were gathered over many years, with some ascribed to Lao Tzu, and others to his disciples. The work is basically a collection of pithy aphorisms or sayings that express the ideas that make up his teachings.

Central Beliefs

The Taoist philosophy is not the easiest to understand. The Taoists rejected the Confucian idea of regulating life and society and said it's better to be concerned with a contemplation of nature. They believed that by doing nothing they could accomplish everything and harness the powers of the universe. Here's a quote from Lao Tzu:

> *The Tao abides in non-action,*
> *Yet nothing is left undone.*
> *If kings and lords observed this,*
> *The ten thousand things would develop naturally.*
> *If they still desired to act,*
> *They would return to the simplicity of formless substance.*
> *Without form there is no desire.*
> *Without desire there is tranquility.*
> *In this way all things would be at peace.*
> *The Taoist sage has no ambitions so he cannot fail.*
> *Those who never fail always succeed.*
> *And those who succeed are all-powerful.*

The Tao has been described as the origin and mother of the Ten Thousand Things—a standard phrase to show that everything exists. One achieves without force. One gives life without possessing the things one has created. This is the essence of naturalness. One cannot grasp this philosophy with the intellect. One becomes aware, but unable to define.

Outside many Taoist temples at the main entrance is an elaborately colored container. It is for joss sticks, which are placed there to be lit. The rising incense symbolizes prayers offered to heaven. On either side of the container will be carved dragons; similarly, there will be dragons on the roof of the temple. These symbolize strength, energy, and life force.

The idea of a personal deity is foreign to Taoism, so is the concept of the creation of the universe. Therefore, a Taoist does not pray as the Christians do, for instance, because they believe there is no god to hear the prayers or act upon them. On the contrary, they feel the way to seek answers is through inner meditation and outer observation. Their beliefs can be thus summed up: The Tao surrounds everyone and everything so everyone must listen to find enlightenment.

Taoists have an affinity for promoting good health. They believe that five organs correspond to five parts of the sky: water, fire, wood, metal, and earth. Each person should nurture the chi (breath) that refers to the spirit, energy, or life force within everything. There are Yoga-style and Tai Chi exercises to help accomplish this.

Followers should seek the Three Jewels of compassion, moderation, and humility.

The art of *wu wei*—action through no action or do without doing—should be practiced. One way of looking at this is to imagine standing still in a flowing river and letting what is opposing do all the work. By standing still one appears to move against the current by not moving against it. To an outsider one would appear to take no action but, in fact, one does take action before others ever foresee such a need. It follows that one should plan in advance and consider what to do before doing it.

A Taoist should be kind to others, if only because doing so leads to reciprocation of the same act. Others are by nature compassionate. The saying implies that if they are left alone this will be exhibited without the need for recompense.

The essential belief of Taoism is that the only permanent thing in life is change. Taoism says that because everything is changing, people are tempted to look ahead to find something that is permanent. Once they do that, a person ceases to be aware of the present. When that happens the tendency is for the present to be interpreted in terms of the past. Taoism says a person should be in the reality of the now—the present moment.

FACTS

Traditional Chinese medicine believes that illness is caused by blockages or lack of balance of the body's chi. The practice of Tai Chi is believed to balance this energy flow. Through the gradual building of one's inner energy, it is discovered how soft overcomes hard. Tai Chi is known as an internal art because of its emphasis on internal Chi power, rather than on external physical power, which helps to restore balance.

The world is as it is. If it is perfect then that is what is, not what people imagine it should be. That being so, any change will make things less than perfect. It is said that the enemy of human perfection is the unnatural, which includes the forced, the premeditated, and the socially prescribed.

Writings

The major piece of literature in Taoism is Lao Tzu's Tao-te Ching (Classic Way of Power—*te* means power, the energy of Tao at work in the world). As stated earlier, it has never been established that Lao Tzu was the sole author. There are no references in the work to other persons, events, places, or even writings that could provide any evidence to assist in placing or dating the composition. The fact that the work can't be authenticated as to its author or place is, again, somehow in keeping with the philosophy of Taoism; the work exists and that is everything.

The essence of the book is pure simplicity: Accept what is without wanting to change it. Study the natural order and go with it, rather than against it. The effort to change something creates resistance. Everything nature provides is free; a person should emulate nature and consider everyone as an equal.

If people stand and observe, they will see that work proceeds best if they stop trying too hard. The more extra effort you exert and the harder you look for results, the less gets done. The philosophy of Taoism is to simply be.

The Tao-te Ching was compiled in an environment that was racked by widespread disorder, wanton self-seeking rulers, and rampant immoral behavior. The popularity of the work has been, and is, widespread. An amazing number of translations have been produced, more than for any other literary work except the Bible. There have been eighty English translations alone.

FACTS

One example of the use of harmony and meditation is the practice of Feng Shui. The literal meaning of Feng Shui is wind and water, which are the natural elements that shape the landscape. A Feng Shui expert can advise on how to get the best results in a home or office by establishing the most advantageous alignment of space and furnishings to allow the most positive and harmonious flow of chi.

Chuang-tzu was a great Taoist sage. He is best known for the book that bears his name, the Chuang-tzu, also known as *Nan-hua Chenching* (The Pure Classic of Nan-hua). It is thought to have originally comprised thirty-three chapters, although there may have been more. Again, as it seems with most works of written religious antiquity, there is controversy over what the author wrote and what others contributed. However, scholars agree that the first seven chapters of the Chuang-tzu were written by the author alone.

He wrote other books highly critical of Confucianism. On the other hand he was seen as being a great influence on the development of Chinese Buddhism. Buddhist scholars considered Chuang-tzu to be the primary source for Taoist thought and they drew heavily from his teachings. Overall he was considered the most significant and comprehensive of the Taoist writers.

He lived around 327 B.C.E., which made him a contemporary of the eminent Confucian scholar, Mencius. All of this confirms yet again how intertwined Taoism, Buddhism, and Confucianism were with each other.

The following example of the value of living naturally comes from Chuang Tzu. He said that a drunk could fall from a moving carriage without hurting himself, whereas a sober person would be injured by the same fall. The reason is that the drunk is "united" and his body reacts naturally. The sober person, perceiving danger, tenses his- or herself and is thus vulnerable.

Apparently, when he was on the point of death, there was talk of an elaborate funeral, dressing of the corpse, and all that. Chuang Tzu dismissed the idea and said that all creation would make offerings and escort him on his way. His disciples replied that they were afraid that the crows and the buzzards might eat him if he wasn't properly prepared.

Chuang-tzu replied, "Above the ground it's the crows and the kites who will eat me, below the ground it's the worms and the ants. What prejudice is this, that you wish to take from the one to give to the other?"

Worship and Practices

Philosophical Taoism developed a Religious Taoism that included rituals, temples, priests, monks, and nuns. The religious element was concerned with immortality. What was sought was the ability to become immortal, and part of this search became involved with magical powers. The search was concerned with chi and its supply, meaning a need to create a greater reservoir of breath (chi). The essence of this was not that persons would get younger but would live longer.

Taoism has strong elements of shamanism seen in its belief in the existence of two worlds: the physical one and the spiritual one. The oldest surviving Chinese religious text is the *I Ching,* which is a divination system. The *I Ching* dates from around 1,000 B.C.E. and is attributed to Confucius. The fighting of ghosts and evil spirits was revered by Taoists until the Communists outlawed the practice.

Fortune-telling is becoming popular again in Taoist and Buddhist temples. A fortune-teller gives advice but not predictions.

How did the Taoists and Confucians get along with each other?
Confucians looked at Taoism as emotional, irrational, and magical.
The Taoists looked at the Confucians as bureaucratic and imperialistic.
But, it was the Confucian system that shaped China for over two
thousand years.

Rituals and Customs

The religious aspects of Taoism are related more to shamanism than
worship in the typical way. Taoist priests usually look after temples in
urban areas. Monks and nuns live in temples located in sacred mountains.
China has many sacred mountains and some of the temples are even
dramatically suspended on the side of them. In general, monks and nuns
are permitted to marry. Their work ensures the worship of the sacred
texts, of which there are some 1,440 books.

In Taoism there is a strong element of the ways and means of
achieving immortality. Throughout life, adherents study and practice
exercises designed to increase the flow of chi energy, and some will
become expert in meditation to the point where they become one with
the Tao. A quote from the Chuang Tzu provides a good clue to the Taoist
attitude toward life and death:

> *Birth is not a beginning; death is not an end. There is existence without*
> *limitation; there is continuity without a starting point.*
> *Existence without limitation is space. Continuity without a starting point is*
> *time. There is birth, there is death, there is issuing forth, there is entering in. That*
> *through which one passes in and out without seeing its form, that is the Portal*
> *of God.*

Birth and Death

Birth is a time for casting horoscopes. A month after the birth a
naming ceremony is held. Death combines elements of Taoism, Buddhism,
and Confucianism in regard to life after death. Funeral rites have to be
performed correctly for the dead to join the family ancestors. There is a

belief that the soul is judged by the King of Hell. After the body is buried, paper models of money, houses, and cars are burnt to help the soul in the afterlife, perhaps by paying for a release from the King of Hell. After about ten years the body is dug up. The bones are cleaned, then reburied at a site often chosen by a Feng Shui expert.

When a Taoist funeral procession passes through the streets on its way to the cemetery, the family and friends of the deceased wear white, the traditional color of mourning in China.

Festivals

Taoists and Buddhists share four major Chinese festivals. In addition, the Taoists celebrate many others throughout the year including the Taoist vegetarian and fasting days.

Chinese New Year is the major festival, which is also known as the "Spring Festival." It is a time of great excitement and joy. It is also a time of wonderful and copious food and of gifts and roving bands of musicians that parade through the streets. Families reunite and give lavish gifts to children. Traditionally, it is the time when new paper statues of the kitchen god are put up in houses. The door gods, who defend the house against evil spirits, are also replaced with new ones and good luck sayings are hung over the doorways.

The high point of the season is New Year's Eve, when every member of every family returns home. A sumptuous dinner is served and children receive gifts of red envelopes that contain gifts of lucky money. Firecrackers and whistling rockets seem to be everywhere.

In preparation for the events, every house is thoroughly cleaned so that the New Year will start off fresh and clean. Hair must be cleaned and set prior to the holiday, otherwise a financial setback would be invited. Debts should also be settled so that the coming year can start off with a clean slate.

Following various religious ceremonies, the eleventh day is a time for inviting in-laws to dine. The Lantern Festival, on the fifteenth day after New Year, marks the end of the New Year season.

The Dragon Boat Festival is celebrated with boats in the shape of dragons. Competing teams row their boats forward to a drumbeat in an effort to win the race. Celebrated in June, the festival has two stories about the history of its meaning. The first one is about the watery suicide of an honest young official who tried to shock the emperor into being kinder to the poor. The race commemorates the people's attempt to rescue the boy in the lake from the dragons who rose to eat him. It is viewed as a celebration of honest government and physical strength.

The other story says the boats raced to commemorate the drowning of a poet on the fifth day of the fifth lunar month in 277 B.C.E. Citizens throw bamboo leaves filled with cooked rice into the water so the fish can eat it rather than the hero poet.

The third great festival is the Hungry Ghosts Festival. Taoists and Buddhists believe that the souls of the dead imprisoned in hell are freed during the seventh month, when the gates of hell are opened. The released souls are permitted to enjoy feasts that had been prepared for them so that they would be pacified and would do no harm. Offerings and devotions, too, are made to please these ghosts and even musical events are staged to entertain them.

The Mid-Autumn Festival is also called the Moon Festival because of the bright harvest moon, which appears on the fifteenth day of the eighth lunar month. The round shape of the moon means family reunion, so, naturally, the holiday is particularly important for members of a family.

One myth says that on the moon were the fairy Chang E, a woodcutter named Wu Gang, and a jade rabbit that was Chang E's pet. In the old days people paid respect to the fairy Chang E and her pet. The custom has ended now, but moon cakes are sold on the month before the arrival of the Moon Festival.

Another story concerns the goddess Sheng O, whose husband discovered the pill of immortality and was about to eat it and become a cruel ruler for eternity. Sheng O swallowed the pill instead, but the Gods saved her and transported her to the moon. She lives there to this day.

CHAPTER 13

Jainism and Baha'i

J ainism is an ethical belief system concerned with the moral life of an individual. While Jainism originated in India and Baha'i originated in Persia (now Iran), such was the commingling of many beliefs and sacred works that they can be summed up in the Baha'i teaching: "The Earth is but one country and mankind its citizens."

The Development of Jainism

Jainism is a religion and philosophy of India that along with Hinduism and Buddhism is one of the three most ancient religions still in existence in that country. It dates back to 3,000 B.C.E. The three have common elements in their beliefs; for instance, all share the idea of karma where the actions of an individual in successive lives affects and determines a future life. Each also has a historical literary heritage. For example, a classical Hindu story was so influential that the Jains and Buddhists retold it. Each also has a tradition of asceticism. Many Jains and Hindus worship images, and there are even places outside India where Hindus and Jains have joined to build a single temple and share worship space.

The name Jainism comes from the Sanskrit meaning "to conquer." Conquer in that context means conquering inner feelings of hate, greed, and selfishness. The object in life for Jains is to renounce materialistic needs, so that they eventually achieve bliss, or *moksha*.

Jainism's influence on Indian philosophy, logic, art, architecture, grammar, mathematics, astronomy, and astrology has in many ways been greater than that of Hinduism and Buddhism, which have far more adherents. However, unlike those two, Jainism hasn't spread as far; the bulk of the adherents are in India, although there are a few small communities in the United States.

FACTS

Jainism split into two factions in the fourth or third century B.C.E.: the Digambaras (sky clad) and the Svetambaras (white-robed). The major difference between them was the degree of asceticism. The Digambaras believed complete nudity was necessary to signify detachment from material things. The Svetambaras held that simple white robes, three of them, would be equally acceptable.

In Jainism twenty-four significant perfected historical figures act as teachers in the search for perfection. These teachers operate in what are believed to be cycles of history. Jains look at time as eternal and formless. So, the teachers, called Tirthankaras, appear from time to time to preach the Jain religious way. Each of the Tirthankaras has attained absolute freedom, because they have broken away from the cycle of rebirths.

Another sixty-four gods and goddesses, great souls, luminaries, and others are involved in the teaching as well.

The core principle of Jainism is *ahimsa*, or nonviolence.

Vardhamana Mahavira

Of the twenty-four Tirthankaras, the most important, and the last of them, was Vardhamana Mahavira. Born in Bharat, India, either in 540 or 599 B.C.E., he is thought to have been an older contemporary of the Buddha; because he is referred to in Buddhist writings. When he was thirty years old he decided to become an ascetic, suffering for twelve years as he wandered naked, living only on the food he received as alms. He frequently stood as still as a statue. When he was in his early forties he received enlightenment and was thereafter known as a Jina (a conqueror). His followers were known as Jains.

Mahavira preached Jainism for about thirty years, and in that time, gathered followers around him who were organized into four groups that became his disciples: monks, nuns, laymen, and laywomen. It is said that he broke through his karma and attained *moksha*. He died at Pavapuri in the state of Bihar when he was seventy years old. Some reports said that he died of voluntary starvation. Pavapuri has become a place of pilgrimage for Jains.

FACTS

Mahatma Gandhi, the world-famous former Indian pacifist, was apparently strongly influenced by Jain philosophy. The foundation of his policy of nonviolence, which was directed against the British, can be seen in the principles of ahimsa.

The Central Beliefs of Jainism

The goal of Jainism is complete perfection and purification of the soul, which Jains can accomplish by seeking liberation and nonattachment to their bodies, in other words, by cleaning up their karma. They believe that during people's lifetimes their actions are bound to their souls and then the souls through reincarnation are bound to new bodies. This legacy gets in the way of freedom for the soul. The soul starts out pure and possesses infinite knowledge, bliss, and power. It's what goes on in life that explains all the trouble with karma. Actions that arise from desire create the shell that binds the soul. To free yourself from karma you must stop new intake of it and eliminate what has been acquired through the stillness and abstention of asceticism. Karmic intake is the consequence of intentional action combined with passionate expression.

Theoretically, it may seem easy, just eliminate taking in bad karma, but in order to make progress, people need to adopt a mode of life that gives them a clear path to follow. Jain ethics suggest the tools of right knowledge, faith, and proper conduct.

Ahimsa

Essential to any virtuous conduct is the principle of ahimsa, or nonviolence. It's a psychological truism as well as a Jain one—thoughts may give rise to action. For example, violent thoughts must precede violent action. Then, violence in thought is the greater and subtler form of violence.

According to Jainism, yoga—the meditative discipline of the monks—is the means to attain omniscience and thus *moksha*, or liberation. Yoga is the way to cultivate true knowledge (or reality), faith, and true conduct.

Jainism counsels adherents to avoid all forms of violence, whether committed by body, mind, or speech. To accomplish such nonviolence, Jains are committed to a strict lifestyle.

Jains are strict vegetarians and see vegetarianism as an instrument for the practice of nonviolence and peaceful, cooperative coexistence. Strict adherents even limit some forms of plants, including root vegetables, figs, honey, and certain fruits because they contain a greater number of minute living beings.

They often chose to be tradespeople because most other jobs involve doing harm to other beings, even unintentionally. For instance, plowing the earth may destroy untold numbers of insects. Monks and nuns are often seen carrying a small brush that they use to gently sweep the earth in front of them in an effort to avoid treading on an insect. Some even wear a mask over their face in case an insect might accidentally fly into their mouth and be harmed.

The Five Principles

A Jain code of conduct—The Five Principles—is made up of five vows and exists as a strict guide. Practicing Jains promise to adhere to the principles of:

1. **Ahimsa:** To protect all life and avoid harm completely
2. **Satya:** To speak the truth deliberately, so as to avoid saying anything painful to others
3. **Asteya:** To refrain from stealing and to avoid greedy behavior and exploitation
4. **Aparigraha:** To be detached from material things and nonpossessive
5. **Brahmacharya:** To be chaste. Monks and nuns must remain celibate, and the rest of the people must adhere to the important principles of monogamy and faithfulness

Holy Writings

The original teachings of the Jain scriptures begin with the sermons of Mahavira, written down by his disciples and contained in fourteen texts— the *Purvas* (Foundation). The oldest of these have been lost. Of all the many remaining scriptures, the best known is the Uttaradhyayana Sutra, which is an anthology of dialogues and teachings believed to be the last sermon of the Mahavira, plus the Kalpa Sutra, which contains biographies of the Jinas (victors).

Other scriptures contain laws for monks and nuns and an authoritative biography of Mahavira. The Jain doctrines about disputes with other Hindu and early Buddhist teachings provide evidence of the close intertwining of the religions of the East.

FACTS

The Digambaras faction of Jainism does not allow women into the ascetic order and thus they are not allowed to attain liberation, *moksha*, without being reborn as a man along the spiritual path. The Svetambara sect accepts spiritual equality between the sexes. Today, there are three times as many nuns as monks in the membership ranks of the Svetambara sect.

Rituals and Customs of Jainism

The life cycle rites of the Jains differ slightly from those of the Hindus. One significant difference is that the Jains object to some postfuneral rites that the Hindus observe concerning the transition of the deceased's soul from one existence to the next.

Weddings

There are similarities with the Hindu tradition in marriage, but a Jain wedding ceremony is far from a quick trip to a registry office. It actually begins seven days before the wedding, with the prewedding ritual that involves invoking the heavenly goddesses. Another ceremony is held seven days after the wedding; its purpose is to thank and dismiss the deities. In the days before the marriage, the skin of the bride and groom is regularly massaged with perfumed oil, turmeric, and other substances to beautify them for the occasion.

The wedding ceremony is performed under a *mandap* or canopy. The four main posts that hold it up must be erected at an auspicious time of day. Since the *mandap* is usually rather large, the construction is done at the bride's home and often moved to a hired place for the ceremony itself. In the United States, it is possible to rent a *mandap* and have it professionally erected and taken down.

An elaborate series of rituals takes place, including the washing of the groom's feet by the bride's parents prior to the beginning of the actual service. At the conclusion of the ceremony, the priest congratulates the couple on their marriage and gives a final blessing. Their parents send the couple to the temple then to the bride's home.

Festivals

Jains celebrate their religious holidays by fasting, worshiping, reciting sacred texts, holding religious discourses, giving alms, taking certain vows, and other such acts of piety. Annual holidays are observed based on the lunar calendar. The most important celebrations are the birth of Mahavira in Caitra (March/April), his death in Kartik (October/November), and the holiday period Paryushana, which is held for eight or ten days in the months of Shravana and Bhadrapada (August and September). During Paryushana confessions are offered, visits are made to home places for the purpose of asking and extending forgiveness, and fastings are held.

FACTS

Festivals are also celebrated on pilgrimages, which can last for several days. There are many Jain holy places, temples, and shrines. Not surprisingly, many of the pilgrimages and festivals revolve around significant events in the lives of the Tirthankaras.

The Development of Baha'i

Baha'i originated in Persia, now Iran, in the mid-nineteenth century. In 1844, Mirza Ali Mohammad of Shiraz, Iran, a descendent of Mohammed, declared he was the messenger of God and dubbed himself the Bab—a title that means gateway—and became the founder of the Baha'i faith.

His growing success, the number of adherents he gained, the boldness of his doctrine, his epistles and commentaries, and his warnings to his followers that they must break free from the Islamic ideology, stirred fear within the established religious and secular establishments. The Islamic leaders reacted against him and argued that he was not only a heretic but also a dangerous rebel. In 1850, he was arrested, beaten, and executed.

The Execution of the Bab

Sir Justin Shiel, Queen Victoria's Envoy Extraordinary and Minister Plenipotentiary in Tehran recorded an eyewitness report on July 22, which he sent to Lord Palmerston in London. During the first attempt to execute the Bab, the shots broke only the ropes that bound him. Dense smoke from the gunpowder obscured the view; some onlookers said that he had ascended to the skies. In fact, he had been whisked away by supporters. But, he was discovered and the second attempt to execute him was successful. His remains were eventually entombed in the Shrine of Bab, Mount Carmel, Haifa, Israel.

Baha'ullah

Soon after his execution, the Bab's followers suffered their first series of persecutions; 20,000 people were killed. But, before his death, the Bab had predicted that a new prophet would appear to carry on his work who would be greater than himself. One of the survivors from the persecutions was Mizra Hussain Ali. He changed his name to Baha'ullah (the Glory of God).

Baha'ullah, who had been an ardent follower of the Bab, was arrested and put in jail after the Bab was executed. While he was there he had a mystical experience that told him he would become "He Whom God Will Make Manifest." After his release from prison he was exiled. In 1863, he declared himself the new prophet, which resulted in his being put under house arrest by the authorities until 1868. He and his family were exiled again, this time to the city of Acre in Palestine, which is in present-day Israel. Acre was a Turkish community for exiled criminals.

During his time in Acre, Baha'ullah set up a community of adherents and used his time to produce a series of books that became the foundation of the Baha'i scriptures, which established the religion. He and his followers were eventually allowed to come out of exile and settle in

Mount Carmel in Israel. His aim was to establish a universal religion that preached peace and harmony. The Baha'ullah died on May 29, 1892.

Before the Baha'ullah died he appointed his eldest son, Abbas Effendi, as the only interpreter of his teachings. The son changed his name to Abdul Baha (servant of God) and for the next thirty years he conducted a missionary crusade throughout the world, including North America and Europe. He expanded his father's writings and died on November 28, 1921.

The Last Leader

The third and last leader was the grandson of Abdul Baha, Shoghi Effendi (the guardian). He established an administrative structure designed to oversee the religion and a supreme legislative body called the Universal House of Justice. He died on November 2, 1957, without leaving a successor.

The faith then underwent a considerable growth, which began in the 1960s. By the late twentieth century, Baha'i had more than 150 national governing bodies and over 20,000 local spiritual assemblies. When the Islamic fundamentalists came to power in Iran in 1979, the government persecuted the indigenous members of the Baha'i faith.

FACTS

Baha'ullah insisted that there was only one human race and it is wrong for any group of people to assert that they are in some way superior to the rest of humanity. Prejudice, whether based on race, ethnicity, nationality, religion, or class, must be overcome if humanity is to create a peaceful and just global society.

The Central Beliefs of Baha'i

The Baha'i faith is the youngest of the world's independent religions. The Baha'ullah is regarded to be the most recent in a line of messengers of God that included Abraham, Moses, the Buddha, Zoroaster, Jesus Christ, and Muhammad. The majority of the central beliefs of Baha'i emanated from the Baha'ullah. He taught that there is one God who is unknowable and whose revelations have been the chief civilizing force in history. Each of the religious messengers has offered essentially the same message of peace and goodwill.

The central theme of Baha'i is that there is one single race and that there is in motion forces that are breaking down traditional barriers of race, class, creed, and nation. Unification is the major challenge and goal. The one religion of God is continuing to evolve; each particular religious system represents a stage in the evolution of the whole.

Among the principles that Baha'i promotes are:

The abandonment of all forms of prejudice.
The assurance to women of full equality of opportunity with men.
The recognition of the unity and relativity of religious truth.
The elimination of extremes of poverty and wealth.
The realization of universal education.
The responsibility of each person to independently search for truth.
The establishment of a global commonwealth of nations.
The recognition that true religion is in harmony with reason and the
    pursuit of scientific knowledge.

One of Baha'ullah's principles was coincidentally very close to that of the late beloved physicist, Nobel Prize winner Richard P. Feynman, who said, "First solve all the problems that have been solved." Baha'ullah said: "Acquire knowledge with your own eyes and not through the eyes of others." He advised followers not to go blindly forward uncritical of traditions, movements, and opinions.

The Baha'i believe in the harmony of science and religion. They attribute any contradictions between the two to human fallibility and arrogance. The Baha'ullah affirms that the result of the practice of unity of science and religion will strengthen religion rather than weaken it.

Since its founding nearly 150 years ago, the Baha'i has taught the equality of the sexes. This faith is the only independent world religion whose founder unequivocally stated that women and men are equal.

The Baha'i literature—hundreds of texts—is based on the writings and spoken words of the Bab, Baha'ullah, Abdul Baha, and Shoghi Effendi. However, the two considered to be most important, written by Baha'ullah, are the Most Holy Book (*Kitab-i-Aqda*) and the Book of Certitude (*Kitab-i-Iqan*). He also wrote the Book of Covenant, which authorized future interpretations by his son. Since the death of Shoghi Effendi no one has been authorized to offer official interpretations of the writings.

Practices of the Baha'i Faith

Professional priests, monastic orders, complicated ceremonial rituals, and initiation ceremonies are not part of the Baha'i faith. Membership in the faith is open to anyone who accepts the teachings of Baha'ullah and professes faith in him.

Private prayer is encouraged; there are many collections to choose from in the works of Baha'ullah and Abdul Baha. At least one of three obligatory prayers should be said each day, in the direction of Acre and Haifa. Baha'i communities hold regular worship meetings under the direction of a respected unpaid person in the community. Readings are carried out from the scriptures.

The Community

Every Baha'i community with nine members or more elects a nine-person administrative body annually on April 21, the date that Baha'ullah announced he was the chosen one. The next administrative level is the National Spiritual Assembly, also elected annually. The final level is the Universal House of Justice, which is elected every five years.

Most meetings take place in people's homes, but some fantastic Baha'i houses of worship have been built according to designs indicated by Baha'ullah: The nine-sided buildings symbolize the nine major faiths that preceded the Baha'i. The number nine, the highest single-digit number, also symbolizes completeness. The Baha'i temples are generally surrounded by beautiful gardens, with various trees and fountains. Other buildings built next to the temple serve educational and social purposes.

The Baha'i community has members from all over the world and numbers about five million souls. These represent 2,112 ethnic and tribal groups who live in over 116,000 localities in 188 independent countries. Baha'i adherents come from diverse religious backgrounds: Buddhist, Christian, Hindu, Jain, Jewish, Muslim, Sikh, Zoroastrian, and nonreligious.

The work of the faith is supported entirely by voluntary contributions from its members. Giving to the Baha'i fund is regarded as one of the privileges of membership.

Religious Festivals

The Baha'i calendar is comprised of nineteen months, with each month having nineteen days, providing a 361-day year. It was established by the Bab and confirmed by the Baha'ullah. The four days (five days in leap year) not included are called intercalary days and are used for giving gifts and providing hospitality. Several annual festivals mark the anniversaries of historically important events—the birthdays of the Bab and Baha'ullah, the anniversary of the death of the Bab, and the ascensions of Baha'ullah and his son.

The most important festival is the Feast of Ridvan held from April 21 to May 2. It commemorates the Baha'ullah's announcement of his mission. The Nineteen-Day Feast is another important occasion. These feasts are held on the first day of each month (according to the Baha'i calendar, each month has nineteen days), and they promote hospitality and communal celebration.

CHAPTER 14
Sikhism

Sikhs reject the assertion that Sikhism is a reform movement of Hinduism and Islam. Instead, they say that it came from the divine inspiration of Guru Nanak and the nine gurus who succeeded him. All sects follow the belief in one God and the teachings and scriptures of the ten gurus.

Origins and Development

Sikhism was founded by Guru Nanak in the Punjab (Panjab), India, in the late fifteenth century C.E. An adherent of the faith is called a Sikh, which means "follower" in Sanskrit. There are roughly nineteen million Sikhs, the majority of them are in the Punjab in the northwestern part of India. About two million have emigrated to live and work in the United States, Europe, or in parts of what used to be the British colonies.

Sikhism, which is, comparatively speaking, a young religion, is a monotheistic one. Sikhs believe in one God called *Waheguru* (great teacher). Scholars have indicated that they think Sikhism evolved as a Hindu reform movement or as a mixture of Hinduism and Islam. The Sikhs reject that theory and claim their religion grew out of the divine inspiration of Guru Nanak and the nine gurus who came after him. Nevertheless, Nanak was born a Hindu in Punjab in 1469. When he was young he worked for a local Muslim politician and it's recorded that he impressed everyone with his wisdom and learning. He was part of a group that would sit by the side of a river to pray and discuss religion.

At one point he was absent from this routine for three days. When he came back, he didn't speak for a day. When he did, he said, "There is neither Hindu nor Muslim, so whose path shall I follow? I shall follow God's path. God is neither Hindu nor Muslim and the path I follow is God's." There are other reports on what Nanak might have said, but the essence of having received enlightenment seems to be reliable.

After his revelation in his late twenties, he left his wife and two sons to travel in search of truth and wisdom. After about twenty years, he acquired farmland and settled in central Punjab where he founded the town of Kartarpur and became Guru Nanak. The Sikh religion was born and Nanak was its first guru.

FACTS

There are stories told about Nanak's childhood and his amazing abilities. At school he was taught the classical lessons in addition to Persian and Arabic languages and Muslim literature. His teacher realized he had reached the point where there wasn't any more he could teach him; he was learning from Nanak.

The Path of Guru Nanak

Guru Nanak followed the not unusual path of the prophets who preceded him. He traveled and taught in far outlying areas and set up communities of followers along the way. He spoke out against what he saw as inequities (the Hindu caste system, for example), and he stressed that all people were equal.

Nanak's childhood friend, Mardan, a professional musician, accompanied him on his travels. Nanak liked to sing and did so in the form of hymns. So, he and Mardan entertained the local populace while getting the message out. As part of his message, Nanak wore a mixture of Hindu and Muslim clothes when he and Mardan, as it were, toured.

Many of the Hindu and Muslim audiences became followers of the fledgling religion. As he gathered followers around him, his spiritual ideas bore fruit until his composed hymns, which were written down, eventually became the core of the Sikh sacred text: the *Adi Granth* (original book).

In the final phases of his life, Guru Nanak returned from all the traveling to his established Sikh community at Kartarpur and settled down with his wife and sons. It was time for him to consider a successor. Most people thought he would appoint one of his sons. But, his insistence on the principle of equality that he had been teaching for years and had made part of the religion made him choose Lehna, a man who had become an ardent disciple. Nanak blessed Lehna and gave him a new name, Angad, and he had him anointed with a saffron mark on his forehead. When Guru Nanak gathered his followers together for prayers, he invited Angad to occupy the seat of the Guru. In that way Guru Angad was ordained as the successor to Guru Nanak.

When his followers lifted the sheet, they found nothing except the flowers, all of which were fresh. The Hindus took theirs and cremated them, the Muslims took theirs and buried them.

The myth of Guru Nanak's death says that Guru Nanak asked for flowers to be placed on either side of him, from the Hindus on his right, from the Muslims on his left. He explained that those whose flowers remained fresh the next day would have their way. He then asked his disciples to pray, and he lay down and covered himself with a sheet. In the early hours of the next morning, September 22, 1539, Guru Nanak merged with the eternal light of the Creator.

Central Beliefs

To understand how the Sikhs developed it helps to get to know The Ten Gurus. The word guru means teacher, but when the Sikhs speak of the Guru they mean God, the Great Teacher. Pieces of Sikh history can be related to a particular guru. Each one of them had an influence on the beliefs of the religion, and some of them had political influence. As we know, the first guru was Guru Nanak who lived from 1469 to 1539. The period from the first to the last, the tenth guru, was, roughly speaking, from the mid-1500s to the late 1600s.

The Ten Gurus in historical order are:

1. **Guru Nanak (1469–1539)**, who founded the Sikh religion.
2. **Guru Angad (1504–1552)** was a Hindu before turning to Sikhism. Born Bhai Lehna, he made pilgrimages every year and became a close and prominent disciple of Guru Nanak, who eventually anointed him. He devised a script that was used for writing the Sikh scriptures. His work is found in the *Guru Granth Sahib*—the Holy Book.
3. **Guru Amar Das (1479–1574)** collected the hymns of Guru Nanak and added his own. He developed the custom of the *langar*, the communal meal, which was devised as a social kitchen to remove caste distinctions and establish social harmony among his followers.
4. **Guru Ram Das (1534–1581)** was the son-in-law of Guru Amar Das. He founded the city of Ramdaspur, now known as Amritsar, which became the Sikh holy city to which he initiated pilgrimages. The construction of the Golden Temple began during his time. He also contributed to the *Guru Granth Sahib*. In particular, he wrote the Sikh wedding hymn.
5. **Guru Arjan (1563–1606)** was the youngest son of Guru Ram Das. He compiled the *Adi Granth*, the most important segment of the *Guru Granth Sahib*, and completed the building of the Golden Temple. He

made the Sikhs very popular and such a presence that the Muslim Mughals came to see the Sikhs as a growing menace. The Emperor had him tortured and killed.

6. **Guru Hargobind (1595–1644)**, the son of Guru Arjan, instilled a sense of Sikh militancy and tried to organize the Sikhs and the Hindus against the Mughals and was imprisoned for a short time. He perfected the dress code introduced by his father and started the tradition of wearing two swords, one signifying his political authority, the other his religious authority.

7. **Guru Har Rai (1630–1661)**, grandson of Guru Hargobind, supported the elder brother of Emperor Aurangzab in a conflict and as a reprisal the Mughals held his son hostage. He had a reputation for medicine and opened hospitals where treatment was provided free.

8. **Guru Har Krishan (1656–1664)**, known as "the boy guru," was the second son of Guru Har Rai and succeeded his father at the age of five when his brother was still being held hostage by the Mughals. The Emperor summoned the boy guru to Delhi and kept him under house arrest. He contracted smallpox and died.

9. **Guru Tegh Bahadur (1621–1675)** was the second son of Guru Hargobind. Tegh Bahadur (brave sword) was not his original name, it was given to him by his subjects because of his resistance to Emperor Aurangzab. He gained a reputation for feeding the hungry, and he wrote many hymns that are now in the *Guru Granth Sahib*. He predicted the coming of the Western powers to the Indian subcontinent and the downfall of the Mughals. He was beheaded after refusing to accept Islam.

10. **Guru Gobind Singh (1675–1708)**, the tenth and last guru, was the most famous after Guru Nanak. He organized the Sikhs to oppose the tyranny of the Mughals and established a military defense group known as the Khalsa (the brotherhood of the pure), which still remains. The Khalsa are considered a "chosen" race of soldier-saints willing to give up their lives to uphold their faith and defend the weak. Guru Gobind Singh gave all Sikhs the name *singh* (lion) for men and *kaur* (princess) for women, to do away with all traces of the caste system. He also decreed that the writings of the *Guru Granth Sahib* would be the authority from which the Sikhs would be governed. The book is treated almost like a human being. Wherever it is

moved, it is attended by five Sikhs who represent the Khalsa. In his efforts to oppose the Mughals, he lost his two sons and was finally assassinated. He has been called "the most glorious hero of our race."

FACTS

Sikhs developed a warrior attitude because of the violence against them by the Mughals. This attitude was reinforced when the Khalsa was founded and the five tenets known as Ks were instituted—*kesh* (uncut hair), *kangha* (comb), *kirpan* (sword), *kara* (steel bracelet), and *kachch* (short pants for use in battle). As a result Sikhs wear long uncut hair with a comb in it and a steel bracelet on the right wrist. The sword and short pants are usually reserved for battle.

Sikhism is based on the discipline of purification and the overcoming of the five vices: greed, anger, false pride, lust, and attachments to material goods. At the end of a person's life, the good and the bad conduct are balanced out and the result determines the family, race, and character of the person when reborn. There is no direct belief in heaven or hell as places, but those who have been selfish or cruel in the current life will suffer in their next existence. Those who acted with compassion and honesty will be better off in their next incarnation. The soul develops as it passes through the many incarnations until it becomes united with the infinite one.

Sikhs are opposed to the idea of austere asceticism; they emphasize the ideal of achieving saintliness as active members of society. Sikhism prohibits idolatry, the caste system, and the use of wine or tobacco. Stress is placed on the importance of leading a good moral life that includes loyalty, gratitude for all favors received, philanthropy, justice, truth, and honesty.

Holy Writings and Worship

There is only one canonical work, the *Adi Granth* (First Book) also known as the *Guru Granth Sahib*, which was compiled by the fifth Guru, Guru Arjan, in 1604. There were at least three versions of the book, but the one recognized as authentic was revised by Guru Gobind Singh in 1704. The *Adi Granth* has about 6,000 hymns composed by the first five Gurus:

Nanak, Angad, Amar Das, Ram Das, and Arjan. Other contributors to the book include Bhakta saints and Muslim Sufis.

The *Adi Granth* occupies a focal point in all Sikh temples. The *gurdwara* (doorway to the Guru) contains a cot under a canopy on which a copy of the *Adi Granth* is placed on cushions and covered by elaborate decorations. All who enter the *gurdwara* in the temple must cover their heads and take off their shoes and wash their feet. Services may take place at any time; there is no special time of worship. Worshipers will bow in front of the *Guru Granth Sahib* and during services prayers will be said, there will be a sermon, chanting of hymns, and finally a communal meal. In accordance with the principles of equality in Sikhism, men and women share the tasks of preparing and serving the *langar* that is made available after most services to anyone who wishes to indulge.

The chief *gurdwara* is the magnificent *Harimandir* (the Golden Temple) at Amritsar in Punjab state. However, in the average *gurdwara* there may be readings, Sikh music, study classes, and even physical activities.

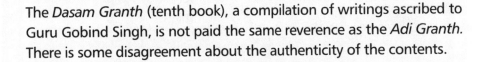

The *Dasam Granth* (tenth book), a compilation of writings ascribed to Guru Gobind Singh, is not paid the same reverence as the *Adi Granth*. There is some disagreement about the authenticity of the contents.

In their homes, most Sikhs will set aside a room to hold a copy of the *Guru Granth Sahib*. The room is also called a *gurdwara*. Daily readings are part of the duties of the household. Many Sikhs will recite verses during their daily activities. Because not every person or family has the accommodations to set aside a separate room for the *Guru Granth Sahib*, they will, instead, have a copy of excerpts, which are known as the *Gutkha*, from which to say morning and evening prayers.

Rituals and Customs

Birth and naming are carried out in different ways by different faiths: The Christians have christening, the Jews circumcision, and the Sikhs have the naming ceremony.

After the birth, the parents take the child to the *gurdwara*. Hymns are sung that express gratitude for the birth of a baby. The *Adi Granth* is then opened at random and the child is given a name beginning with the first letter of the first word on the left page. The parents take some time to think about it, then they chose what they want the name to be. Then more hymns are sung.

Marriage

Marriage can still be an arrangement between the families of the bride and groom. But, Sikhs now accept the right of the men or the women to reject the person chosen for them. However, marriage is still seen as the joining of two families.

Traditionally, the bride wears red and gold; her head is covered with a red scarf, her hands and feet decorated with patterns, and she wears lots of gold jewelry. The groom wears a colored turban and scarf, and carries a long sword.

The Sikh conducting the marriage ceremony will explain the ideals of marriage to the couple. The father of the bride will pass one end of the groom's scarf to the bride. This signifies the passing of responsibility for the care of his daughter to the bridegroom.

A wedding hymn, the *Lavan* of Guru Ram Das, is sung. While that is happening, the couple will walk around the *Guru Granth Sahib* four times. As they finish each circuit they will bow to the holy book. The families will follow the couple to show support for them. The bride and groom are then free to go to their new home.

Death

Death could be a new beginning for a Sikh because they believe in the cycle of reincarnation. They are taught, therefore, that it is not necessary to mourn excessively since the deceased lives on in another body.

Hymns may be read by family and friends from the *Guru Granth Sahib* and prayers for the peace of the soul will be said, followed by evening prayers. The period of mourning usually lasts ten days. During that time, relatives may visit to make their condolences.

The body will have been washed and dressed before the service. In India, it may be cremated on a funeral pyre, but taking the body to the crematorium is also acceptable. The ashes are usually scattered in a river or the sea. If the ceremony takes place in India, the ashes are scattered in a sacred river, such as the Ganges.

Festivals and Ceremonies

Many ceremonies are held to celebrate the birth and death of the ten gurus, two to commemorate the deaths of martyrs, and a festival for the anniversary of the *Baisakhi*, the date the Khalsa was founded, which was originally a harvest festival. The five major observances include *Baisakhi*, the birthdays of Gurus Nanak and Gobind Singh, and the martyrdom of Gurus Arjan and Tegh Bahadur.

All the Sikh festivals are marked by continuous forty-eight-hour readings of the *Guru Granth Sahib*.

Diversification into Modern Society

The history of the development of the Sikhs over the past 500 years has, at times, been tumultuous and bloody. The involvement of the British only propagated the violent fighting between the Sikhs and the Hindus. The subcontinent was partitioned into India and Pakistan in 1947. The Sikh population was divided equally on both sides of the boundary line.

In 1984, Indian troops attacked the Golden Temple where militants had established their headquarters. There was considerable damage and the militants were driven out. It was believed that the angry reaction of the Sikhs led to the assassination of the Indian Prime Minister Indira Gandhi by Sikh members of her bodyguard later that year. The reaction to that dreadful event led to riots and the massacre of many Sikhs.

The separatist movement has the establishment of an independent Sikh state to be called Khalistan (Land of the Pure) as its goal.

CHAPTER 15
Shinto

Shinto is the religion of Japan. The word "shinto" came from the Chinese words *shin tao* (the way of the gods/ spirits), a translation of the Japanese phrase *kami-no-michi*. *Kami* is the spiritual essence that exists in gods, human beings, animals, and even inanimate objects. The Shinto believe that the world is created, inhabited, and ruled by *kami*.

Origins and Development

The Shinto religion is as old as the Japanese people. It has neither a founder nor sacred scriptures. Adherents believe that the world is created, inhabited, and ruled by *kami*.

There's no real way to describe *kami* other than the emotions it evokes: wonder, fear, and awe. Buddhists regard the *kami* as a manifestation of various Buddhas, but the Shintos believe that the Buddha is another *kami* or nature deity.

Shinto is one of two religions practiced by the Japanese people, many of whom are also followers of Buddhism. The two faiths have not always seen eye-to-eye with the other's doctrine, but the differences didn't alter their peaceful coexistence.

Shinto has been affected by the influx into Japan of Confucianism and Buddhism in the sixth century. Unlike the migration of other religions to foreign locations, this one did not cause conflict and disruption, at least for some years. Instead, both arrivals melded into the culture and a cross-fertilization of religious and cultural influences took place.

During the first century of Buddhism in Japan, it had a great influence on the arts, literature, and sciences and was the dominant religion of the upper classes. Buddhism evolved and merged with many aspects of Shintoism to incorporate the worship of *kami*. Buddhist priests then began to run many Shinto shrines and Shinto priests were demoted to the lower steps of the ladder of the hierarchy.

From the earliest recorded times until the later part of the nineteenth century, Shinto and Buddhism coexisted without incident. In fact, it would have been difficult to tell the two apart. So, the Shinto priests started to assert their own ancient traditions in contrast to the foreign, more sophisticated Buddhist practices.

Despite the general coexistence of Shinto and Buddhism, Shinto could not coexist with Catholicism, that arrived in the form of European missionaries in the sixteenth century. Initially, the guests were accepted and welcomed. However, the influx of more missionaries and their message proclaiming loyalty to a pope in faraway Rome began to anger the Shinto. The Japanese government began to suspect their motives, and, in 1587, Christian missionaries were banned from Japan. For the next fifty years, many initiatives were enacted to abolish Christianity from the islands of Japan.

FACTS

The intermingling of Buddhism and Shinto extended to sharing some rituals. For instance, Buddhists supervised the preaching and conducting of funeral services; Shinto priests oversaw the birth and marriage rituals. This didn't last forever, of course; eventually the Shinto priests wanted to establish and preserve their own identity.

In 1868, things changed. The Emperor Meiji ascended to the throne and put Shinto shrines and priests under governmental control; State Shinto became the national religion. Then, the discord started. Buddhist estates were seized, temples were closed, and Buddhist priests were persecuted.

The Emperor used Japan's myths—linking the sun goddess to the emperor—to promote his being worshiped as a living God. The state was divided into two: Shrine Shinto (*Jinja* Shinto) and Sectarian Shinto (*Kyoha*). *Jinja* was the largest group of the two and was the original form of the religion going back to prehistory. A third sect called Folk Shinto (*Minkoku*) also developed; it was not an organized sect and was centered in agricultural and rural families. Shinto has had a proclivity to form sub-sects; all together, there are more than six hundred of them. However, when State Shinto evolved it promulgated nationalistic and racist overtones. In State Shinto priests became civil servants. Many of them opposed the regime, but to no avail; State Shinto became mandatory throughout Japan.

State Shinto played a very significant role in Japanese society during their involvement in the Second World War. It wasn't until the defeat of Japan that it was officially discredited and banned by decree of the Allied occupation forces. Nevertheless, many Shinto followers apparently still held that the emperor was divine and a direct descendent of the sun goddess Amaterasu.

After the Second World War, Shinto was completely separated from the state and returned to being a nature-based, community-oriented faith. The shrines no longer belonged to the state, but to the Association of Shinto Shrines.

FACTS

The act of hara-kiri is suicide by cutting one's stomach. A person who commits hara-kiri does it to prove his or her loyalty after having failed to meet the Shinto code of conduct.

Central Beliefs

Shinto is very deeply rooted in the Japanese culture and traditions. It is an optimistic faith, that believes all humans are fundamentally good, and that evil is caused by evil spirits. Its rituals are directed toward avoiding evil spirits through rites of purification, offerings, and prayers. Shinto does not have a fully developed theology. It has no concepts that compare to Christian or other beliefs of the wrath of God, or the dogma of separation from God due to sin; the general concept of good and evil does not exist. All humanity is regarded as *kami*'s child, and so all life and human nature is sacred.

The absolute essence of Shinto philosophy is loyalty. It is of greater importance for a follower of Shinto to demonstrate loyalty than to do good deeds for others. A follower is absolutely loyal to the family, his superiors, his job, and so on. But, that doesn't mean that Shinto followers don't think about others. On the contrary, they would see the philosophy of loyalty as being the ultimate thought for others.

The family is the main method by which traditions are preserved. A love of nature is sacred. Close contact with nature is equated to close contact with the gods. Natural objects are worshiped as sacred spirits; for instance, rocks, birds, beasts, fish, and plants can all be treated as *kami*.

Physical cleanliness is paramount, which is why followers of Shinto frequently take baths, wash their hands, and rinse out their mouths. Japanese people are considered to be the cleanest people in the world.

The sun goddess Amaterasu is the closest that Shinto comes to having a deity; there are many others that are conceptualized in many forms.

There are three Shinto sects—Shrine Shinto, Sectarian Shinto, and Folk or Popular Shinto. Shrine Shinto is centered around the more than 100,000 shrines throughout Japan. Sectarian Shinto has five sub-sects: Pure, Confucian, Mountain, Purification, and Redemptive. The Purification Shinto performs rites of purification to purify a person's soul, mind, and body from evil. But, all the sects are concerned with the environment and the cleansing of pollution. Pure Shinto fosters nationalism and is opposed to foreign influences. Loyalty to the state is a central element. Confucian Shinto follows the ethics of Confucianism. Redemptive or Faith-Healing Shinto believes in a divine source such as the sun goddess.

The most diverse form of Shinto, Folk, involves superstition, the occult, and ancestor worship. Thousands of deities are part of Folk Shinto and many adherents have rituals that are centered on the *kami-dana* (*kami* shelf), a small shrine used for daily worship. Memorial tablets made from wood or paper are inscribed with the names of an ancestor. At special life-cycle events such as births, marriages, and anniversaries, candles are lit and the head of the family offers food and flowers to the deities.

QUESTIONS?

Which sacred mountain in Japan is the most famous?
Mount Fuji is world famous and at 12,388 feet, the highest mountain in Japan. Its volcano has been dormant since 1707. Considered a sacred mountain, it is surrounded by temples and shrines, even at the edge and bottom of the crater. Today, crowds of more than 100,000 a year go there during the climbing season from July 1 to August 26.

Parishioners of a shrine believe in their *kami* as the source of life and existence. All the deities cooperate with each other. To live a life in accordance with the will of a *kami* is believed to give mystical power to the recipient and provides power and the approval of the particular *kami*.

Sacred Texts

There are no holy writings as such in Shinto. But, they do have about 800 myths, some of which have been enshrined. Shinto literature tends to be based on the interpretation of mythology.

Two major texts form the basis of the Shinto sacred literature: the *Kojiki* (Records of Ancient Matters) and the *Nihon* (Chronicles of Japan) written in 712 and 720 C.E., respectively. They came from oral traditions and were passed on and compiled. Apparently, because of the lack of a Japanese alphabet at that time they were written in Chinese characters to represent Japanese sounds.

FACTS

In some shrines, statues of the *kami* are present, but images are not commonly found. The foremost Shinto shrine in Japan is the grand shrine of Ise. It is Amaterasu's chief place of worship. The most common representation of the *kami* in a shrine is a mirror, which is what Amaterasu left behind to represent her presence.

The *Kojiki* contains myths, legends, and historical information on the imperial court. The entire writings were re-evaluated by Moto-ori-Norinaga, who wrote the complete Annotation of the *Kojiki* in forty-nine volumes.

Of all the myths' subjects, the most famous and important one is about the sun goddess Amaterasu Omikami (Great Divinity Illuminating Heaven). One myth states that she was born from the god Izanagi when he used water to purify his left eye after a visit to the nether world. Another says she was born after intercourse between Izanagi and Izanami (Nihon Shoki 720 C.E.). She was the sun goddess and assigned to rule the High Celestial Plain. Later, she sent her grandson, Ninigi no Mikoto, to pacify the Japanese islands, having given him a sacred mirror, sword, and jewels that became the Imperial Regalia. Her great-grandson became the first Emperor Jimmu.

Worship and Practices

Shinto does not have a schedule of regular religious services. Followers make up their own minds when they wish to attend a shrine. Some may decide to go when there is a festival, of which there are many, or on the first and fifteenth of each month. Of course, some Shinto go every day. Japan has over 80,000 Shinto shrines. Some, particularly in outlying districts, are tiny, others are elaborate and large. The small shrines seldom have a priest; the local people look after the shrine, opening the shrine doors at dawn and closing them at dusk.

A devotee attending a shrine follows a ritual. First, he or she must cleanse the mouth and hands (purity is a vital part of Shintoism). If a person has been in contact with blood—for instance, a menstruating woman—he or she is forbidden to enter. When a person enters the shrine area, she or he passes through a *Tori* (bird), a special gateway to the gods that demarcates the finite world from the infinite world of the gods. Once inside the shrine, worshipers can buy a prayer board; some have prayers printed on them or a depiction of an animal. Adherents believe that animals are messengers of the gods.

Once approaching the shrine, the worshipers clap their hands together to let the *kami* know of their presence, then make an offering of money, which is put into a box in front of the shrine. It is appropriate to bow twice deeply, clap the hands twice, bow deeply once more, and pray. When a priest is present in the shrine, he will bang a drum to alert the *kami* of his presence. In a purification ceremony, the priest will deliver prayers and then pass a purification stick over the head of the worshiper to draw out all the impurities.

Rituals and Customs

Shinto priests perform the rituals and are usually supported by young ladies (*miko*) in white kimonos. The young ladies must be unmarried; often they are daughters of priests. There are also a few female priests.

A newborn child is taken to a shrine to be initiated as a new adherent somewhere between thirty and 100 days after the birth. When boys are five years old and when girls are three years and seven years of age, they go to the shrine to give thanks for *kami's* protection and to pray for healthy growth. This is done at the *Shichi-go-san* (Seven-Five-Three) festival on November 15. Another festival for young men to commemorate their twentieth year is celebrated on January 15.

FACTS

As the majority of Japanese are both Shinto and Buddhist, they have their funerals in the Buddhist manner. Only those who adhere exclusively to Shinto will follow the Shinto ceremony and services.

Festivals

Japanese festivals are designed to express pride and patriotism. The New Year festival requires much preparation. Houses are cleansed of evil influences and the *kami-dana* is provided with new tablets, flowers, and other items. Special foods are prepared, and houses are decorated with flowers, straw, paper, pine branches, and bamboo sticks.

A Girl's Festival is held each March 3; it is intended to honor family and national life. The Boy's Festival is held each May 5 and is meant for families to announce to the community their good fortune in having male children.

A festival of the dead called Bon is held in the middle of the year in which souls of dead relatives return home to be fed by their families. At the conclusion of the feast, farewell fires are lit to light the way for the relatives on their journey home.

The most famous Japanese festival is the ancient Cherry Blossom Festival. It is held in the early spring. Obviously, it is the celebration of the cherry blossom trees, which can frequently be seen on the grounds of shrines or on holy mountains. This festival is another example of the Shinto reverence for nature.

New Year's Day is the largest festival. It draws millions to shrines all over the country. There will be much praying and the asking for blessings of the *kami*. It is believed that the celebration will mark the beginning of an auspicious new year.

CHAPTER 16

Lesser Known Faiths

The faiths explored in this chapter could be said to share a charismatic flavor. Their followers tend to be fervent in their beliefs and some are given to actively seeking to convert nonbelievers to their faiths. While they are not major religions, they are well dispersed throughout the world and illustrate the wide mosaic of faiths that exist.

Hare Krishna

Hare Krishna, also called the International Society for Krishna Consciousness (ISKCON), was founded in the United States in 1966, which makes it one of the world's youngest religions. Krishna was the eighth and principal avatar of Vishnu in the Hindu religion and this religious sect has strong Hindu affiliations. The initial appeal of the movement was to counterculture youths, many of whom were runaways. They became a common sight on the streets dressed in Hindu clothes with shaven heads and smiles on their faces. They were often chanting and playing Indian finger cymbals. The chants are called a mantra which is a repeated vibration of sound that many believe cleanses the mind. Their main activity was soliciting contributions from passersby, something many people called begging. They were frequently prohibited from public areas, particularly airports.

The movement is an authoritarian one with an emphasis on religious enthusiasm. The movement claims that it is for anyone, whatever their religion, ethnic background, or sex; there are no initiation fees.

People are thought of as souls composed of Krishna's highest energy. To achieve peace and happiness, adherents are urged to seek Krishna. Krishna consciousness is not imposed on the mind, rather it is already inside waiting to emerge. Followers are advised that chanting "Hare Krishna" is a way of seeking Krishna directly.

The official seven-point goal of the Hare Krishna consciousness movement were given by Srila Prabhupada at the time of ISKCON's incorporation in July 1966 in New York City. They are:

To systematically propagate spiritual knowledge to society at large and to educate all people in the techniques of spiritual life, in order to check the imbalance of values in life and achieve real unity and peace in the world.

To propagate consciousness of Krishna, as revealed in Bhagavad-Gita and *Srimad-Bhagavatam*.

To bring the members of society together with each other and nearer to Krishna, the prime entity, thus developing the idea within the members, and humanity at large, that each soul is part and parcel of the quality of Krishna.

To teach and encourage the *snkirtan* movement, congregational chanting of the holy names of God, as revealed in the teachings of Lord Sri Caitanya Mahaprabhu.

To erect for the members and for society at large, holy places of transcendental pastimes dedicated to the personality of Krishna.

To bring members closer together for the purpose of teaching a simpler and more natural way of life.

With a view towards achieving the aforementioned Purposes, to publish and distribute periodicals, magazines, books, and other writings.

FACTS

Caitanya explained that real god consciousness does not depend on caste or church membership. He was opposed to any social, religious, or racist prejudice. The purpose of the chanting of the name Krishna was a method to enable anyone to become Krishna conscious.

Srila Prabhupada

Srila Prabhupada was born in Calcutta in 1896 and died in 1977. In 1922, he met his spiritual master, Srila Bhaktisddhanta Sarasvati Thakur and became his initiated disciple. Meanwhile, he formed a successful pharmaceutical business to maintain his family.

In 1950, he left his home and family and dedicated the rest of his life to teaching. In 1959, he renounced material life and wrote three volumes of the *Srimad-Bhagavatam* in English.

He became convinced that the United States would be the best marketplace to accept his preaching, so he moved there. Eventually, he rented a small storefront at 26 Second Avenue in New York City. Devotees began to gather, which led to the incorporation of the movement. He held chanting sessions and gave lectures. He distributed *prasadam* (food that has been offered to the Supreme Lord; devotees eat only what has been offered first to the Lord because to do otherwise would be to ingest sin), and he started the first Sunday feasts.

Once the New York devotees became established, Srila Prabhupada moved to San Francisco, where the hippies flocked to join the movement.

They were attracted by the philosophy of spreading spiritual love and peace. Some of the devotees became disciples and were sent to preach the message in other parts of the world and to establish Krishna Conscious centers. They went first to London, England, and then spread out to Berlin and India. Meanwhile, the belief was spreading throughout America.

Srila Prabhupada died in 1977. By then, he had built a foundation and aided the expansion of a religion that encompassed well over 100 centers throughout the world and was said to have written more than fifty volumes of transcendental literature. He established a publishing house (The Bhaktivedanta Book Trust), which has become the world's largest publisher of Vedic literature. He also built a scientific preaching academy (The Bhaktivedanta Institute).

Central Beliefs

Reincarnation is a pillar of the faith. Hare Krishnas believe that our current lives are not the only ones we will live and that what we contain within—the soul or self—has no beginning and no end; this essence within moves from one incarnation to the next. They propose that during life we move from childhood to middle age to old age, but only the body changes, not the inner self or the soul.

Death is only a transition; we continue the cycle with birth in another body. How we behave in one life will affect what we become in the next.

FACTS

Hare Krishna adheres to the Vedic tradition of spiritual masters going back to the Lord Krishna. There are many different interpretations of the Vedic faith, including Hinduism, Buddhism, and Jainism. Caitanya's teachings, based on the Hindu ideology, included the ethic of not depending on caste. One argument was that the Brahmin status is determined by aptitude, rather than birth.

The official statement of the faith proposes a society that moves toward a more natural economy with smaller, self-sufficient economic units based on simple living and high thinking. They envisage an environment that reduces the urge to excessive exploitation, thus leading to the nonmaterial happiness of the soul. They feel that without raising desires from the materialistic to the spiritual, the basic impetus toward environmental destruction will remain.

Holy Writings

The original Bhagavad-Gita forms the basis of Hare Krishna's required study; however, Srila Prabhupada produced his own translations and editing of the work. He wrote and published fifty volumes of transcendental literature. His major books include *Bhagavad-Gita As It Is* and *Srimad Bhagavatam*. Adherents are encouraged to read Srila Prabhupada's selected literature daily.

Adherents of ISKCON are vegetarians and serve vegetarian meals in their restaurants, temples, and through the Food for Life programs for the homeless, hungry, or disadvantaged. The society has sold over 10 million copies of its vegetarian cookbooks.

QUESTIONS?

Do Hare Krishnas have churches?
Not as such, they have temples that essentially are communes. Unmarried men and women live separately. Married couples have other quarters. Members support the temples by soliciting funds and selling publications. Spiritual masters initiate new members and oversee the spiritual life of the temples. Members of the temples dress in Hindu clothes.

Pentecostalism

Probably the most common words that come to mind when one thinks of Pentecostalism is the phrase "speaking in tongues," as well as the names Aimee Semple McPherson and, more recently, Oral Roberts.

The origins of Pentecostalism go back to the Bible and the Jewish pilgrimage festival of Pentecost. Early Christians believed that Pentecost commemorated the day the Holy Spirit descended in fulfillment of the promise of Jesus. In Acts 2:2–13 it is written:

And suddenly a sound came from heaven like the rush of a mighty wind, and it filled all the house where they were sitting. And there appeared to them tongues as of fire distributed and resting on each one of them. And they were filled with the Holy Spirit and began to speak in other tongues, as the Spirit gave them utterance. Now there were dwelling in Jerusalem Jews, devoted men from every nation under heaven. And at this sound the multitude came together, and they were bewildered, because each one heard them speaking in his own language. And they were amazed and wondered, saying, "Are not all these who are speaking Galileans: And how is it that we hear, each of us in his own language?"

And all were amazed and perplexed, saying to one another, "What does this mean?" But others mocking, said, "They are filled with new wine."

Pentecostalism arose out of Protestantism in the twentieth century due to dissension with the rigid manner in which the established churches preached and organized the delivery of their way of interpreting the Bible.

Pentecostalists endorse a more literal interpretation of the Bible than mainstream Christians. Many churches have adopted specific passages as their guiding force. One such passage is found in Mark 16:15–20 where it is reported that those who receive baptism and find salvation will "cast out devils, speak in strange tongues; if they handle snakes or drink deadly poison they will come to no harm; and the sick on whom they lay their hands will recover." There are some churches that include the handling of deadly snakes and the drinking of poison as part of their worship services.

The new sect didn't think the way of the true Christians was memorizing prayers and creeds and adhering to hard and fast rules within an unwavering structure. The Pentecostalists sought a direct experience of

God that would produce a sense of ecstasy, known as the baptism of the Holy Spirit. This baptism was seen as a second blessing.

Speaking in Tongues

It was in Topeka, Kansas, in 1901 at a service being conducted at the Kansas Bible College by Charles Fox Parham that the movement—it is more than a denomination—got the first demonstration of a strange happening. A female participant was praying and suddenly began speaking what seemed to be a foreign language. Apparently, she was unable to speak English for three days afterward. This event had a dramatic effect not only on Parham but also the entire congregation. The demonstration was taken as a sign from God and the word quickly spread.

Coincidentally, at the same time in Los Angeles a black preacher, William Joseph Seymour, started preaching at a mission and it wasn't long until he and his parishioners were speaking in unknown tongues. A church was founded on Azusa Street in Los Angeles, and it grew rapidly as services began to be held on a regular basis.

Women became active members in the Pentecostal movement. One of them, Aimee Semple McPherson, generated a big following from her tabernacle where she produced theatrically dramatic versions of biblical stories from the stage.

The speaking in tongues, known as glossolalia, was not universally accepted; in fact, it was quite the reverse for a lot of people. As in the Biblical story in Acts, many people thought the speakers were drunk. It wasn't just the fact of speaking in an unintelligible tongue that upset listeners, it was the emotional overtones that went with the delivery. The term "holy rollers" was ascribed to practitioners who were actually rolling in the aisles of the church in their ecstasy. Adherents believed that speaking in tongues and the actions that accompanied this were a way of communicating directly with God. However, no reliable sources have established that an actual language was or is being uttered during glossolalia.

Expansion

Pentecostalism is now one of the fastest growing religious movements in the world. In the United States alone it claims nine million adherents; worldwide, the figure goes up to 400 million. It is sometimes referred to as "the third force of Christianity."

The movement first drew members from among the poor, not the establishment; the promise of equality for all was particularly attractive to the unfortunate. Thus, the movement became associated with the Bible Belt in the Southern states among poor whites and urban blacks. It then became increasingly popular with the middle classes around the country, and once the movement spread to the mainstream of society, members of churches such as the Episcopal, Lutheran, and Presbyterian adopted it, often in addition to their own religion.

FACTS

In 1913, at a Pentacostal meeting in California, John G. Scheppe announced that he had experienced the power of Jesus. Enough people accepted his statement for them to proclaim that true baptism can come only in the name of Jesus and not the Trinity. The justification for this, they said, could be found in the Bible, John 3:5 and Acts 2:38.

The controversy split the movement and led to the formation of new sects within Pentecostalism. Three main movements evolved: Pentecostalism, Fundamentalism, and Evangelicalism. Other sects, particularly throughout the rest of the world, are emerging.

Beliefs, Worship, Writings, and Rites

Pentecostalism has not united into a single denomination in spite of believing in baptism of the spirit and common beliefs in selected doctrines of the Christian faiths. It has strong beliefs in the literal interpretation of the Bible and healing by the spirit.

The history of Pentecostalism shows that many adherents either added it to their original faith or left the original faith entirely. Literature is being gathered from Roman Catholics who have become committed to Pentecostalism.

Catholics tend to investigate Pentecostalism with a view of trying to distinguish what is different about it today from its historical standpoint. With the growth of Pentecostalism, the charismatic experience, as it is called, has expanded its presence into many parts of the world to such an extent that it is being looked at by some as a new era of the spirit. The Pentecostalists envision the movement sweeping whole countries, cultures, and religions, including Catholicism, with a promise of changing Christianity. They have even coined a new name: Catholic Pentecostals. The Pentecostalist viewpoint is that there is confusion not only in Catholicism, but also in Christianity. This opinion is not shared by the Roman Catholic Church and other Christian denominations.

FACTS

On Father's Day in 1995, at the Brownsville Assembly of God in Pensacola, Florida, a revival was held. During a prayer service congregants began falling about and shaking. It was reported that one minister touched another on the forehead and that man fell to the ground struck dumb as if by the Holy Spirit. Thousands began to arrive, either to indulge or to watch.

Opponents of the movement say that Pentecostal-style religion is not easily captured in a denominational form because it stresses the impulse of the moment and behavior such as speaking in tongues. Many point out that similar evangelical outpourings that took place in the 1980s ended with the disgrace of people like Jimmy Swaggart and Jim and Tammy Faye Bakker.

Pentecostalists describe themselves as believing in exorcism, speaking in tongues, faith healing, and seeking supernatural experiences.

As with other developing religions, many schisms have occurred that resulted in the setting up of separate sects with their own variations of the basic belief. Here are some of the best known Pentecostal sects:

Church of God in Christ
International Church of the Foursquare Gospel Church of God

Church of God of Prophecy
Pentecostal Holiness Church
Fire-Baptized Holiness Church
Pentecostal Free-Will Baptist Church
The Assemblies of God
The United Pentecostal Church

Rastafarianism

Origins of Rastafarianism go back to Marcus Garvey who was born in the late 1880s in Jamaica. Garvey preached that members would be going back to Africa; he founded the movement and preached that a future black African king would lead the people.

In 1930, Ras Tafari Makonnen was crowned king of Ethiopia. He claimed the title Emperor Haile Selassie I (Lion of the Tribe of Judah, Elect of God, and King of Kings of Ethiopia). Thus, Haile Selassie fulfilled the prediction of a black king. As far as the Rastafarians were concerned, he was the living God for the black race. They believed that he was the Jesus Christ that Christianity speaks of, that the white man tricked the world into believing that Jesus was a white man.

FACTS

Jamaica was sighted by Christopher Columbus in 1494; years later it was colonized by the Spanish, and subsequently by the British. The slave trade, which was introduced by the Spanish, continued on until the 1830s when it was abolished. In 1959, Jamaica became an independent country within the British Commonwealth.

It was after Haile Selassie was crowned that Rastafarianism came into being. One of its early leaders was Leonard Howell, who was later arrested by the Jamaican government for preaching a revolutionary doctrine. Here are his six principles:

Hatred for the white race.
The complete superiority of the black race.

Revenge on whites for their wickedness.

The negation, persecution, and humiliation of the government and legal bodies of Jamaica.

The preparation to go back to Africa.

Acknowledging Emperor Haile Selassie as the Supreme Being and only ruler of black people.

On April 21, 1966, Haile Selassie visited Jamaica. Two things resulted from his visit: April 21 was declared a special holy day, and Selassie strongly advised Rastafarians not to immigrate to Ethiopia. He said they should liberate the people of Jamaica first. Many people have since wondered about his motive for discouraging immigration.

Rastafarians (sometimes called Rastas) do not accept that Haile Selassie is dead. They believe that his atoms have spread throughout the world and live through individual Rastafarians. The Rastafarian name for God is Jah.

Central Beliefs and Holy Writings

The original belief system was so vague that what was acceptable doctrine was largely a matter of individual interpretation. Rastafarians accept the Bible, but with reservations. They think that much of the translation into English has produced distortions so that while the basic text may be in order, it should be viewed in a critical light. They have no holy scriptures, apart from the Rastafarian interpretation of the Bible.

The doctrine of Rastafarians has similarities to Christianity in that they believe that God revealed himself in Moses, their first savior, followed by Elijah and then Jesus Christ. But sources differ. One of them, as has been claimed above, asserted that Rastafarians believed that Haile Selassie was actually Jesus Christ. Others believe that the devil is actually the god of the white man.

There is an expression "I and I" that is frequently heard in the Rasta dialect. It means that all are absolutely equal. This means that people wouldn't say "you and I," but "I and I."

We now get to the two major symbols that exemplify the Rastafarians, as well as identify them: dreadlocks and *ganja* (marijuana). Dreadlocks symbolize the Rasta roots. They are the antithesis of the blond look of the white man and his establishment. The way the hair grows and is tended represents the Lion of Judah (Haile Selassie). By association this has come to represent priesthood. As is probably well known, dreadlocks have been adopted by many black people even though they may not be adherents of Rastafarianism. It is not commonly known if those wearers are adapting to a current fashion in hair or are actually members of the belief. *Ganja* is the Rasta name for marijuana; it is used for religious purposes. Its religious justification is based on different verses from the Bible:

"He causeth the grass for the cattle, and herb for the service of man."
    (Psalms 104:14)
"Thou shalt eat the herb of the field." (Genesis 3:18)
"Eat every herb of the land." (Exodus 10:12)
"Better is a dinner of herb where love is, than a stalled ox and hatred
    therewith." (Proverbs 15:17)

Apparently the use of the herb is extensive, and not only for religious ceremony. The Nyabingi celebration, for instance, uses the herb for medicinal purposes, such as for colds.

The use of *ganja* for religious rituals started in a cult commune set up by Leonard Howell in the hills of St. Catherine called Pinnacle, which overlooked the city of Kingston.

The growth of Rastafarianism is attributed to the worldwide acceptance of a reggae artist, Bob Marley, who became a prophet of the belief in 1975. The movement spread, mainly to black youth throughout the Caribbean, many of whom saw it as a symbol of their rebelliousness. The expansion also found believers in England and the United States.

Scientology

Scientology developed in the 1950s as an extension of a bestselling book, *Dianetics: The Modern Science of Mental Health,* by science fiction author L. Ron Hubbard. The book detailed Hubbard's new form of psychotherapy.

L. Ron Hubbard, founder of Scientology, attended George Washington University, School of Engineering from 1930 until 1932 and withdrew without attaining a degree. He died in 1986.

The words "god," "sacred deity," "holy deity," or any similar descriptive name does not appear in any text that is part of Scientology literature.

The Church of Scientology was formally established in the United States in 1954. It was subsequently incorporated in Great Britain and other countries. It is considered a religio-scientific movement.

The movement has generated considerable controversy, even extreme anger, with accusations of being dangerous and vicious, fleecing its members, and harassing those who disagree with its philosophy and manner of operation.

On the official Web site of Scientology, a section titled *What Is Scientology?* says, in part:

Comparing specific Scientology doctrines and practices with those of other religions, similarities and differences emerge which make it clear that although Scientology is entirely new, its origins are as ancient as religious thought itself.

. . . And because the principles of Scientology encompass the entire scope of life, the answers it provides apply to all existence and have broad ranging applicability.

The Church of Scientology and its officers have had many private lawsuits brought against it. The government prosecuted the movement for fraud, tax evasion, financial mismanagement, and conspiracy to steal government documents. The church claimed that it was being persecuted by government agencies. Former members testified that Hubbard was guilty of using a tax-exempt church status to build a thriving, profitable business.

Central Beliefs

The core of the movement is based on a system of psychology and the way the mind seems to work. The word engram is part of the Scientology nomenclature; it means a memory trace that is supposedly a permanent change in the brain that accounts for the existence of a memory that is not available to the conscious mind. However, it remains dormant in the subconscious, and can be brought into consciousness when triggered by new experiences. These new experiences are supplied in what Scientology calls an audit, which is conducted by an auditor in a one-on-one session with a potential devotee where the auditor confronts the engram in order to bring it to the surface and clear, or free, the devotee's mind of it. The purpose is to free the mind of engrams and thus allow the devotee to achieve improved mental health and outlook. Those people familiar with the techniques originated by Dr. Sigmund Freud might find similarities.

To quote again from official statements: "An auditor is a minister or minister-in-training of the Church of Scientology. Auditor means one who listens, from the Latin *audire* meaning "to hear or listen." An auditor is a person trained and qualified in applying auditing to individuals for their betterment. An auditor works together with the preclear (a person who has not yet completed the clearing process) to help him or her defeat his or her reactive mind.

The officially stated Scientology meaning of the word engram is, "A recording made by the reactive mind when a person is unconscious." An engram is not a memory, it is a particular type of mental image that is a complete recording, down to the last accurate details, of every perception present in a moment of partial or full unconsciousness. "To become 'clear' indicates a highly desirable state for the individual, achieved through auditing, which was never attainable before Dianetics. A Clear is a person who no longer has his own reactive mind and therefore suffers none of the ill effects that the reactive mind can cause. The Clear has no engrams, which when restimulated, throw out the correctness of his computations by entering hidden and false data."

In addition to the personal mental freeing that supposedly takes place, Scientology lays great stress on a universal life energy, what they call thetan.

L. Ron Hubbard has described his philosophy in more than 5,000 writings and in 3,000 tape-recorded lectures. *Dianetics: The Modern Science of Mental Health* has been described by the movement as marking a turning point in history. There are no sacred texts.

Worship and Practices

The movement appoints its own ministers. Scientology ministers perform the same types of ceremonies and services that ministers and priests of other religions perform. At a weekly service a sermon may be given that addresses the idea that a person is a spiritual being.

Scientology congregations celebrate weddings and christenings with their own formal ceremonies and mark the passing of their fellows with funeral rites.

The Chaplain also ministers to Scientologists on a personal level. Apparently such aid can take many forms. It is stated that Scientology is a religion where, ultimately, everyone wins. An escalating fee structure for services rendered is stringently applied.

Shamanism

A shaman is a man or a woman of any age who can be benevolent or harmful. Shamans deal with supernatural spirits. They have gained their reputation mainly for healing and curing illnesses, including mental illnesses, which are sometimes thought to be the result of evil spirits. The province of dealing with evil spirits and what they can cause is generally associated with native shamans. They will usually occupy a position of high respect and even power in a village. Shamans look just like anyone else.

It is almost certain that the history of shamanism goes way back to prehistory. Even though the practice has strong elements of sorcery and magic, most scholars agree that it also has religious characteristics in that a shaman deals in identification with the supernatural, particularly as it relates to calling up and working with spirits.

The word shaman is said to have originated in Siberia. It is a name and sometimes a verb, it is not a religion as such, but is frequently part of, or an adjunct to, a religion, especially in Eastern religions and in developing countries. In fact, shamans can be found virtually anywhere in the world. With the popularity of the New Age movements in the 1960s, shamanism gained considerable attraction and gave birth to a growing number of western shamans.

Typically, shamans have a strong bond with animals, as spirits often take animal form. Masks depicting whichever animal the shaman has as a guide, as we shall see, is part of the initiation of becoming a shaman; it comes at the end of the quest to contact and take control of an animal's spirit and lets the people know which animal is the shaman's guiding spirit.

The Shaman's Position in the Tribe

Just as doctors do today, shamans tend to specialize. As one would consult a modern doctor whose specialty treats one's particular complaint, the same goes for the shaman of choice. In both professions there are also general practitioners. However, shamans have absolutely no medical qualifications, although they would no doubt proffer their spiritual power as the absolute qualification. Their diagnoses, too, will be vastly different. For instance, a doctor might prescribe an analgesic for consistent headaches; a shaman would find out what was possessing the patient, perhaps an evil spirit that needs to be cast out.

As do our doctors, even native shamans in tribal regions charge for their services, often a barter for a spear or a good meal. Bartering as payment was not uncommon for medical doctors in the rural United States who were paid with a chicken or having his horse reshod.

Even though shamans are often members of a tribe, they rarely hold a position that could be considered synonymous to that of a prophet. The tribal chief could occupy such a position, but the shaman—or medicine man in some regions—does hold a position of authority, and if consistently successful, awe. Historically, shamans may have been itinerant, going from village to village, particularly if they had built up a good reputation.

Shamans use their power to cure illnesses. They do not typically cause harm. The power of a shaman will be directly related to the power of his spirits. Some shamans may also be consulted to influence the weather, getting the rain to start or stop depending on the agricultural needs of the client.

FACTS

Original shaman masks are hanging in many of the finest museums and art galleries. They are considered excellent examples of native art. Copies are readily available for purchase from a large number of vendors, including several on the Internet.

Central Beliefs

The supernatural is the domain of shamans. While they may inherit the position, they must train to become one.

Once the decision, or "call," has come about, the supplicant has to embark on a period of intensive training that leads to initiation. Many myths describe the process. One is that in order to become a great healer, the supplicant has to journey to the underground, suffer, and nearly die. He or she would often have an out-of-body experience and ascend to the sky. Essentially, this is accomplished by going into a trance. The shaman thus masters the ability to go beyond the physical body.

Another training method involves going with a mentor deep into the woods to carry out an animal quest. This quest can last days and would involve prayers and fasting. Elaborate oaths have to be made to the spirits, as if making a contract with them. Part of the contract will be a listing of the various illnesses the shaman intends to heal. Once the spirit animal has been chosen, the shaman-to-be will take on that animal's persona by making animal sounds and even imitating it physically. The shaman may go on repeated quests to build up his or her power. Each time, the soul of the animal becomes a spirit of the shaman and each time another mask is fashioned.

The initiated shaman will display the appropriate accouterments, including masks, drums, and rattles, all of which are important elements of his or her image for the patients. Similarly, a modern day doctor wears a white coat with a stethoscope hanging out of a pocket.

Shamans are able to move outside their physical bodies and into other spheres. Such journeys, as they are called, may take the shaman to other levels of existence. A shaman is the link between this world and other worlds and between the past and the future. This ability is considered a sacred trust to be used for the benefit of all. Shamans frequently fulfill the role of priest, magician, healer, and guide. A shaman lives on the edge of other realities. To accomplish these duties takes a person of exceptional strength and courage, one who is prepared to undergo personal deprivations.

FACTS

Shamanism forms a major part of the religious life of Eskimos. Healing is a predominant part of the shaman's way of life in the Arctic. The shaman is called an *angakok* in the Arctic, and it is said that their journeys have taken them to the moon in magic flight. Some *angakok* claim to have flown around the earth.

While believers hold to the power of the shaman, skeptics attribute any healing success to the placebo effect, even though they agree that altered states of consciousness exist. However, the placebo effect accounts for 30 percent of responses to all medication and suggestion.

Shamanism has grown considerably in the western world, particularly in the United States, due in part to the growth of the New Age movements based in California.

Yoruba

The Yoruba are a semi-independent people who live in the southwestern part of Nigeria in Africa. They number about 15 million, divided into many tribes. Rather than being a cohesive nation, they are loosely linked by geography, language, and most particularly by history. Archaeologists estimate that their ancestors may have lived in the region since prehistoric times. The majority live on the edge of a forest belt. Some live in the kingdom of the powerful Old Oyo kingdom (Katunga), which is on the fringes of the northern savanna grasslands, just north of a sacred city called Ife, which is believed to be the birthplace of humankind. Ife may have been named after the god of divinity Ifa. Ife, which dates from 850 C.E., is recognized as the oldest and most ritually important Yoruba city. The rival city Oyo, just north, was founded around 1350 C.E. The kings of both are still the most highly respected in Nigeria. Old Oyo, along with a city called Benin, became the seats of important political significance.

The slave trade to the Americas dramatically altered not only the Yoruba but also the whole of West Africa. Remnants of the Yoruba culture can still be found in parts of the Americas, Cuba, and Brazil. When a local king tried to raid Ife for slaves in 1793, the severe internal resistance led to a series of wars that destroyed the Oyo empire. Eventually, in the late 1880s, with the help of a British mediator, a treaty was signed among the various warring factions. In 1901, the land was colonized by the British.

FACTS

The spiritual head of the Yoruba has custody of the sacred staff of Oranmiyan (a king of Benin), which is an 18-foot granite monolith in the shape of an elephant's tusk. The Ife museum houses a collection of bronze castings and terra cotta sculptures that were found during excavations in 1939.

In 1961, Obafemi Awolowo University (formerly the University of Ife) was founded. It became one of Nigeria's major universities. It operates a teaching hospital and has a major library. There is the Institute of Agricultural Research and Training, which operates the Moor Plantation for agricultural research and the country's largest specialized agricultural library. In short, tremendous efforts were made and much was accomplished.

Customs and Central Beliefs

The indigenous traditional religions are still very much in evidence. There is an elaborate hierarchy of deities numbering in the hundreds. Because the major national product is predominantly agriculture, many of the deities are related to the land—mountains, streams, and so on are frequently considered divinities. Most Yorubas live in cities and commute to their farms. The Yoruba believe that higher modern education is the pathway to success, and the private sector provides the bulk of the nation's elite: educated politicians, judges, and wealthy traders.

It has been in this mix of the old with the new that the Yoruba religion has changed and developed. Under European rule many of the Yoruba practices were severely restricted, including polygamy and incestuous marriages. The ritual of burying the dead in the house, where it was thought there was communion between the live and dead relatives, was banned and replaced by the use of communal graveyards.

Traditionally, when a child is born a diviner will be consulted as to the deity the child should follow. According to oral tradition, the mighty gods descended from the sky to create the earth. It is the descendants of these gods that are said to have spread the Yoruba religious practices. When the child is grown, he or she may well decide to honor several of these deities.

The Yoruba call their deities *orisha*, and the high god is Ogun (spellings may differ, source to source). While there are no organized priesthoods or shrines to honor the gods, their spirits are invoked for blessings and to give thanks. The Yoruba believe that when they die they join their ancestors and that they still have influence on earth. All deceased members of a lineage are honored with a yearly sacrifice. The major gods include: Ifa, the god of divination; Eshu, the trickster; Shango, the god of thunder; and Ogun, the god of iron and modern technology.

Worship and Practices

Apart from retaining many of the cult practices within their own tribes, many Yorubas follow the religion the Europeans brought—Christianity.

The indigenous beliefs vary tremendously from tribe to tribe. In one tribe, the same deity may be male in one village and female in the next. Many myths were created and passed by word of mouth from one generation to the next. In spite of that, it has been said that all the faiths are a sort of diffused monotheism, meaning that the overall belief is in a single omnipotent creator who rules over the universe, along with the several hundred lower gods.

An example of how the culture of a faith is an integral part of its religion is shown by the reverence given to the most important god: Ogun. Art and, in particular, metal smithing, along with pottery, weaving, and bead working, form a major part of a highly artistic society. Ogun serves as the patron deity of blacksmiths, warriors, and all who use metal in their work. In court, devotees of the faith swear to tell the truth by kissing a machete sacred to Ogun. The Yoruba believe that if anyone breaks a pact in Ogun's name, his retribution will be fearsome.

FACTS

Yorubas have no written history. Nevertheless, they greatly respect their past and their ancestors. A few tribes believe that with death comes the possibility of assuming the persona of a true deity, thus becoming a demigod.

Yorubas believed that Ifa mediates between the gods and humans. The gods communicate their motives through the process of divination and suggest actions for individuals to avert misfortune. These suggestions can extend to an individual or to a whole town. Solutions can be obtained to difficult problems and to restore good relations between the believers and the gods.

Like many African nations, Nigeria has, and is, undergoing regular periods of civil unrest and violence. In several parts of the country there have been ethnic-religious conflicts between Christians, Muslims, and the Yoruba. In very recent times there were demonstrations that resulted in numerous casualties throughout the area.

CHAPTER 17
Ancient Faiths

Ancient faiths have often influenced the growth of faiths that succeeded them. For instance, Zoroastrianism influenced Judaism, Christianity, and Islam. The learned Druids have been linked to an ancient Indo-European priesthood allied to the Hindu Brahmin.

One of the Oldest Religions

Zoroastrianism is a small religion and has been diminishing over the years. Today, about 150,000 members practice the faith in Iran and India. In India, the belief is called Parsiism. Nevertheless, the religion had a large impact on Judaism, Christianity, and Islam. Pinpointing the date of origin of the religion has been difficult. But, scholars now estimate it occurred during the sixth century B.C.E. Some sources date its founder's birth as 660 B.C.E. Thus, it is one of the oldest religions still in existence.

The founder was Zoroaster or Zarathushtra (Zarthosht in India and Persia). He was born in Persia, now known as Iran, and legend says that he predicted the birth of Jesus. During his childhood, several miracles happened to him: Instead of crying at birth, he laughed; later a stallion stood by him and protected him from runaway horses.

Once more there are interesting parallels with Jesus Christ, who arrived after Zoroaster. For example, it is believed that Zoroaster's mother was a virgin and conceived following a visit by a shaft of light. It is said that the boy helped his father tend cattle. Nothing else seems to be known about him until he was thirty years of age. It may also be remembered that the birth of Buddha is also shrouded in myth: His mother had a dream that a silver elephant entered her womb through her side.

Zoroaster

Zoroaster was educated as a priest and wandered the wilderness where he practiced meditation. One day, when he stood on the banks of the sacred river Daiti, an apparition appeared to him of the ancient God of Iran, Ahura Mazda (The Wise). Mazda taught him the principles of a true religion and continued instructing Zoroaster during subsequent revelations.

Zoroaster then returned from the desert to preach his gospel. At first, he was greeted with hostility from the establishment. They accused him of being an arch-heretic who denounced the current beliefs, and of founding astrology and magic. It took him ten years of preaching before he made his first convert, a cousin. Eventually, when he was forty-two years of age, Zoroaster tried to convert a powerful monarch, King Vishtaspa. One of the king's prize horses was paralyzed and Zoroaster cured him. That was the breakthrough he needed; the king, his queen, and his court became converts and helped to introduce the religion in Persia, and even as far away as China.

Zoroaster then became established and accepted and went on to crusade for the next twenty-five years. His death at the age of seventy-seven came about in the great war of Arjasp when a soldier in the army of the infidel King of Turania stabbed him. At the moment of Zoroaster's death he hurled his rosary at the soldier and killed him. After his death Zoroastrianism became widespread throughout Persia.

After the fall of the Sasanian Empire (651 C.E.), Persia was converted to Islam. A small group of Zoroastrians remained in the area of present-day Iran, but most went to India to seek asylum. They've been there ever since and became known as the Parsi. The Parsi took on many of the customs and rituals of the Hindus.

FACTS

Myth states that the chief priests of King Vishtaspa practiced dark magic and superstition and that Zoroaster was subjected to a duel of wits with them. The magicians of the court asked him thirty-three questions over three days, called the "Terrible Conflict." Zoroaster passed it. The beaten priests then tried to bribe a servant to plant incriminating evidence of witchcraft against him, but they failed.

The Beliefs of Zoroastrianism/Parsiism

Ahura Mazada became the supreme god of the religion, supplanting the original polytheistic theology that included many gods and devils. Zoroaster looked at humanity as a constant struggle between good and evil. Good and evil were represented by the offspring of Ahura Mazda: Spenta Mainyu, the good, and Angra Mainyu, the evil. They represented symbols of the moral judgments that humans must face during their lives.

The all powerful God Ahura Mazda was opposed by the evil spirit of violence and death, Angra Mainyu. So the ethical dualism—the theory that the forces of good and evil are equally balanced in the universe—contained in the religious belief was established.

Zoroaster preached the ethic of "good thoughts, good words and good deeds." In the struggle between good and evil humans have the option of free choice.

At death a person is judged according to choices he or she made during life's passage. On the morning following the third night after death, the soul leaves the body and must cross the Chinvat Bridge. Those whose lives have been exemplary cross the bridge without a problem and enter into heaven. But, for those who had led sinful lives, the bridge narrows to the width of a razor's edge and the person falls into hell. There is no atonement; eternal salvation is earned throughout life—good thoughts, words, and deeds provide their own reward.

The Zoroastrian overview of the history of cosmology—the science or theory of the universe—encompasses their philosophy of dualism. There is a wonderful mythical story that revolves around Ahriman (the destructive Spirit) and Ormazd (Ahura Mazda, the supreme God) that illustrates this view.

Ormazd created the world as a battlefield because he knew that the fight against Ahriman would be very lengthy; in fact, it would last 9,000 years divided into 3,000-year segments. During the entire period the attacks and defense initiated the process of creation. The process is a complicated one that involves demons and the creation of Infinite Light seen as a form of fire, out of which all things were to be born, including Primal Woman and Primal Man.

FACTS

From 550 to 330 B.C.E., the magnificent city of Persepolis was the capital of the Zoroastrian empire. At that time the religion spanned Asia, Africa, and Europe. The Persian capital city was burnt down and destroyed by Alexander the Great in 330 B.C.E.

Ahura Mazda (Ormazd) created the first humans for the purpose of helping him trap Ahriman. Each time humans resist temptations of Ahriman, his strength would wane, until Ahura Mazda would defeat him, which has been predicted to occur at the end of the last 3,000 years. Then, Ahura Mazda will finally triumph and reign supreme.

Holy Writings

The Holy Texts of Zoroastrianism are contained in the *Avesta*. The *Avesta* is not the original text, those were much longer and were destroyed by Alexander the Great, conqueror of Persia. The current texts were assembled from pages that were recovered and put together in the third to seventh centuries C.E.

The *Avesta* has four distinct parts. (Some scholars insist there were five.) The major part is a series of five hymns written by Zoroaster called the Gathas. These are abstract sacred poetry directed to the worship of one god. They focus on the understanding of righteous and cosmic order, the promotion of social justice, and the individual choice of good and evil. Also contained are references to the afterlife and its possible ramifications.

The other parts, not written by Zoroaster, concern the laws of ritual and practice and the traditions of faith. Included in those parts is the Khorde Avesta, known as the Little Avesta. It is a group of minor texts, hymns, and daily prayers.

FACTS

Prayers are made to Ahura Mazda and verses are recited from the *Avesta*. Particular attention is paid, in prayers, to the environment: the sky and the earth. The four elements of air, water, earth, and fire are held in great esteem.

Worship, Practices, and Rituals

Worship includes prayers and symbolic ceremonies, which are carried out before a sacred fire. Fire is holy because it is a symbol of God, and plays a prominent role in Zoroastrianism. The Zoroastrian temples are generally built as terraces, towers, or square rooms. They were depicted on coins, which showed a replica of a fire-altar. Fire is ranked according to its use. For instance, the fire of artisans and traders has a lower rank of importance when compared to the three great eternal fires of Persia. Fire is the symbol that is core to the Zoroastrian belief system, and in adherents' homes it must be lit at all times. To put the fire out is a great sin.

Most ceremonies, for instance, the Jashan Ceremony, can be held in any clean place: temples, meeting houses, or private homes. A priest would be present, sometimes even two, one being senior to the other. Priests typically wear snow-white vestments; white is the color of purity and holiness. They also wear a cylindrical white cap and during chanting a mask-cloth will be placed in front of the face. This ancient custom prevents breath and saliva, which are thought to be ritually impure, from defiling the fire. The ceremony will be elaborate and include specially selected flowers accompanied by chanting. The entire ceremony can take up to an hour.

An initiation ceremony is held for children when they are between seven and ten years of age. They pledge their devotion to the belief and promise to be responsible for Zoroastrian duties. In marriages and funerals cleanliness is, again, of the absolute essence, even to the point that those who have come into contact with a corpse must perform a cleansing ritual. In ancient times the body would be left in the sun and exposed to vultures. Today, the nude body is typically placed in a cement box so that dirt doesn't fall on the body.

Pious Zoroastrians will wear the ancient clothing—a sacred garment and a sacred tie-around belt—under their clothing. The principle of wearing white is never deviated from because of its symbolism of purity.

Religious Festivals

Because the Zoroastrian/Parsi religion is so small, their festivals are not highly visible, neither do they feature public ceremonies or music. Most of the festivals are celebrated within the community, confined to homes, community centers, or temples.

Generally speaking, it could be considered that every day of the year is a special day. However, the Zoroastrian year has six seasons with one major festival in each season. The Zoroastrian feasts are elaborate occasions.

The Druids

The Druids and the Romans have a common bond, in that the Druids were under the domain of the Roman Empire. Originally, the Druids were in Brittany in Gaul (now France) until they were suppressed by Tiberius (14–37 C.E.) and in the British Isles where they were invaded by the Romans. The Romans didn't get as far as Ireland, which became a sanctuary for the Druids for a time. In other parts of Great Britain their only option was death or conversion.

Julius Caesar is the main source of information about the Druids, backed by other scholars, especially Poseidonius. Knowledge about them dates back as far as the third century B.C.E. Druid means "wise oak" and comes from the Celtic expression "knowing the oak tree." The Druids were inhabitants of the Celtic nations, which comprised Scotland, Wales, Ireland, Cornwall, the Isle of Man, and Brittany. Their language was called Gaelic, which evolved into separate dialects: Manx in the Isle of Man, and Scottish, Irish, and Welsh Gaelic.

By all accounts, the Druids were the intellectuals of their time; they have been called the first environmentalists. They studied astronomy, philosophy, law, poetry, and music. Because of persecution by the Romans and Christians, they went underground and became a secretive people. They tended to live in the countryside close to nature, and out of this probably came their expertise in the magical powers of healing, prophesy, controlling the weather, levitation, and the ability to change themselves into the forms of animals.

FACTS

While the Druids could be called priests, the Romans never used the title because the Druids didn't have congregations. However, they did believe that the soul was immortal and at death went from one person to another.

The Central Beliefs of the Druids

Education was paramount with the Druids, and they became judges, doctors, mystics, mathematicians, astronomers, scholars, and teachers. Because they didn't indulge in warfare, Caesar let them pay tribute (taxes) to Rome, instead of being required to fight. Naturally, this attracted many people to join them to take advantage of the privilege. The Druids formed schools for students who wanted to become true Druids. Their education was lengthy, sometimes as long as twenty years in training.

The Deities

The Celtic deities included Lugus, whom the Greeks identified with the sun god Apollo. Another god, Cernunnos, was staghorned and

known as the Lord of the Animals. Stags feature strongly in Celtic literature as do ravens, bulls, and boars, all of which were considered divine. Goddesses were a powerful force, particularly the crow goddess Morrigan, the great queen, who, together with the mare goddess Rhiannon, ruled over fertility, death, and rebirth.

The Celtic worship was directed to the other world with special emphasis on the land and water. The Druids believed that natural elements were inhabited by guardian spirits, generally females. The other world was thought to be a group of islands across or under the Western ocean. Irish tales tell of heroes lured away by women from these islands, creatures that are reminiscent of Homeric sirens.

Trees were a central part of Celtic ritual and were considered sacred, so much so that, as was said above, the Druids took their name from the word meaning "knowing the oak tree." Mistletoe, which grows on the oak tree, was collected with a golden pruning hook and used in ritual sacrifices and feasts.

Stonehenge

Perhaps the most fascinating puzzle connected to the Druids is the proposition that they built Stonehenge. Stonehenge is a gigantic structure in the county of Wiltshire in England. Basically, it is a circle of large stones that has a so-called Altar Stone, Slaughter Stone, two Station Stones, and the Heel Stone; there are many other stones in the construction. It was a work in progress thought to have started in prehistoric times around 3100 B.C.E. and proceeded in three stages over centuries to be finally extended and completed around 1100 B.C.E.

Nobody knows why it was built, although it may have been a place of worship. Another theory is that it had something to do with astronomy, because the northeast axis aligns with the sunrise at the summer solstice. The mystery is how whoever built it transported the stones to the site. Some of the stones weighed 4,860 kilograms and were 30 feet long. There are no similar stones near the site: It is estimated that they were brought 240 miles either by sea, river, or overland from Wales.

In 1963, United States astronomer, Gerald Hawkins, said that Stonehenge was a complicated computer for predicting lunar and solar eclipses. However, R. J. C. Atkinson, an archaeologist from the University College, Cardiff, Wales, said, "Most of what has been written about Stonehenge is nonsense or speculation. No one will ever have a clue what its significance was."

Most scholars dismiss the idea that the Druids had anything to do with the construction because they weren't in the area until long after the final stage was completed. But, many put that aside and have other ideas. In fact, in the eighteenth century in England there was tremendous enthusiasm when the idea that the Druids built Stonehenge was first proposed.

Druid Festivals

Druid festivals have become incorporated into Christian festivals. Their four major celebrations always begin at sundown the previous evening, and include bonfires and revelry that's allied to the season. In Ireland, the year was divided into two periods of six months by Beltane and

Samhain. Each of those periods was equally divided by the feasts of Imbolc and Lughnasadh. The four festivals are:

Samhain, October 31.
Christians call this All Saints' Day. It honors the beginning of the winter half of the Druid year.
Imbolc, February 2.
Christians call this Candlemas. It signals the first signs of spring.
Beltane, May 1.
Christians call this May Day. It is the beginning of the summer half of the Druid year. Maypole dances are held.
Lughnasadh, August 1.
Christians call this Harvest Festival, as do the Druids. It was also the feast of the god Lugh.

Druids follow the phases of the moon very closely. A new venture should start only when the moon is waxing, an old one consummated only when it is waning. The night of the full moon is a time of rejoicing. The night of the new moon is a solemn occasion and calls for vigils and meditation.

Diversification into Modern Society

Like Wicca, there has been a resurgence of interest in Druidism. In England there is an organization called the Order of Bards, Ovates, and Druids. Students can take up the study in much the same way that the original Druids did. One aspect that obviously appeals is the respect given to the environment. It is recorded that Druids are growing in numbers dedicated to preserving the wisdom from the Druid history.

CHAPTER 18

Native American and African Faiths

S uch is the vastness of the American and African continents that it is impossible to generalize about their religions. Each tribe had, and in some cases, still has, its own spiritual ceremonies and beliefs. The spread of missionaries and the influx of Western thought did much to diminish the wisdom of these ancient peoples. Nevertheless, their influence on modern religious study continues.

Native American Religions

It is not possible to examine Native American religions as a whole because of their amazing diversity. Knowledge about the development of religion in the Native American tribes is imprecise. In fact, the word religion had no equivalent in any of the 300 Native American languages that existed at the time Columbus arrived on the continent. Their origins have been traced back some 60,000 years, but there is little in the way of early written material to provide reliable data. The various teachings, ways of life, and stories were passed on orally with all the drawbacks that are inherent in that way of communicating, becoming tainted and more and more unreliable with each telling.

There are common elements, though. Religions (used here in the sense that the immigrant Christians and Roman Catholics knew) were very closely related to the natural world, which included supernatural and sacred spiritual worship and power. Ceremonial rituals were directed at protecting local communities and tribes. The very core of the Native American philosophy was, and is, grounded in the natural world where no distinction between natural and supernatural entities is made. The goal is wholeness and harmonious balance to fulfill the cycles of life, and to walk in beauty.

The Influence of Outside Forces

The invasion of settlers from Europe during the nineteenth century wrecked the existing customs and the native people. Whole ways of life were radically changed, destroyed, or lost. For example, during the Gold Rush days in California, in spite of the treaties made by the federal government providing clearly defined reservations, the miners would hold "Sunday shoots," where crowds of whites would attack Indian villages and kill as many people as they could; whole tribes were massacred.

Today, young Native Americans who wish to revitalize their culture have great difficulty because the older people—the carriers of the oral tradition—are dying off or gone forever.

Christianity, when it arrived, was frequently forced on the natives, with reprisals if it wasn't embraced. Although some of the natives accepted the religion voluntarily, many may have done so for the sake of expediency:

Become a Christian and survive. Once the threat of physical survival was no longer a factor, there was a melding of beliefs, as happened with many other religions that came under the power of an invader or those who relocated to different cultures where they embraced local customs and rituals. Thus, the beliefs in fixed doctrines, sacred texts, and moral codes and customs that were part of the European religious system were taken by Native Americans and made part of their beliefs and values.

FACTS

The Lakota were nomadic, equestrian plains Indians who hunted buffalo and lived in tepees. They became famous for destroying Custer's forces at the Battle of the Little Bighorn in 1876. They followed the Seven Sacred Rites: the sweat lodge, the vision quest, ghost keeping, the sun dance, the making of relatives, puberty ceremony, and throwing the ball. With the exception of throwing the ball, which has been replaced by a practice known as *yuwibi*, all are still used in worship.

Central Beliefs

Again, individual beliefs were peculiar to individual tribes. However, it is possible, without becoming overly simplistic, to look at the generalities that existed

As has been said, the knowledge of past information was passed on verbally, one generation to another. Tradition, therefore, was a vital element specific to each tribe. Many tribes would actually record events. The known method was by using a specially prepared buffalo hide. Each year a figure or symbol illustrating the most memorable event would be painted on the hide. In time the hide would become filled and it would be maintained for as long as there were people who could remember what the figures and symbols meant. For instance, in one year there might have been a very good harvest of berries, in another the tribe might have moved to another location.

But, there was a limit as to how much material could be painted on any one hide, so oral communication was the standard method of passing on stories, customs, and rituals. There might be a ceremony at which these teachings were told to the other members of the tribe, particularly the young. No doubt the recounting of the exploits of local warrior heroes was popular.

In the belief system there was one great advantage in not having a tribal religion: There was no controversy between competing beliefs nor religious schisms within groups/tribes, as was common among established religions. The geographical vastness of the country and the sparse population also played a role.

FACTS

The Apache occupied the southwestern part of the United States. They embraced the concept of supernatural power and carried out shamanistic ceremonies. Four is a sacred number; their songs and prayers occurred in quartets. Rites lasted for four successive nights. Their life-cycle rites included the rite for a child's first steps and a girl's puberty rite.

Native American Practices

The Native American Church, which became institutionalized in the twentieth century, has accepted some of Christianity's beliefs and it has spread from coast to coast. In some instances, traditional languages have been incorporated into Christian worship. It has received government support, particularly in the establishment of Indian schools.

The church is also known as Peyote Religion. Peyote comes from the name of a cactus—eating it produces an hallucinogenic effect. It was used extensively throughout many of the tribes. In 1997, the Native American Church estimated that there were about 225,000 adherents.

Peyote, when used in a ritual, is usually chewed and eaten. The rite can take place in a tepee with an earthen altar mound in the center of it, plus a sacred fire. The ceremony is generally an all-night affair, led by a peyote chief, and includes singing, prayers, water rites, and meditation. The ceremony concludes with a Sunday morning breakfast. The church's ethics includes brotherly love, family care and support, and the avoidance of alcohol.

Peyote produces visions during trance states, which were part of a Ghost Dance. Songs were sung and the person in the trance might have a vision of an eagle or crow guiding him or her to the world of the dead. Part of the Ghost Dance provided information about the traditional culture that the individual sought to retrieve. Those who are familiar with the books by Carlos Castaneda and the *Teachings of Don Juan* will recognize the ritual.

Rituals

The majority of Native American rituals revolved around the calendar and the lunar and solar observations. Others were allied to the various subsistence needs; for example, hunting and harvesting. The Native American environment was symbolized by the ritual of the six directions: North, South, East, West, the Zenith, and the Nadir. The Zenith was Grandfather (day). Sky is represented by Father Sun and the Thunderbirds. The Nadir is Mother or Grandmother Earth. Grandmother Moon was female.

A series of thankful rituals related to entities of the earth:

Maple: thankful for the maple.
Sun: thankful for the sun.
Thunder: thankful for the thunder, and so on.

Different tribes had different rituals; nevertheless, the principle throughout the majority of the tribes was closely tied to nature and existence. For instance, the spirits and power of mountains, springs, lakes, clouds, flora, and fauna were seen as sacred.

The sweat lodge, fasting, and the sun dance were all part of Native American rituals. A sweat lodge is a structure made from saplings and covered by animal skins that generates moist air, like a sauna. There is a depression dug in the center of the lodge where hot rocks are placed; water is thrown on them, which makes the steam. Sweat lodges vary in size; some can hold as many as a dozen people. The purpose is for purification, or spiritual renewal.

The Sun Dance

Fasting rituals are, naturally, self-explanatory, but the Sun Dance is spectacular. A religious ceremony that originated with the Plains Indians, most notably the Sioux, the Sun Dance was generally held once a year in the early summer. It was held to celebrate and reaffirm beliefs about the universe and the supernatural.

Sometimes the dance was done by individual tribes; other times a group of them would come together. There were elaborate preparations and after the Sun Dance itself was under way it continued for several days and nights. Dancers didn't eat or drink during the dance and many ended up in a frenzy of exhaustion; some even indulged in self-torture and mutilation. In 1904, the U.S. government outlawed the Sun Dance. Some tribes have tried to revive the dance in its original form.

Death

Birth, marriage, and death do not fit into a universal set of beliefs and rites. The various rites are meant to be indulged in by the relatives and the community. However, death is considered a transition. It is believed that many outcomes are possible following death. Some believe in reincarnation, others that humans return as ghosts, and others that the spirit goes to another world.

FACTS

The Navajo live on the Navajo nation, a reservation in northern Arizona and New Mexico. They believe in powerful holy people, with whom they can live harmoniously. Twenty-four Navajo chants have been identified. One of the central chants is the Navajo creation myth that recounts what happened after their emergence on earth.

The Native American Church Today

Many Native Americans still cling to and express the values and traditions they were taught by their forefathers. Today, many tribes of Native Americans are continuing their legal measures to reclaim lands they feel they have title to. Original languages are virtually extinct, but the Native American Church and its congregations are endeavoring to keep them alive and to re-establish a culture that has been virtually destroyed by its invaders.

A great and proud Indian warrior chief made a statement after a long, hard, and bitter war with the enemy was lost. Everything was lost: their horses, cattle, and personal possessions, their land; and their freedom. The tribe was the Nez Perce, who came under the heel of General Sherman, whose policy was no leniency or charity. The saying, "The only good Indian is a dead Indian," was attributed to him.

The words from the proud Indian warrior chief Joseph of the Nez Perce have now become world famous, although their sentiments are rarely emulated: "Hear me my chiefs, I am tired; my heart is sick and sad. From where the sun now stands, I will fight no more forever."

African Religions

Attempting to analyze religions in the vast continent of Africa is an awesome task. Africa is the second largest continent in the world after Asia and contains more than fifty countries. It has an amazing geographical variation and cultural diversity. Each of its countries has its own history, ethnic group, and language. Many of the religious beliefs, customs, and rites evolved due to the environment in which the followers were born, grew up, and survived. Environmental factors have strongly influenced how the various faiths developed. For example, Jewish dietary laws illustrate how religious, political, and environmental factors influenced the creation of practices that became traditional to the faith.

While there is no single body of religious dogma for the continent, many similarities are found among all the countries. The simple common denominator is the belief in a single god or creator who is somewhere else. Even though, in some cases, there is a collection of gods, there is usually one top god, who has domain over all. These other spiritual beings can be nature spirits and ancestors and are often called the Children of God. Sacrifices to lesser spiritual beings are believed to go to the supreme being. Many of the religious groups in various parts of the continent are on the decline.

The largest religious influence in Africa has been Islam, which came first to North Africa. The Arabs then brought the faith into the Sahara, which is why a lot of western African people embraced Islam.

FACTS

To make a relationship of sizes, it might be noted that the total land area of North America is 9,355,000 square miles, making it the third largest continent in the world. The total land area of Africa is 11,724,000 square miles. Interestingly, the population of Africa is only 10 percent of the world's population. North America, also, only contains 10 percent of the world's population, but then they have about 2,369,000 fewer square miles to move around in.

Many people mistakenly think of African religions as being mainly concerned with animism, sorcery, and various tribal rituals. This is not actually true. First of all, one has to consider that Africa is virtually divided in two at the Sahara Desert. (It is cut almost equally in two by the equator, meaning it is bound in the north by the tropic of Cancer and in the south by the tropic of Capricorn.) Islam took hold in the north. Christianity at one time was in the Sudan and it's still active in Ethiopia, which is the only African kingdom with a Christian state church. Christian missions have spread throughout most of the areas south of the Sahara.

In the dense tropical forests ancient traditional beliefs are still active, except where missionary zeal has made a presence in a country. In those cases, the majority of peoples has followed the customs and beliefs of the imported religion. Even so, it is highly probable that there has been an intermingling of the traditional with the new.

Central Beliefs of African Religions

Religion has always played a major part in the different cultures in Africa. Each locale has many varied stories that tie them directly to either a god or the gods they worshiped. However, there is a strong similarity to the stories. First, the god would create the earth, then the animals, and, lastly, the humans.

Because of the lack of a written language, very little written religious history is available. Mostly, what is known came in two ways: orally from parents to children, and the results gathered from the extensive work of archeologists, which revealed a tremendous amount of evidence not only of religious practices and ways of life but also how those lives evolved over the years. The traditions were so strong that even today's religious practices provide valuable insight into the way they were conducted years ago.

E

FACTS

In the Central African Republic about two fifths of the population are Christians, mainly Roman Catholics plus some Protestant denominations. Sunnite Muslims are a growing minority. The remainder are either adherents of traditional religions or have no religious affiliations.

Some of the common elements in African religions are that the cosmos is populated by divine beings, that there are sacred places and spaces (for instance a mountain that a god or sacred spirit inhabits), that males and females are both parts of the cosmic scheme, and that the idea of society was organized around the values and traditions from early beginnings. Africans have taken strong steps over the years to stave off the influences of foreigners onto existing traditions and beliefs in an effort to preserve indigenous cultures. These efforts have not always been successful.

Many scholars believe that those African countries that have remained most stable into the twenty-first century are those that retained their traditional ways of life and religions. African religions don't have a dogma insofar as they strictly follow laid-down religious laws. Their entire philosophy is directed to nurturing a proper relationship with the divine and how the divine relates to the earth, life, and community. Their rituals revolve around means of establishing and maintaining a relationship with the spiritual forces in nature and with the gods.

This relationship is accomplished by prayers, offerings, and sacrifices made to shrines and altars. A sacrifice often means the shedding of blood; it is believed that the ritual of sacrifice releases the vital force that sustains life. In some parts of Africa, a blood sacrifice must be made to the gods. These would certainly include the earth gods. In other parts of the continent, earth gods are seen as the punishers of sin. Today, it is animals that are sacrificed; it wasn't always that way. Typically, a goat or chicken is consecrated, ritually slain, and then either burnt or buried. It's never eaten as a meal for the devotees. The purpose of many sacrifices is to assuage the wrath of the gods, which can be exhibited by drought, pestilence, epidemic, famine, or other dire happenings.

The shrines don't have to be imposing edifices; they can be insubstantial little structures placed wherever seems appropriate. They don't even have to be permanent.

Ancestors play an important part in the beliefs; they act as the go-betweens for spiritual access. People don't automatically become ancestors when they die; to do that they had to have lived a good life—a moral life that has contributed to the community. When a person gets seriously ill, it's believed that the cause is some kind of emotional or social conflict, and it is the ancestor, who has been watching over the person, who delivers the reprimand of illness.

The Rituals of African Religions

There is a general linking thread that is common throughout Africa in the rituals performed, at least as far as they are concerned with progress throughout life.

QUESTIONS?

How many religions are there in Africa?
No one knows. Africa has been a hub for missionaries. So, in addition to the traditional beliefs and independent churches, the Roman Catholic Church made considerable inroads, as did the Baptists and other Protestant denominations. The Ethiopian Church, formed in 1892, had connections with the African Methodist Episcopal Church in the United States.

Birth

An expectant mother is an important person. As in the United States where a child may grow up to be president, so in Africa a male child may grow up to be a chief. The actual birth rarely takes place in the presence of a man. The child is anointed by a priest. Naming the child is very important and usually consists of a given name, followed by the name of the father, then the grandfather's name. After the ceremony there will be songs, dancing, and a feast.

Puberty

Both circumcision and clitoridectomy are performed. The justification for what some people call mutilation, is that it is an important means of establishing gender—that there should be no indication of androgyny. Boys often have their faces painted in preparation for the coming-of-age rite of circumcision.

Some tribes initiate girls in what we, in the west, would call domestic science. This even extends to sexual etiquette and the religious significance of womanhood and female power.

Boys may be led by the wise men in the village to a specially secluded place and stay there for up to a year while they learn secret information about becoming a man.

Marriage

A woman who is to be married is seen as very powerful; she may give birth to a warrior or chief. In some areas, after the wedding has been planned, the groom's family must move to the bride's village. Gifts will be exchanged and in some cultures an offering is made to the gods. Sometimes a sacrifice will be made, too.

The actual wedding ceremony will include both families, and sometimes the entire village. Not surprisingly, there will be much celebration. For several weeks after the consummation of the marriage the couple will continue their celebrations.

Death

Death is not seen as the final stage of life, but as going to a place to be with deceased loved ones. The corpse is cleaned and dressed, then placed with special artifacts to aid in the journey. The corpse will be buried and afterwards there will be an exchange of gifts, and an animal sacrifice.

Witches are not given burial rites because of their earthly practices. They are disposed of in a secret place.

African religious beliefs and customs have traveled, particularly to the United States, where elements of the indigenous faiths have frequently remained and/or been absorbed into the local religions. The lasting picture of religion in Africa is one of amazing historical development in that rituals and customs from ancient times have continued into the twenty-first century and commingled with a variety of imported religions.

CHAPTER 19

Pacific Rim Faiths

One of the central beliefs of these religions is in their mystical heritage. For example, the Australian Aborigines had their belief in dreaming about the powerful beings who arose out of the land. The Maoris of New Zealand and the Polynesians had similar attachments to natural phenomena, particularly the sea and the stars.

Australian/Aboriginal Faiths

Aborigines first traveled to Australia about 40,000 years ago. At that time there was a land bridge between Asia and Australia. Over the years the sea levels rose and Australia became an island. By the time the English arrived in 1788 and colonized the east coast, called New South Wales, there were well over a million Aborigines and more than 200 different languages were spoken. The English planned to convert the natives to Christianity from what they considered paganism and superstition.

Because the Aborigines did not cultivate crops or domesticate animals, apart from the dingo (a kind of wild dog), they were essentially nomads. The typical results of being invaded by foreigners were diseases against which they had no immunity, enforced labor, and even murder; collectively these sharply reduced the population. Then, the missionaries arrived and, in 1821, the first Wesleyan Missionary Society established a presence, and spread throughout the land.

QUESTIONS?

Did the Aborigines believe in a god?
Historically, the answer is no. Today, those who are Christians do.

There was no cohesive element among the Aborigines and so nothing came anywhere near an established organized national identity. While there was sporadic resistance against the colonists by various tribes, as the English called them, not much came of the efforts and evangelical Christianity became accepted. Today, more than two thirds of Australian Aborigines are considered to be Christians.

Beliefs of the Aborigines

The colonists concluded that the Aborigines had no actual religion until they discovered something called Dreamtime. The thrust of the Aboriginal existence was their relationship with the environment and handed-down oral beliefs. Like all peoples, they asked themselves the universal questions: Who am I? Where did I come from? What am I doing here? Where do I go when I die?

Aborigines believed that when their heroic ancestors died, they went into a spiritual place where they created, through Dreamtime, everything that was: the earth; the land they occupied; every plant, animal, insect, and reptile; and the sky above; everything. It was during Dreamtime that their creators made men and women. Birth was seen as the result of what the creators did; their power was present at every birth, not only of people but also everything else. In addition, some of the tribes believed that spirit children and spirit animals gained life by entering a female's body.

The most important thing to an Aborigine was spiritual heritage. After death the person's spirit was believed to return to its spirit place. That belief gave rise to burying a corpse to face the direction of its spirit home.

The creators taught men and women how to hunt and gather food, and how to make the tools to carry out those duties. As the generations came and went, the belief in Dreamtime was passed on by living a life known as Dreaming—the person lived in the same way as their forebears.

Ceremonies

Puberty rituals for a boy generally took place once he had started to grow facial hair. When that happened, he was ready for the initial rituals. Initiation was a symbolic re-enactment of death and rebirth, which was seen as the way to a new life as an adult. The novice would leave his camp and the women would begin to wail. This symbolism was a prelude to the religious beliefs in which all men participated. Circumcision was an important part of the rites and was considered as a secret sacred ritual. There were other rites, which included piercing the nasal septum, pulling teeth, hair removal, scarring, and actually playing with fire.

The puberty of girls did not have a universal ritual; in some tribes, it was celebrated by either total or partial seclusion and taboos on certain foods. In some areas defloration and hymen cutting were practiced.

As Christianity became well ingrained in the land, the Aborigines adopted the ceremonies of the Christian Church to which they had been converted. What tended to take place, certainly in the early days, was a mixture of Christian ceremonies and indigenous ones, which, although the indigenous ones were looked on by the colonists as secular, they were sacred to the Aborigines.

There has been much research into whether or not the Aborigines actually had what could be called a true religion. The consensus was that for that to be established there must be evidence of a god. However, there was not even a suggestion of one in the Dreamtime myths.

Historically, the marriage ceremony involved the ritual of the man arriving in the camp of his wife-to-be and catching or hunting food, which was presented to his future father-in-law and other members of the family. The prospective wife would often build a new hut for her prospective husband and herself. She then prepared a meal for her husband-to-be and when the meal had taken place, the couple was considered to be married. However, the ceremony was not looked upon as a religious occasion.

In Today's World

In modern times, Aborigines have had problems similar to those of the Native Americans regarding land rights. The Aboriginal people have strong feelings of having been dispossessed. Dreamtime is still a part of their heritage as is their landscape, which was formed by their ancestors and is still believed to be alive with their spirits. The Aborigines say that those spirits are as much a part of the land as they themselves are part of its creation.

Steps are being taken to find a just solution. Nevertheless, on Australia Day in January 2000, the words of reconciliation by Governor Sir James Gobbo did nothing to diminish the anger of a group of Aboriginal activists who labeled Australia Day a day of mourning; they burnt the Australian flag in protest.

The Aboriginal flag is divided horizontally into two equal halves of black (top) and red (bottom), with a yellow circle in the center. The black symbolizes Aboriginal people and the yellow represents the sun, the constant renewer of life. Red depicts the earth and also represents ochre, which is used by Aboriginal people in their ceremonies. The flag was designed by Harold Thomas and was first flown at Victoria Square, Adelaide, on National Aborigines' Day on July 12, 1971. It was used later at the Tent Embassy in Canberra in 1972. Today, the flag has been adopted by all Aboriginal groups and is flown or displayed permanently at Aboriginal centers throughout Australia.

In the late 1770s, Captain Cook said, ". . . in reality the Aborigines are far more happier than we Europeans, being wholly unacquainted with the superfluous conveniences so much sought after in Europe . . . they live in a tranquility which is not disturbed by the inequality of Condition."

The Maori Faith

The Maoris are indigenous to New Zealand, which comprises two islands in the South Pacific below Australia. New Zealand was one of the last lands on earth to be populated by humans. Originally, it was settled by Polynesians. The people had no name for themselves until they adopted Maori (which means "normal") to distinguish themselves from the Europeans, who had become more numerous following the discovery of the two islands by the English Captain Cook in the late 1700s.

With the English came a series of diseases to which the Maori had no initial resistance, mainly measles and influenza, which led to a decline in the local population. After Great Britain annexed the country in 1840, there was an appreciable increase in the number of Europeans. Today, New Zealand is populated mainly by people of European descent; the Maoris are in the minority.

The north island is the area of economical success, the hub of which is the city of Auckland. The south island is the most dramatic with a stretch of alps 300 miles long with Mt. Cook as its pinnacle; at 12,349 feet it is the highest mountain in New Zealand.

The Maoris have a wonderfully rich mythical origin that began with Ranginui, the sky father, and Papatuanuku, the earth mother. The sky father and earth mother prevented light from reaching the world because they were always in such a close embrace. Their offspring decided to separate them and thus allow light to come into the world.

But, there was a war about the separation of the parents. Tawhirimatea (god of the winds) won over Tane (god of forests) and Tangaroa (god of seas). However, Tumatauenga (god of war) came to defeat all of them. Thus, the world developed with wars and violence.

The British came seeking profit and the Maori chieftains eventually took exception and became involved in the bargaining of their land for sale. Not everyone agreed with that policy and more violence took place within the Maoris. At last, by 1872, the fighting came to an end; the result by then was that the Maori culture had become decimated and the struggle was how to retain the customs and rituals that had existed before the invaders arrived.

QUESTIONS?

Who owns or operates Easter Island?
Easter Island is the odd one out in the Polynesian Triangle in that it is the only island controlled by a Latin American country, Chile. While some people still speak Polynesian, the majority speak Spanish. Only one third of the residents are from Chile.

Spiritual Movements of the Maoris

The most spiritual movement in New Zealand, Ringatu, was founded in 1867 by the Maori guerrilla leader Te Kooti. It embraced a benign philosophy, including faith healing. Services were held on the twelfth day of each month and on Saturdays. Generally, they were held in meeting houses, and love feasts and communion (without bread or wine but including Bible verses, songs, chants, and prayers) were all part of the services. Te Kooti, who had been pardoned in 1883, was elevated to the status of a prophet and martyr. A liturgy produced in the 1960s, *The Book of the Eight Covenants of God and Prayers of the Ringatu Church,* may have originated orally from Te Kooti.

In the twentieth century, Christianity had become entrenched and many of its customs and rituals had been incorporated into the Maori traditions. Concurrent with this, the Maoris had become politically active in parliament.

The Ratana Church

A Methodist farmer, Tahupotiki Wiremu Ratana, founded the Ratana Church. He had established a reputation as a mystical faith healer, which drew the crowds. He preached of moral reform and of one God: the God of the Bible. By a process of political and religious pressure, the Ratana movement disassociated itself from other denominations. The New Zealand Anglican bishops denounced the church; they weren't too taken with their practices of faith healing and the taking of medicines.

By becoming politically involved and gaining some support, the church eventually, in the 1960s, got back together with the other New Zealand Christian churches. The Ratana church by then was not solely Maori, but had attracted many white members to the congregation.

The Maoris have no official, established religion; in fact, many of them have no adherence to any religion, although the Maori version of Christianity is practiced in the Ratana and Ringatu churches.

Most of New Zealand is comprised of the English-speaking population; even so, about a third of Maoris speak their native language. In fact, the Maori language is taught in selected schools.

Ethnic and Religious Mix of New Zealand

New Zealand is a predominantly Christian country comprised of Anglicans, Presbyterians, Roman Catholics, Methodists, some other Protestant groups, and Eastern Orthodox, with a few Jewish congregations.

In New Zealand, the majority of inhabitants are of British Isles or other European country descent. Other ethnic groups include Pacific Islanders, Chinese, and Indians. The actual Maori population is in the minority, which has produced an element of racial tension, but nowhere near that found in other countries.

The Maori literary production since World War II has gained a tremendous reputation. The majority, although written by Maoris, are in the English language. The highest point in literature was Keri Hulme's *The Bone People* (1983), which won the Booker Prize, Great Britain's most prestigious literary award, in 1985.

The development of Maori arts and the proliferation of Maori life in the arts now forms a large part of Maori achievement. This has fostered a returning to the roots of the Maori culture.

Polynesian Religions

The world of Polynesia and its many religions and beliefs is an exotic but complicated place. Polynesia is a collection of islands over the central area of the Pacific Ocean that roughly forms a triangle, with the Hawaiian Islands to the northeast, French Polynesia to the southeast, and New Zealand on the southwestern side. The name Polynesia is derived from the Greek words *poly* (many) and *nesoi* (islands). There are, in fact, thousands of islands of varying sizes.

Many of the islands are the result of volcanic action over the centuries. The island of Tonga, for example, was formed by being the summit of a chain of undersea volcanic mountains that were raised above the sea by continued volcanic eruptions.

The geological action of the environment of Polynesia has been a major contributing factor to the development of the religions and customs of the entire area. In addition to all of that, Polynesia had been immensely affected by its extensive European contact. Many of the islands suffered under various political factions, although now most are free of all that and operate under their own political systems. Hawaii is the fiftieth state of the United States and American Samoa is still an American territory. Only six other entities are under the umbrellas of Western powers.

If you travel to Polynesia today, keep in mind that there are remnants of magical practices still around, even though they may appear to be local social customs. Good manners may be based on the tradition of *mana*.

Central Beliefs of the Polynesian Religions

In the nineteenth century, the word *mana* was understood to mean supernatural force or power. It was applied to people, spirits, or even inanimate objects. Polynesian chiefs were said to have great *mana*, so great that if another person even touched the chief's shadow, the only way that error could be corrected was by the death of a subject. Everyday life became like a maze through which people had to negotiate to avoid offending *mana*. It got to the point where almost everything was believed to have the *mana* of a great person or god. When men prepared for battle they had to go through a ritual of purification that meant eating certain foods, avoiding women, and going away on their own to avoid defilement.

The violation of certain acts such as disturbing the bones of the dead could evoke supernatural punishment. Magic became an important part of society practiced in order to ward off the vengeance or wrath of *mana*. This situation gave birth to specialists in magic who were available, for a price, to offer rituals that had to be performed to protect the people.

The belief in gods of varying power, called Tangaroa, Tu, or Lono, gave rise to the necessity to worship them. Sometimes this worship required human sacrifice, sexual orgies, and extensive fasts and chanting.

Eventually, all of this became too much, and *mana* itself was challenged. With the growing belief in Christianity, brought to the islands by missionaries, the meaning of *mana* was revised to mean the personal attributes of only people in powerful positions, like a clergyman or senior government official. The belief that supernatural aspects of *mana* were floating around in almost anything was discarded.

While Christianity is the predominant religion in Polynesia, there are smatterings of other religions. In Tonga, for example, about 50 percent belong to the Free Wesleyan Church, 14 percent belong to the Free Church of Tonga, 9 percent are Mormon, and the remainder belong to other denominations.

Polynesians are a family- and group-orientated society, and religion forms an important, integral part of their makeup. Like the Maoris, the Polynesians are, in the main, Christians and follow the teachings of the Bible.

CHAPTER 20

New Age and Other Beliefs

All these beliefs have one thing in common: a seeking for respect from the traditional religions just as they, in turn, respect the beliefs of those peoples (even though they do not adhere to them). Here you will find the what and why of alternative beliefs, and perhaps, a greater understanding of them.

Agnosticism and Atheism

Mention agnosticism or atheism to a deeply religious person and the odds are you will be in for an argument that could become very contentious. People who are agnostics or atheists tend to be very careful whom they tell. Many of them complain that once the word is out, religious devotees treat them as if they should sit in the back of the religious bus. The one plus, they say, is that at least if you keep your beliefs to yourself, you can't be identified by the way you look. To understand what this is all about, it's best to know exactly what the words mean and what it entails to believe in their philosophies.

Agnostics

Agnostics are often accused of sitting on the religious fence. The word is from the Greek and means "not knowing." It was originally coined in 1869 by a British biologist, Thomas Huxley, whose scientific fame came from discovering, in 1845, a new membrane in the human hair sheath that became known as Huxley's layer.

The dictionaries and encyclopedias say that agnosticism is the doctrine that the existence of God and other spiritual beings is neither certain nor impossible. It should be noted that agnosticism sharply differs from atheism, which completely denies the existence of God and other spiritual beings.

The basis of the modern belief arose out of the works of two philosophers: David Hume, who was British, and Immanuel Kant, who was German. Both of them pointed out that there were logical fallacies in the arguments for the existence of God and of the soul. One can see how this doesn't go down too well with those who believe in God.

If a person did some in-depth research into the beliefs, or nonbeliefs, it would become apparent that they overlap, which, of course, leads to the confusion in the minds of many people regarding their differences. For instance, even Huxley rejected as false the typical view about God and what happens after a persons dies. Not that he didn't know, but that he dismissed the propositions. A coworker of Karl Marx is on record saying that Huxley and his colleagues were, in fact, atheists.

The Catholic Church states: "The Agnostic does not always merely abstain from either affirming or denying the existence of God, but crosses over to the old position of theoretic Atheism and, on the plea of insufficient evidence, ceases even to believe that God exists. While, therefore, not to be identified with Atheism, Agnosticism is often found in combination with it."

In 1876, a British mathematician and philosopher of science, W. K. Clifford, wrote in *The Ethics of Belief*: "It is wrong always, everywhere and for everyone to believe anything upon insufficient evidence." Later in 1889, Huxley wrote in an essay, ". . . that it is morally wrong not to believe certain propositions, whatever the results of strict scientific investigation of the evidence of these propositions."

Some critics expounded the idea that agnosticism actually had a religious, as opposed to secular, outlook. Buddha (Gautama) was cited as being someone who didn't answer the Christian propositions of the certainty of God and divine scheme of things being necessary to salvation, but put his own very different spin on the whole question.

The Roman Catholic Church says, "The Agnostic denial of the ability of human reason to know God is directly opposed to Catholic Faith. The Council of the Vatican solemnly declares that 'God, the beginning and of all, can by the natural light of human reason, be known with certainty from the works of creation.'" In short, it might be reasonable to say that what agnostics believe is there is something out there, but they are not sure what.

Atheism

Atheism might be looked at as the hard core of religious disbelief. The definition of religion according to the encyclopedias is when a human becomes conscious of a power above and beyond the human, and recognizes a dependence upon that power, then religion has become a factor in his or her being. Atheism rejects that concept, together with belief in all spiritual beings; in other words it rejects religion.

The base of Christianity and Judaism is the belief in a God who created everything out of nothing and has absolute control over all. Adherents of these religions have accepted that they were born sinners and rely on their religious leaders—priests, ministers, and rabbis—to interpret the holy writings, customs, and rituals that it is believed their god requires their believers to obey. Atheism rejects the whole package.

For someone to worship, he or she has to have some understanding of what is being worshipped. The atheist would ask to be shown this god who is being worshipped. As there is no concrete entity provided, the atheist would take the stance that only myth is being worshipped.

Nevertheless, just because a person does not believe in a god, it doesn't mean that they are devoid of morals, ethics, or love for their relatives, friends, and people in general, or that they don't try to live good lives.

New Age Spirituality

Unlike most traditional religions, the New Age movement has no organized base; it is a network, you might say, of people who have different spiritual approaches to life. Many New Age followers are members of an existing religion, with the New Age philosophy an adjunct to their central beliefs. Other members have discarded their traditional religion in favor of a more free-flowing, nondogmatic belief.

The movement has no holy text, clergy, or creed. While there are, of course, no sermons preached, meeting places exist where seminars on various aspects of New Age philosophy and new developments are delivered. A large number of New Age bookshops that sell a wide variety of books on the subject frequently act as meeting places for followers. However, the movement did set up communities, often called communes, where members followed the new lifestyle.

The movement came about in the 1970s and was strongly influenced by Eastern religions and philosophy (particularly Buddhism and Hinduism), Western psychology, Carl Jung's teachings and his concept of the collective unconscious, and Native American beliefs and rituals. With the advances in science the belief also included a pseudoscientific association with an interpretation of quantum physics.

Adopting beliefs from various sources and integrating them into the New Age movement gives an indication of the thrust of the movement—a search for a new paradigm. While not a registered religion, it is certainly a spiritual movement. Its development is said to be linked to the social changes that preceded it—for instance, the Beat generation, the Hippie culture of the 1960s, and the anti-Vietnam War groups. Its rise might have been a reaction to the general disillusionment of many people within the established churches and governments.

FACTS

There are no reliable demographics available on how many people may actually practice New Age philosophy. However, the indications are that far more women than men embrace the movement, and that the majority of the followers are Caucasian. Men tend to be limited to the roles of gurus, educators, healers, guides, and writers.

Beliefs

The followers were looking to a New World Order that would produce an end to wars, famine, pollution, poverty, and discrimination. The new order would usher in what was termed "the dawning of The Age of Aquarius." The Age of Aquarius was based on the belief that a new sign of the zodiac came along every 2,000 years. The previous sign was said to be Pisces, the fish, which came at the time a new religion called Christianity was emerging. Interestingly, the symbol of the fish indicates Christianity; a metal representation of the symbol can often be seen on the trunks of automobiles.

The central belief of the movement is that the universe and all that exists within it are one interdependent whole. This means that every existing entity, from atom to galaxy, is rooted in the same universal, life-creating reality. All people, whatever their race, creed, sex, caste, or color, are invited to participate as individuals, or within collective environments that share in these basic beliefs and understandings. The movement claims that it imposes no dogmas, but points toward the source of unity beyond all differences—devotion to truth, love for all living things, and commitment to a life without personal judgment of others.

How do I go about joining a New Age group?
You could take a look at some of the New Age Web sites on the Internet or locate a New Age/Spiritual bookstore. The staff are usually New Agers, low key and kind, and they probably will be the best source.

Practices

Attached to the expressed philosophy of the movement are a number of esoteric practices, many of which have been ridiculed by skeptics and scientists. A lot of the practices have strong health applications.

Crystals are believed to have healing energy. Based on the idea that their molecular structure can be shaped to vibrate at a specific frequency, crystals can positively affect a person's well-being and good health.

Astrology is based on the theory that at the exact time of a person's birth the planets were in a unique position. Interpreting those positions in the constellation, which is a highly complicated endeavor, can predict a person's personality and future events. (New Agers aren't the only people who believe in astrology.) The widespread belief by New Agers in astrology is thought to have given birth to the opening gambit, frequently made in bars: "What's your sign?"

The human potential movements, also known as the Emotional Growth Movement, which include Esalen Growth Center, EST, Gestalt Therapy, Primal Scream Therapy, Transactional Analysis, Transcendental Meditation (made famous by the Beatles), and Yoga (an integral part of many Eastern religions), can thank New Agers for their widespread acceptance and application. Essentially, human potential groups are involved in therapeutic methods designed to help people advance spiritually. Many of the movements have declined in popularity.

Aromatherapy, which has been practiced since the beginning of civilization, has been embraced by many New Agers as a therapeutic health adjunct. The oils can be applied directly to the skin, used in baths, or inhaled. They are not inexpensive. As with television advertisements for drugs, these may not be for you, and you won't get very far consulting your doctor about them.

There are almost countless other therapies and techniques aimed at either improving one's health and/or mental equilibrium. Obviously, many of the practices and ingredients used present a wonderful opportunity for the skeptics. Nevertheless, the placebo effect some people obtain from them can't be discounted. It should be added that the marketing of the many New Age accoutrements has produced a multibillion dollar business.

Books

The New Age movement has no holy writings, but three books among thousands of New Age books have made a lasting impression on many followers.

The first of eight books by the same author came out in the late 1960s—*The Teachings of Don Juan: A Yaqui Way of Knowledge* became a cult book. People who have read it say it transformed them and became their manifesto. The author, Carlos Castaneda, is a former anthropologist who became a sorcerer's apprentice, psychic visionary, and original philosopher.

Admirers credit Castaneda with introducing to popular culture the traditions of shamanism, including entering the nonordinary realms of spirit powers in order to restore balance and harmony to body, soul, and society. The book and its message were ready-made for the fast-growing New Age market.

The second book, created by Dr. Helen Schucman, is a series of workbooks collectively called *A Course in Miracles*. She claimed the words came through a process of inner dictation directly from Jesus. It is supposedly a Christian-based interpretation of the Bible. The work comprises a three-volume curriculum consisting of a text, workbook for students, and a manual for teachers. When the book was being produced, Dr. Schucman was a tenured Associate Professor of Medical Psychology at Columbia University. Her department head assisted her in its production. Dr. Schucman learned shorthand in order to take the dictation, which, it is reported, took eight years. The book states, "that its goal for you is happiness and peace." The book offers a one-year training program; it begins with the process of changing the student's mind and perception. According to the Preface, "at the end, the reader is left in the hands of his or her own internal Teacher Who, will direct all subsequent learning as He sees fit."

FACTS

A nonprofit organization founded in 1978 established a networking center for a Course in Miracles students. They publish a periodical called *The Holy Encounter* and offer free services for students of the course to help them connect with others and understand and integrate the principles into their lives. As has been said, this is not the easiest study course to take.

The *Workbook for Students* is 365 pages long, with an exercise for each day of the year. The entire publication is written to express a nonsectarian, nondenominational spirituality. It does not claim to be a religion. As one teacher has said, "There is within each of us a center where we can retreat and find rest from the activities of the world. Love calls to each of us to slip effortlessly through the open door and leave behind our guilt from the past and fear of the future."

The third set of publications is the *Conversations with God* series written by Neale Donald Walsch. The content of all three books is a record of a series of the author's conversations with God. According to the record, Mr. Walsch called out in anguish, "What does it take to make life work? And what have I done to deserve a life of such continuing struggle?" His questions kept coming and he wrote them down on a yellow legal pad; the list looking like an angry letter to God. Then, he heard a reply in his mind coming from a voiceless voice, a voice Mr. Walsch felt very strongly was that of God, who said, "Do you really want an answer to all these questions, or are you just venting?" That was the start of it all.

Prayer and Healing

It isn't too often that science, religion, and politics meet. But, in the field of prayer and healing, The National Institutes of Health has funded research into the effectiveness, or not, of prayer on the healing of the sick, including patients with cancer and AIDS.

Spiritual healing has been going on for centuries and is one of the oldest religious customs in the world. Today, there are many healing centers set up in churches all over the country where people may go for advice about praying for an ill loved one. To the members of any religion or belief, the power of prayer, the laying on of hands, and the recordings of miracles is, therefore, nothing new.

Reaction of Today's Society

In today's society a medical scientist would have grave doubts about the recordings of miracles ascribed to Christ in the Bible. The scientist

would have to follow a medical protocol in order to establish the process and validity of the disease, its symptoms, possible treatment, and outcome. But these facts are not available for miracles; the scientist would have to put down the whole affair, and others, as being apocryphal. The assertion that the "proof of the pudding is in the eating" wouldn't wash.

The closest a scientist might come to account for someone whose disease went away without medical treatment would be spontaneous remission, which is often brought into play when there doesn't appear to be a logical answer as to why a patient suddenly appears to be cured. This attitude isn't taken to protect the medical profession so much as it is to protect members of society from being taken in by charlatans, out to make money from the vulnerable.

The ultimate reliance on the ability to heal by an unknown power, as opposed to the medical establishment, is exhibited by some members of established religious faiths, for instance: Christian Scientists say that healing comes through scientific prayer, or spiritual communion with God. It is specific treatment. Prayer recognizes a patient's direct access to God's love and discovers more of the consistent operation of God's law of health and wholeness on his or her behalf. It knows God, or divine Mind, as the only healer. Apparently, a transformation or spiritualization of a patient's thought changes his or her condition.

FACTS

The British medical journal, *The Lancet*, took a poll. The results indicated that 73 percent of people believed that praying for someone else can help cure their illness; 75 percent of patients wanted their physicians to address spiritual issues; 50 percent of hospitalized patients wanted their physicians to pray with them; and 28 percent believed in the ability of faith healers to make people well through their faith and touch.

In 2000, the American National Institutes of Health, after often contentious arguments, approved research funds for distant healing and mind/body connections in an effort to establish the merits of or discrediting of alternative healing practices. Serious high-tech studies were also made by other medical research institutions around the country. All of this research is ongoing.

Spiritual healers believe that it is possible to channel a healing energy to a patient by praying to God. Eastern religions believe that the spirit, mind, and body have to be in harmony or balance to sustain good physical and mental health. Disease is said to begin in the spirit and mind; therefore, the healing must begin there.

Most people who belong to a church are well aware of the practice of the priest or minister making requests for prayers for those in need. The members of the congregation don't need to know the patient personally, nor does the recipient even have to know that prayers are being made on his or her behalf.

Experiments and Research

Reliable research into such topics as ethical distant healing is difficult because many factors need to be controlled. Scientific research often uses the double-blind method to control variables. For example, when a pill is given to selected patients in a study group, none of them knows who is getting the real thing or the sugar pill. At the same time none of the researchers knows whether they are giving the real thing or a sugar pill to the subjects. (They are both blind to the identification of which is which and to whom it's delivered.)

A second very important element is the size of the study group. A drug company isn't going to get too far with the Federal Drug Administration if their study groups are small, usually they're in the hundreds to thousands range. In addition, for any scientific research to claim validity the results have to be replicated, time and time again, not only by the original researchers but also by other scientists. That's a golden rule in scientific research, made in an endeavor to cancel out luck, happenstance, or bias. All of that is why scientists look askance at Biblical and other reports of miracles and healings.

In 1988, a cardiologist, Randolph Byrd, carried out a well-designed, double-blind experiment in an effort to determine if prayers had any effect on patients in the Coronary Care Unit in San Francisco General Hospital. A computer randomly selected who of the 383 newly admitted patients would be prayed for and who would not. The experiment was carried out over a ten-month period. The results were remarkable. Those prayed for were five times less likely to require antibiotics, three times less likely to develop complications, and none had the need for an endotracheal intubation (a tube inserted into the patient's throat), whereas twelve on the nonprayed-for patients list needed that procedure.

FACTS

The reaction to the experiment from the medical establishment was mixed because, it was claimed, the experiment had holes in it (although no mention was made as to how many of the prayed-for patients would agree with that finding). Actually, the reaction was a good thing because it prompted researchers to hone their experimental procedures. Dr. Byrd's findings were, in fact, replicated: prayers seemed to work.

Sorcery

Entering the world of sorcery can be intimidating. To start with, learning to become a sorcerer can take an immense amount of dedicated concentration and time, part of which, as you'll see, is learning a new language. To provide a clue as to what one might be encountering, it is helpful to know that Kralori mysticism is restricted to Kralorela, and is very difficult for outsiders to learn. Apparently, sorcery was originated by the Brithini and Vadeli who had a direct link to Malkion, who was the lawgiver and prophet of the Brithini back in the age of logic. It seems that trouble arrived in the shape of the world breaking apart. The sun went out, the Ice Age began, and chaos crept into creation.

Central Beliefs

Witches insist that witchcraft and sorcery have two completely different outlooks and methods of operation. Witches call on supernatural forces, and generally do good acts; sorcerers need magical power and can cause harm to others, although, in many cultures, it is believed that sorcerers can do good, particularly as healers.

Different cultures have different views of what witches can and cannot do, and what sorcerers do. The New World countries, particularly, contain cultures that believe in sorcery—for instance, Native American tribes and peoples in North and South America.

The world of sorcery is full of apocryphal stories about the ability of sorcerers to kill people. One of them says that first a sketch of the victim should be drawn in the ground. Next, the sorcerer places medicine over where the pain is required. The victim is then instantly felled. Most people know about the voodoo practice of making a doll likeness of a person he or she wants to harm and sticking pins in it—this is the same general idea.

The Brithini are amoral atheists who do not believe in an afterlife. They reject everything that is not part of their ancient way. They worship the invisible god and pay no heed to the law of Malkion. They are said to be the most famous magicians in the world.

In many cultures in the developing nations, sorcerers are feared. It is believed that they can cause death by taking something of the potential victim, such as a piece of clothing, some hair, or even a cigarette end, applying magic to any of those things, and then either burning or burying the item, resulting in the death of the victim. Scholars, however, tend to believe that suggestion plays an important part of the sorcerers' power. Nevertheless, there are many accounts of elaborate magical rituals that have resulted in something awful happening to the victims.

Learning Spells

Learning a spell is not easy. First, you need an instructor and a lot of time. To get the grasp of a new spell will take about fifty hours of training; learning how to use the skill can take another ninety hours. Along the route you may earn points, as it were; there are negative skill values and positive ones. You can also earn magic bonuses.

Once a person has gone through some training, he or she learns about range. Range is the distance over which a spell can be cast or sent. The caster must be able to see the target. As students of sorcery progress, they can take vows after they have mastered all the basic arts.

It would be an easy matter to dismiss both witchcraft and sorcery, but many peoples in all kinds of cultures take both practices very seriously.

Spiritism

Spiritism should not be confused with Sprititualism. Spiritism means the belief and practice of communication with the spirits. Spiritualism is a doctrine of belief in a spiritual order of beings who are as real as the material world and belief that the soul is a spiritual substance.

Spiritism goes way back in history. In spite of the assertions of traditionally religious people that the Bible strictly forbade attempts to communicate with the dead through spirit mediums, there is a very clear indication in the Bible that such an attitude was not followed by everyone. For instance, 1 Samuel 28: 7–19 reads, in part: "Then said Saul unto his servants. 'Seek me a woman that hath a familiar spirit, that I may go to her, and inquire of her.' Saul puts on a disguise and goes to the woman. He says to her: 'I pray thee, divine unto me by the familiar spirit, and bring me him up, whom I shall name unto thee.'" (He was seeking out Samuel.)

While there are many examples of adherents of one religion being violently opposed to another, many go as far as to say that Spiritism is the worship of the devil.

The woman prevaricates and points out that those with familiars and wizards have been punished—something she could do without. Saul assures her she won't suffer. The woman does her stuff and Samuel appears to Saul whereupon they have a conversation in which Saul asks Samuel's advice. The scene concludes with the woman making some unleavened bread for Saul and his men.

Of course the Bible, being such a wonderful scriptural book, can be searched for almost any justification anyone might seek, and, as far as that goes, one can generally find what one is looking for. Nevertheless, that Biblical scene from Samuel is exactly what any modern-day Spiritist would attempt to do.

Many religions indulge in one form or another of Spiritism, including Yoruba, Native North Americans, and sects in Haiti. Other religions, while adhering to their traditional beliefs and practices, also dabble in Spiritism. It is estimated that there are at least 20 million people who are Spiritists, although it's hard to know how that figure was determined.

Modern Spiritism

Modern Spiritism is said to have begun in the home of the Fox family in Hydesville, New York, in 1848. They heard strange "knockings" and pieces of furniture were moved as if by invisible hands. Eventually, whoever was doing the knockings and moving the furniture about began to answer questions. Other disturbances of the same kind were reported in the house of a Presbyterian minister, the Rev. Dr. Phelps. Naturally, none of these happenings could be objectively confirmed, but that did not lessen the public's enthusiasm.

Around the same time in Europe, the Swedenborgian movement reported a whole series of table-turnings. This news spread across the Channel to England and was adopted by mediums who started to hold séances. The outcome was that a number of serious people, including scientists, became interested.

Beliefs and Customs

Those who profess to be serious Spiritists believe that God is the supreme intelligence and the primary cause of all things. God is eternal, immutable, unique, and supremely just and good. The universe is God's creation and encompasses all beings. They believe that beyond the physical world is a spiritual world, which is the habitation of incarnate spirits. All the laws of nature are divine moral laws and man is an incarnate spirit in the material body.

The relationship of spirits with man is constant and has always existed. The good spirits tend to lead us toward goodness and aid us in our troubles. While humans have free will they must take responsibility for their own actions.

Prayer forms an essential part of the belief, as it helps humans to improve and become stronger against the temptations of evil. The good spirits come as a result of prayer and help humans. Help is never denied to those who ask with true sincerity.

There is no ministry within the belief; neither are there vestments, altars, banners, candles, processions, talismans, amulets, or sacraments.

Probably the most important and most used Spiritist practice is trying to get in touch with those who have died. Disbelievers often base their mistrust of Spiritism on their experience of the many tricksters and confidence artists who lack the skills, but try to cash in on people's vulnerability.

Communication with the spirit world manifests itself in various psychical ways: telepathy, clairvoyance, and trance speaking. Physical phenomena include levitation, automatic writing, poltergeists, and the mysterious substance called ectoplasm. And in between is reading of auras, which are a sort of invisible dressing around our bodies that can be seen only by a person versed in reading auras. An aura is made up of various colors and hues; by reading them the medium is able to describe personality and illnesses.

Psychical research institutions throughout the world have carried out investigations into such phenomena. The research is ongoing. So far, it seems, no results have been scientifically validated. The major traditional religions are quick to cite these results, just as the Spiritists are quick to point out that there is no scientific evidence to validate the spiritual claims of traditional religions.

Spiritualism

There is no starting point when Spiritualism can be said to have begun. In prehistoric times, the people were motivated to seek out unseen and unknown entities who controlled things. Hence, a sun god or rain god was created and worshipped because the sun and the rain were essential to well-being. Other gods were instituted to suit the needs of the people, who had no direct control over events. If things went wrong, the people felt they had displeased the gods somehow; one way of dealing with that was to make offerings and sacrifices. Not too much has changed; nobody has come up with a way to prevent earthquakes, for instance, or drought, fire, and floods. They can only combat them. Today, most people pray in times of adversity.

Both Plato and Aristotle could be considered Spiritualists, if for no other reason than they cogitated about the soul of man. In short, the soul was considered to be a source of activity that was distinct from the body, but operating from within it. Spiritualists, and other beliefs, give the soul another name: spirit.

Encyclopedias tell us that Spiritualism is a philosophy that is characteristic of any system of thought that affirms the existence of immaterial reality imperceptible to the senses. This might lead some of us to conclude that there is something going on out there, but what?

QUESTIONS?

How does a person become a Spiritualist?
You could start with a book: *Teachings and Illustration as They Emanate from the Spirit World* by Mary T. Longley. Or, you could write to the National Spiritualist Association of Churches in Lily Dale, New York. The association has been in existence since 1893.

Beliefs

Spiritualists believe that there are other planes of existence. For example, the next plane up is similar to our earthly one but operates at a higher rate of vibration and luminosity. One method of service in spirit is to communicate and help illuminate those who are living on the earthly plane.

Mediums in the spirit world and mediums in the physical world adjust their vibrations to enable communication between the two planes to take place. There is an absolute belief that life moves in a gradual state of evolution, culminating in the arrival in the spiritual realm. Like Spiritism, Spiritualism believes that the understanding gleaned on the earthly plane continues to the next level; what is left behind are the pains, struggles, and frustrations. Life is about continuous growth, and consciousness never dies because it is part of God and the infinite.

Human beings are considered spiritual beings, an indivisible part of the Divine. God is the spirit within everyone. One of the purposes of Spiritualism is to awaken a person to consciously accept and activate that spirit within. Free choice and personal responsibility are paramount, and Spiritualism offers a set of principles to assist world travelers, as they are called, to proceed upward toward the light.

Spiritualists affirm that modern beliefs mean following natural laws: God's laws of growth, love, and the seeking of truth in a religion that incorporates science as part of its philosophy. True Spiritualists believe in the core philosophy that each human is a soul clothed in a material body through which mental and spiritual faculties function, and that it is within this material body that the spiritual or etheric body resides.

The Spiritualists Declaration of Principles is published, not as a creed that is binding, but as a consensus on the fundamental teachings of Spiritualism by Spiritualists. In part, it says:

We believe in infinite intelligence.
We believe that the phenomena of nature, both physical and spiritual, are the expression of infinite intelligence.
We affirm that communication with the so-called dead is a fact.
We affirm that the precepts of prophecy and healing are divine attributes proven through mediumship.

It is said that the study of natural law is beneficial to all and that natural law is like a kind teacher who understands that we learn by doing. Most natural laws are ones that any person would instinctively know, but others, for instance, the Law of Vibration, the Law of Adhesion/Cohesion, and the Law of Mind, would take some effort to understand.

Practices

A medium is a person whose body is sensitive to vibrations from the spirit world. Because of that sensitivity the medium is able to participate in prophecy, clairvoyance, clairaudience, laying on of hands, visions, revelations, healing, and a host of other esoteric actions.

The declared object of Spiritualism is, "To teach and proclaim the science, philosophy, and religion of modern Spiritualism. To protest against every attempt to compel humanity to worship God in any particular or prescribed manner. To encourage every person to reveal understanding of new truths and leave all people free to follow the dictates of reason and conscience in spiritual as in secular affairs."

Many philosophical beliefs are said to be compatible with Spiritualism as long as they permit a reality that is independent from and superior to matter. While statistics on Spiritualism are not known, there is no question that the belief is evident, in many guises, throughout the world.

Wicca and Witchcraft

In 1692, an infamous trial was held in Salem, Massachusetts. Nine-year-old Elizabeth Parris the daughter, and eleven-year-old Abigail Williams, the niece of a Salem Village minister began to exhibit strange behavior, such as blasphemous screaming, convulsive seizures, and so on. Several other Salem girls began to demonstrate similar behavior. Physicians concluded that the girls were under the influence of Satan.

Pressured to identify some source of their afflictions, the girls named three women, and warrants were issued for their arrests. The women were examined and found guilty of witchcraft. This set in motion hysteria among the populace, which resulted in the death of twenty-four people accused of being witches; nineteen were hanged, the others died in prison. Today, the Salem Witch Museum and other local sites and documents can be visited and studied.

Witchcraft and sorcery are frequently misunderstood; the two are separate entities. A Witch is someone who has innate magical powers. (The term Witch applies to both men and women; "warlock" is now considered to be derogatory.) A sorcerer is someone who uses potions and spells to get their way.

Throughout history the calamities that people are subject to are often blamed on someone else, when all the time it's his or her own doing. This common fault in human nature was, and is today, the basic motivation of prejudice: Find a scapegoat and blame someone else for what's wrong. The Christian witch hunts back in the sixteenth and seventeenth centuries were a time when thousands of alleged witches were persecuted and executed, usually by burning them to death. While it's difficult to believe, it's recorded that between 1994 and 1995 over 200 people in South Africa were burnt to death after being accused of witchcraft. Even today, the Harry Potter books, which have given wonderful pleasure to thousands of children and adults, have been condemned by certain Christian fundamentalists. Why do witches get such a bad rap? Perhaps the Wicked Witch of the West in *The Wizard of Oz* with her long, hooked warty nose and old-fashioned broomstick didn't help.

Central Beliefs

Wicca is said to derive from an ancient Celtic society, which is older than Christianity. Other sources say the religion is a modern one that does not have a long historical connection. Either way, they were, and are, seen by the churches as having ties to Satan. This they did, and still now strongly deny, insisting that Wiccans are no more like Satanists than Buddhists, Hindus, or Muslims. Modern Wiccans maintain that present-day Wicca was created by the merging of some of the ancient Celtic beliefs, deity structure, and seasonal days of celebration with modern material from ceremonial magic.

The general belief is that Wicca arose as an important movement in England during the 1950s. The movement has claimed a fast-track expansion into North America and Europe. Some estimates put the number of adherents at 750,000. That's at best an estimate because Wiccans are, understandably, reticent about telling people of their beliefs. Imagine someone at a company meeting standing up and saying he had to go because he was late for a meeting at his coven, essentially announcing he was a Witch. Not quite the same as being late for a meeting of the Sunday school choir.

If the adherent figures are true, that would make Wicca one of the largest and fastest growing minority religions in the United States. However, it is doubtful if the correct figures will be ever be known or substantiated.

Covens

Some Wiccans worship in a coven. Traditionally, a coven consists of thirteen people who are emotionally connected. The thirteenth member will be the High Priestess or Priest. Generally, there are no rules about the group; it can be mixed gender or not. However, some covens do have one gender, for instance, Dianic Witches. Typically, covens meet in private homes or meeting rooms. On some occasions, holidays in particular, they meet outdoors. Nights of the full or new moon are times of choice.

Covens don't advertise for members; they come through word-of-mouth recommendation and have to be unanimously approved by all the members of the coven before they become full members themselves. So how does one find a coven? Basically, through networking, which raises the question of: Does one turn to the person on the next seat in a coffee bar and ask, "Hi, there, are you a Witch by any chance?" Of course, one stands a good chance of getting a swift reply to such a question. Seriously, today the first step might be to go on the Internet and make some searches. As usual with the Internet, one has to be very circumspect.

FACTS

A recent development allows Witches and covens to become legally recognized. Churches, seminaries, and antidefamation leagues have been formed.

As an alternative to trying to find a coven, a person might prefer to learn about becoming a solitary Witch. Many prospective adherents do this. Once a person feels well informed and confident enough, he or she could perform a spell to act as a kind of personal beacon to draw others of like mind. Traditional Celtic jewelry could also be worn—for instance, crescent moon earrings or a Celtic pentagram.

Practices

Witchcraft members adhere strictly to an ethical code called "Wiccan Rede." They believe that whatever they do comes back to them threefold. Thus, if they did harm they would get harm back to the power of three. Therefore, they have no incentive to curse anyone; the curse would come back to haunt them three times over. Witches may practice some form of ritual magic, which must be considered "good magic." Their ethical code is spelled out in the saying: "An' it harm none, do what thou wilt."

The Council of American Witches write in paragraph 8 of their Principles of Belief: "Calling oneself 'Witch' does not make a witch, but neither does heredity itself, or the collecting of titles, degrees and initiations. A witch seeks to control forces within her/himself that make life possible in order to live wisely and well, without harm to others, and in harmony with nature."

QUESTIONS?

How do Witches cast spells?
Typically, a Witch will start a spell with casting a circle, burning some incense, lighting a special candle, then doing some rhythmic chanting. An analogy has been made between a Witch casting a spell and a person being in a church, a sacred place, as the circle is to a Witch. The churchgoer hopes his prayers are answered; the Witch hopes that a good spell is cast.

A deep respect for the environment features strongly in Wiccan religious activity. So, too, does the value of femininity, and the need to balance what many women, Witches or not, consider the overly oppressive practice of masculine domination in traditional religions.

Witches generally worship a god and goddess, seen as different aspects of the same deity. The deity is known as the ultimate omnipotent god force in the universe and is the same God most people worship. However, Witches relate better to both a mother and father figure, which is why the name goddess figures predominately in the craft.

The Handfasting Ritual

Wiccans have many rituals; one of the most charming is called Handfasting. The ceremony was derived from the medieval wedding practices used in Scotland, Wales, and Ireland. Handfasting is basically a marriage ceremony, although it may not be permanent unless a valid marriage license has been obtained and a licensed and legally certified priest is present at the ceremony.

Originally, the ceremony was not considered a wedding, but a declaration of intent to marry. If, after a year and a day, the couple are still committed to each other, then they would be legally married at an official ceremony.

Before the ceremony can begin, the area chosen is traditionally swept free of debris and negativity by the Maiden of the Broom; once that's done the ceremony commences. The actual ceremony is fairly traditional, although like Christian marriages, for instance, the couple may personalize it. The Wiccan ceremony starts with the High Priestess circling three times and incanting:

Three times round,
Once for the Daughter,
Twice for the Crone,
Thrice for the Mother,
who sits on the throne.

Everything proceeds with the giving of the vows, the placing of wedding bands, and thanks to the elements. The ceremony ends with the opening stanza being repeated.

Wiccan Festivals

Based on the Celtic calendar, the Wiccan calendar recognizes two seasons, winter and summer, each of which begins with a celebration. The eight major holidays are called the Eight Sabbats. Some covens may follow the festivals, others may have alternatives. Minor holidays are called The Lesser Sabbats.

Note that the dates given in the list below may vary:

Yule. The Winter Solstice, late December. The Sun God is born at Yule.

Imbolg (also called Imbolc), February 2. The first signs of waking up from winter (also known as Groundhog Day).

Ostara. The Vernal Equinox, late March. The magical times when day and night are equal.

Beltane, May 1. A great fertility celebration (also known as May Day).

Litha, late June. The Summer Solstice (also known as Midsummer and St. John's Day) is the halfway point of the year.

Lughnasadh, August 1. The beginning of the harvest season.

Mabon, late September. The Autumn Equinox. A time to give thanks for the earth's bounty.

Samhain, October 31. Samhain is the Celtic New Year's Day. It is also known as Halloween.

APPENDIX A
Source Material

Close to 1,200 authoritative source pages of data were consulted to produce this book. These included pages accessed from the Internet and transcript pages from personal interviews. The scholarly sources from encyclopedias, dictionaries, and such are listed on page 276.

As to those accessed from the Internet, readers are advised that to do this for themselves, all that's required is to enter the name of the religion or belief they want to read about into a search engine; the return will produce a plethora of entries per search. However, one should be careful what one accepts from Internet sources; the author tended to discard those written by individuals professing personal views, as these obviously expressed biased opinions and could not be satisfactorily verified. In all cases, the sites created by the actual religions or beliefs were studied; the built-in biases were taken into consideration.

Following is a list of the books that were consulted. All of them were the work of highly informed contributors or groups of contributors. There is no question that the author owes a deep sense of gratitude to these hundreds of people, without whose knowledge this book would not have been possible.

Bowker, John Westerdale. *World Religions*. New York: DK Publishing, 1997.

The Concise Oxford Dictionary of World Religions. Oxford: Oxford University Press, 2000.

Breuilly, Elizabeth; O'Brien, Joanne; Marty, Martin E.; and Palmer, Martin. *The Religions of the World: The Illustrated Guide to Origins, Beliefs, Traditions, and Festivals*. New York: Checkmark Books, 1997.

The Catholic Encyclopedia, New Advent Version.

Columbia Encyclopedia. Columbia University Press New York.

Crim, Keith R.; Bullard, Roger A.; and Shimm, Larry D. *The Perennial Dictionary of World's Religions*. San Francisco: Harper San Francisco, 1990.

Electric Library. www.encyclopedia.com

Encarta Encyclopedia. www.clever.net/cam/encyclopedia.html

Encyclopedia Americana. http://ea.grolier.com

The Encyclopaedia Britannica. Encyclopaedia Britannica, Inc.

The Holy Bible, Authorized King James Version.

Levinson, David. *Religion: A Cross-Cultural Encyclopedia*. Oxford: Oxford University Press, 1998.

Merriam-Webster's Encyclopedia of World's Religions.

Smith, Huston. *The Illustrated World's Religions: A Guide to Our Wisdom Traditions*. San Francisco: Harper San Francisco, 1995.

Sourcebook of the World's Religions. New World Library. Navato, California.

Stanford Encyclopedia of Philosophy. Stanford University, California.

Timeline of Important Dates

What follows is an overview cal-endar of some of the impor-tant dates in the history of religion. It is not meant to be exhaustive, but it should provide a general reference to the emergence of important people and events. It should also provide a good indi-cation of the dissension between religions that took place over the centuries. Please note that the dates given in the B.C.E. time period are, even among scholars, fre-quently educated guesstimates.

B.C.E.

2000–1501—Stonehenge, England, is the center of religious worship.

1500–1001—Moses is given the Ten Commandants on Mount Sinai.

1100–500—The *Veda*, sacred texts of the Hindus, are compiled.

800–701—Isaiah teaches of the coming of the Messiah.

600–501—Confucius, Buddha, Zoroaster, Lao Tzu, and the Jewish prophets are at their height.

540–468—Mahavira establishes Jainism. Siddhartha Gautama, the founder of Buddhism, is born.

450–401—The Torah becomes the moral essence of the Jews.

200—The Bhagavad-Gita is written.

The year 1—Believed to be the birth of Jesus of Nazareth, founder of Christianity.

C.E.

30—Probable date of the crucifixion and death of Jesus Christ.

51–100—St. Peter, disciple of Jesus, is executed. First four books of the New Testament, the gospels according to Matthew, Mark, Luke, and John, believed written.

570—Muhammad, the founder of Islam, is born.

622—Muhammad flees persecution in Mecca and settles in Yathrib (later Medina). Marks year one in the Muslim calendar.

625—Muhammad begins to dictate the Koran.

632—Buddhism becomes the state religion of Tibet.

695—Persecution of the Jews in Spain.

936—Traditional date of the arrival in India from Iran of the first Parsi (followers of Zoroastrianism).

1054—The split between the Roman Catholic Church and Eastern Orthodox Church becomes permanent.

1200—Islam begins to replace Indian religions.

1229—The Inquisition in Toulouse, France, bans the reading of the Bible by all laymen.

1252—The Inquisition begins to use instruments of torture.

1306—The Jews are expelled from France.

1309—The Roman Catholic papacy is seated in Avignon, France.

1349—Persecution of the Jews in Germany.

1483—Martin Luther, who becomes leader of the Protestant Reformation in Germany, is born.

1491—Ignatius Loyola, founder of the Jesuit Order of Roman Catholic priests, is born.

C.E. (CONTINUED)

1492—The Jews are given three months by the Inquisitor General of Spain to accept Christianity or leave the country.

1507—Martin Luther is ordained.

1509—John Calvin, leader of the Protestant Reformation in France, is born.

1509—Emperor Maximilian I orders the confiscation and destruction of all Jewish books, including the Torah.

1531—The Inquisition in Portugal.

1549—Only the new Book of Prayer allowed to be used in England.

1561—French Calvinist refugees from Flanders settle in England.

1611—The authorized version of the King James Bible published.

1620—The Pilgrim fathers leave Plymouth, England, in the Mayflower for North America. They land at New Plymouth, MA, and establish the Plymouth Colony.

1642—George Fox, English founder of the Protestant Society of Friends (the Quakers), is born.

1703—John Wesley, English founder of the Protestant movement that later became the Methodist Church, is born.

1716—Christian religious teaching banned in China.

1859—Charles Darwin, English naturalist, publishes *Origin of Species*.

1869—Meeting of the first Roman Catholic Vatican Council, at which the dogma of papal infallibility is advocated.

1869—Mohandas K. Gandhi, who helped his country achieve independence from Britain and sought rapprochement between Hindus and Muslims, is born.

1933—The persecution and extermination of European Jews, known as the Holocaust, by Adolf Hitler's Nazi party begins.

1948—The independent Jewish state of Israel comes into existence.

1952—The Revised Standard Version of the Bible reaches number one on the nonfiction bestseller lists.

1962—Meeting of the second Roman Catholic Vatican Council, at which changes were made in the liturgy and greater participation in services by lay church members was encouraged.

1983—The World Council of Churches establishes new levels of consensus in regard to Christian faith and worship. The Council holds a historic interdenominational Eucharist.

1990—The New Revised Standard Version of the Bible is published.

Index

Clitoridectomy in African religions, 239
Columbus, Christopher, 206, 230
Condoms in Orthodox Judaism, 139
Confession
    in Catholicism, 30
    in Orthodox Church, 65
Confirmation
    in Catholicism, 32
    Christianity on, 23–24
    in Orthodox Church, 65
Confucianism, 145–153, 156
    Confucian literature, 148–149
    diversification into modern society, 152–153
    Han, 153
    Japanese, 153
    Korean, 153
    origins and development, 146
    rituals and customs, 150
        birth, 150–151
        death, 151–152
        marriage, 151
    schools of, 153
    Shinto and, 190, 193
    Singapore, 153
    Taoism and, 156, 158
Confucius, 146–148, 278
    reputation of, 149–150
    teachings of, 147–148
Congregationalists, 44–45, 52
Congregational Praise, 45
Conservative Judaism, 142–143, 144
    central beliefs in, 142
Constantine, 26
Constantinople, 26
Constitution on the Sacred Liturgy, 27
Contemporary Neo-Confucianism, 153
Conversations with God (Walsch), 258
Cosmology, 222
Council of American Witches, 272
A Course in Miracles (Schucman), 257–258
Covens, 270–271
Cranmer, Thomas, 37
Creed, 16–17
    Apostles', 17, 38, 53
    Nicene, 17, 38–40, 53
Cremation
    in Hinduism, 104
    in Sikhism, 187
Cromwell, Oliver, 52, 71
Cumberland Presbyterian Churches, 52

D

Darwin, Charles, 279
Dasam Granth (tenth book), 185
Dating and Courtship, 50
David, 128
David, Ferenc, 75
Day of Atonement (Yom Kippur), 139
Day of Judgment, 86
Dead Sea Scrolls, 10
Death
    African religions on, 240
    Buddhism on, 120
    Catholic Church on, 32–34
    Christianity on, 24
    Confucianism on, 151–152
    Hinduism on, 104
    Judaism on, 135
    Native American religions on, 234
    Sikhism on, 186
    Taoism on, 164–165
Decalogue, 127
Deism, 57–60
    central beliefs in, 58–59
    diversification into modern society, 60
    holy writing in, 59–60
Dhammapada, 115
Dharma, 97, 122
Dhikr, 87
Dianetics: The Modern Science of Mental Health (Hubbard), 208–209, 211
Dickens, Charles, 2
Digambaras, 168, 172
Divali, 105
Divorce, in Islam, 85
Doane, Marguerite, 41
Donne, John, 21
Dragon Boat Festival, 166
Dreadlocks, 208
Dreamtime, 242–243, 244
Druids, 224–228
    central beliefs in, 225–226
        deities, 226
        Stonehenge, 226–227
    diversification into modern society, 228
    festivals, 227–228
Dualism, 222

E

Easter Island, 246
Eastern Orthodox Church, 26, 65, 278
Eddy, Mary Baker, 42–43

Effendi, Abbas, 175
Effendi, Shoghi, 175, 177
Eid ul-Adha, 87
Eid ul-Fitr, 87
Eightfold Path, 115
Einstein, Albert, 57
Eliezer Ba'al Shem Tov, 140
Elizabeth I, 37
Emotional Growth Movement, 256
Engram, 210
Episcopal Church, 38, 40
Esalen Growth Center, 256
Esau, 124
Essenes, 10–11
EST, 256
Ethical monotheism, 129
The Ethics of Belief (Clifford), 253
Ethiopian Church, 238
Eucharist. *See also* Last Supper; Lord's Supper
    in Anglican Church, 22, 38
    in Catholicism, 22, 32
    in Orthodox Church, 22, 65
Evangelical and Reformed Church, 45
Evangelical Friends International, 74
Evangelicalism, 204
Evangelical Lutheran Church of America, 61
Extreme Unction, 32

F

Family History Library, 51–52
Fasting, 80
Fatima, 78
Feast of Ridvan, 178
Feng Shui, 162
Festivals
    in Baha'i faith, 178
    Christian, 24
    Druid, 227–228
    Hindu, 105
    Islamic, 86–87
    in Jainism, 173
    in Judaism, 135–136
    Shinto, 196
    in Sikhism, 187
    in Taoism, 165–166
    witchcraft, 273–274
    in Zoroastrianism, 224
Feynman, Richard P., 176
Fire-Baptized Holiness Church, 206

THE EVERYTHING SERIES!

BUSINESS

Everything® **Business Planning Book**
Everything® **Coaching and Mentoring Book**
Everything® **Fundraising Book**
Everything® **Home-Based Business Book**
Everything® **Leadership Book**
Everything® **Managing People Book**
Everything® **Network Marketing Book**
Everything® **Online Business Book**
Everything® **Project Management Book**
Everything® **Selling Book**
Everything® **Start Your Own Business Book**
Everything® **Time Management Book**

COMPUTERS

Everything® **Build Your Own Home Page Book**
Everything® **Computer Book**
Everything® **Internet Book**
Everything® **Microsoft® Word 2000 Book**

COOKBOOKS

Everything® **Barbecue Cookbook**
Everything® **Bartender's Book, $9.95**
Everything® **Chinese Cookbook**
Everything® **Chocolate Cookbook**
Everything® **Cookbook**
Everything® **Dessert Cookbook**
Everything® **Diabetes Cookbook**
Everything® **Indian Cookbook**
Everything® **Low-Carb Cookbook**
Everything® **Low-Fat High-Flavor Cookbook**
Everything® **Low-Salt Cookbook**
Everything® **Mediterranean Cookbook**
Everything® **Mexican Cookbook**
Everything® **One-Pot Cookbook**
Everything® **Pasta Book**
Everything® **Quick Meals Cookbook**
Everything® **Slow Cooker Cookbook**
Everything® **Soup Cookbook**
Everything® **Thai Cookbook**
Everything® **Vegetarian Cookbook**
Everything® **Wine Book**

HEALTH

Everything® **Alzheimer's Book**
Everything® **Anti-Aging Book**
Everything® **Diabetes Book**
Everything® **Dieting Book**
Everything® **Herbal Remedies Book**
Everything® **Hypnosis Book**
Everything® **Massage Book**
Everything® **Menopause Book**
Everything® **Nutrition Book**
Everything® **Reflexology Book**
Everything® **Reiki Book**
Everything® **Stress Management Book**
Everything® **Vitamins, Minerals, and Nutritional Supplements Book**

HISTORY

Everything® **American Government Book**
Everything® **American History Book**
Everything® **Civil War Book**
Everything® **Irish History & Heritage Book**

Everything® **Mafia Book**
Everything® **Middle East Book**
Everything® **World War II Book**

HOBBIES & GAMES

Everything® **Bridge Book**
Everything® **Candlemaking Book**
Everything® **Casino Gambling Book**
Everything® **Chess Basics Book**
Everything® **Collectibles Book**
Everything® **Crossword and Puzzle Book**
Everything® **Digital Photography Book**
Everything® **Easy Crosswords Book**
Everything® **Family Tree Book**
Everything® **Games Book**
Everything® **Knitting Book**
Everything® **Magic Book**
Everything® **Motorcycle Book**
Everything® **Online Genealogy Book**
Everything® **Photography Book**
Everything® **Pool & Billiards Book**
Everything® **Quilting Book**
Everything® **Scrapbooking Book**
Everything® **Sewing Book**
Everything® **Soapmaking Book**

HOME IMPROVEMENT

Everything® **Feng Shui Book**
Everything® **Feng Shui Decluttering Book, $9.95 ($15.95 CAN)**
Everything® **Fix-It Book**
Everything® **Gardening Book**
Everything® **Homebuilding Book**

All Everything® books are priced at $12.95 or $14.95, unless otherwise stated. Prices subject to change without notice.
Canadian prices range from $11.95–$31.95, and are subject to change without notice.

Everything® **Home Decorating Book**
Everything® **Landscaping Book**
Everything® **Lawn Care Book**
Everything® **Organize Your Home Book**

EVERYTHING® KIDS' BOOKS

All titles are $6.95

Everything® **Kids' Baseball Book, 3rd Ed. ($10.95 CAN)**
Everything® **Kids' Bible Trivia Book** ($10.95 CAN)
Everything® **Kids' Bugs Book** ($10.95 CAN)
Everything® **Kids' Christmas Puzzle & Activity Book** ($10.95 CAN)
Everything® **Kids' Cookbook** ($10.95 CAN)
Everything® **Kids' Halloween Puzzle & Activity Book** ($10.95 CAN)
Everything® **Kids' Joke Book** ($10.95 CAN)
Everything® **Kids' Math Puzzles Book** ($10.95 CAN)
Everything® **Kids' Mazes Book** ($10.95 CAN)
Everything® **Kids' Money Book** ($11.95 CAN)
Everything® **Kids' Monsters Book** ($10.95 CAN)
Everything® **Kids' Nature Book** ($11.95 CAN)
Everything® **Kids' Puzzle Book** ($10.95 CAN)
Everything® **Kids' Riddles & Brain Teasers Book** ($10.95 CAN)
Everything® **Kids' Science Experiments Book** ($10.95 CAN)
Everything® **Kids' Soccer Book** ($10.95 CAN)
Everything® **Kids' Travel Activity Book** ($10.95 CAN)

KIDS' STORY BOOKS

Everything® **Bedtime Story Book**
Everything® **Bible Stories Book**
Everything® **Fairy Tales Book**
Everything® **Mother Goose Book**

LANGUAGE

Everything® **Inglés Book**
Everything® **Learning French Book**
Everything® **Learning German Book**
Everything® **Learning Italian Book**
Everything® **Learning Latin Book**
Everything® **Learning Spanish Book**
Everything® **Sign Language Book**
Everything® **Spanish Phrase Book, $9.95 ($15.95 CAN)**

MUSIC

Everything® **Drums Book (with CD), $19.95 ($31.95 CAN)**
Everything® **Guitar Book**
Everything® **Playing Piano and Keyboards Book**
Everything® **Rock & Blues Guitar Book (with CD), $19.95 ($31.95 CAN)**
Everything® **Songwriting Book**

NEW AGE

Everything® **Astrology Book**
Everything® **Divining the Future Book**
Everything® **Dreams Book**
Everything® **Ghost Book**
Everything® **Love Signs Book, $9.95 ($15.95 CAN)**
Everything® **Meditation Book**
Everything® **Numerology Book**
Everything® **Palmistry Book**
Everything® **Psychic Book**
Everything® **Spells & Charms Book**
Everything® **Tarot Book**
Everything® **Wicca and Witchcraft Book**

PARENTING

Everything® **Baby Names Book**
Everything® **Baby Shower Book**
Everything® **Baby's First Food Book**
Everything® **Baby's First Year Book**
Everything® **Breastfeeding Book**

Everything® **Father-to-Be Book**
Everything® **Get Ready for Baby Book**
Everything® **Getting Pregnant Book**
Everything® **Homeschooling Book**
Everything® **Parent's Guide to Children with Autism**
Everything® **Parent's Guide to Positive Discipline**
Everything® **Parent's Guide to Raising a Successful Child**
Everything® **Parenting a Teenager Book**
Everything® **Potty Training Book, $9.95 ($15.95 CAN)**
Everything® **Pregnancy Book, 2nd Ed.**
Everything® **Pregnancy Fitness Book**
Everything® **Pregnancy Organizer, $15.00 ($22.95 CAN)**
Everything® **Toddler Book**
Everything® **Tween Book**

PERSONAL FINANCE

Everything® **Budgeting Book**
Everything® **Get Out of Debt Book**
Everything® **Get Rich Book**
Everything® **Homebuying Book, 2nd Ed.**
Everything® **Homeselling Book**
Everything® **Investing Book**
Everything® **Money Book**
Everything® **Mutual Funds Book**
Everything® **Online Investing Book**
Everything® **Personal Finance Book**
Everything® **Personal Finance in Your 20s & 30s Book**
Everything® **Wills & Estate Planning Book**

PETS

Everything® **Cat Book**
Everything® **Dog Book**
Everything® **Dog Training and Tricks Book**
Everything® **Golden Retriever Book**
Everything® **Horse Book**
Everything® **Labrador Retriever Book**
Everything® **Puppy Book**
Everything® **Tropical Fish Book**

All Everything® books are priced at $12.95 or $14.95, unless otherwise stated. Prices subject to change without notice.
Canadian prices range from $11.95–$31.95, and are subject to change without notice.

REFERENCE

Everything® **Astronomy Book**
Everything® **Car Care Book**
Everything® **Christmas Book, $15.00**
    ($21.95 CAN)
Everything® **Classical Mythology Book**
Everything® **Einstein Book**
Everything® **Etiquette Book**
Everything® **Great Thinkers Book**
Everything® **Philosophy Book**
Everything® **Psychology Book**
Everything® **Shakespeare Book**
Everything® **Tall Tales, Legends, &**
    Other Outrageous
    Lies Book
Everything® **Toasts Book**
Everything® **Trivia Book**
Everything® **Weather Book**

RELIGION

Everything® **Angels Book**
Everything® **Bible Book**
Everything® **Buddhism Book**
Everything® **Catholicism Book**
Everything® **Christianity Book**
Everything® **Jewish History &**
    Heritage Book
Everything® **Judaism Book**
Everything® **Prayer Book**
Everything® **Saints Book**
Everything® **Understanding Islam**
    Book
Everything® **World's Religions Book**
Everything® **Zen Book**

SCHOOL & CAREERS

Everything® **After College Book**
Everything® **Alternative Careers Book**
Everything® **College Survival Book**
Everything® **Cover Letter Book**
Everything® **Get-a-Job Book**
Everything® **Hot Careers Book**

Everything® **Job Interview Book**
Everything® **New Teacher Book**
Everything® **Online Job Search Book**
Everything® **Resume Book, 2nd Ed.**
Everything® **Study Book**

SELF-HELP/ RELATIONSHIPS

Everything® **Dating Book**
Everything® **Divorce Book**
Everything® **Great Marriage Book**
Everything® **Great Sex Book**
Everything® **Kama Sutra Book**
Everything® **Romance Book**
Everything® **Self-Esteem Book**
Everything® **Success Book**

SPORTS & FITNESS

Everything® **Body Shaping Book**
Everything® **Fishing Book**
Everything® **Fly-Fishing Book**
Everything® **Golf Book**
Everything® **Golf Instruction Book**
Everything® **Knots Book**
Everything® **Pilates Book**
Everything® **Running Book**
Everything® **Sailing Book, 2nd Ed.**
Everything® **T'ai Chi and QiGong Book**
Everything® **Total Fitness Book**
Everything® **Weight Training Book**
Everything® **Yoga Book**

TRAVEL

Everything® **Family Guide to Hawaii**
Everything® **Guide to Las Vegas**
Everything® **Guide to New England**
Everything® **Guide to New York City**
Everything® **Guide to Washington D.C.**
Everything® **Travel Guide to The**
    Disneyland Resort®,
    California Adventure®,

    Universal Studios®, and
    the Anaheim Area
Everything® **Travel Guide to the Walt**
    Disney World Resort®,
    Universal Studios®, and
    Greater Orlando, 3rd Ed.

WEDDINGS

Everything® **Bachelorette Party Book,**
    $9.95 ($15.95 CAN)
Everything® **Bridesmaid Book, $9.95**
    ($15.95 CAN)
Everything® **Creative Wedding Ideas**
    Book
Everything® **Elopement Book, $9.95**
    ($15.95 CAN)
Everything® **Groom Book**
Everything® **Jewish Wedding Book**
Everything® **Wedding Book, 2nd Ed.**
Everything® **Wedding Checklist,**
    $7.95 ($11.95 CAN)
Everything® **Wedding Etiquette Book,**
    $7.95 ($11.95 CAN)
Everything® **Wedding Organizer,**
    $15.00 ($22.95 CAN)
Everything® **Wedding Shower Book,**
    $7.95 ($12.95 CAN)
Everything® **Wedding Vows Book,**
    $7.95 ($11.95 CAN)
Everything® **Weddings on a Budget**
    Book, $9.95 ($15.95 CAN)

WRITING

Everything® **Creative Writing Book**
Everything® **Get Published Book**
Everything® **Grammar and Style Book**
Everything® **Grant Writing Book**
Everything® **Guide to Writing**
    Children's Books
Everything® **Screenwriting Book**
Everything® **Writing Well Book**

Available wherever books are sold!
To order, call 800-872-5627, or visit us at everything.com

Everything® and everything.com® are registered trademarks of F+W Publications, Inc.